Herbert Mortimer Luckock

After Death

An Examination of the Testimony of primitive Times respecting the State of the

faithful Dead, and their Relationship to the Living

Herbert Mortimer Luckock

After Death

An Examination of the Testimony of primitive Times respecting the State of the faithful Dead, and their Relationship to the Living

ISBN/EAN: 9783337187255

Printed in Europe, USA, Canada, Australia, Japan

Cover: Foto ©ninafisch / pixelio.de

More available books at **www.hansebooks.com**

AFTER DEATH

By the same Author

Second Edition. Crown 8vo. 6s.

THE BISHOPS IN THE TOWER. A Record of Stirring Events affecting the Church and Nonconformists from the Restoration to the Revolution.

'We most heartily commend this delightful volume. It is full of original research and clear and broad grasp of situations; it is written by one with the historical faculty richly developed.'—*Literary Churchman.*

Second Edition. Crown 8vo. 6s.

STUDIES IN THE HISTORY OF THE BOOK OF COMMON PRAYER. The Anglican Reform—The Puritan Innovations—The Elizabethan Reaction—The Caroline Settlement. With Appendices.

'The subject of this present volume is inexhaustibly attractive; and many, we hope, will be glad to retrace the lines of our liturgical Church history in company with so accomplished and sympathetic a guide. . . . If we have ventured to criticise some details in this able and helpful book, which might be reconsidered in another edition, we are not the less desirous of recommending it emphatically to all educated members of the entire Anglican communion.'
Church Quarterly Review.

'We heartily commend Dr. Luckock's very interesting and very readable book.'
The Guardian.

Third Edition. Crown 8vo. Two Vols. 12s.

FOOTPRINTS OF THE SON OF MAN, AS TRACED BY ST. MARK. Being Eighty Portions for Private Study, Family Reading, and Instructions in Church. With an Introduction by the late Bishop of Ely.

'His book is designed "for private study, family reading, and instructions in church." For one or all of these three purposes we heartily recommend it. . . . The frequent references to the Talmud and Mishnah, as illustrating the Gospel record, form a peculiarly valuable feature of the book.'—*Church Quarterly Review.*

'We will undertake to say that there is not a church in England in which the congregation would not be greatly benefited and advanced in religious knowledge by listening to these addresses.'—*Guardian.*

RIVINGTONS, WATERLOO PLACE, LONDON.

AFTER DEATH

AN EXAMINATION OF

THE TESTIMONY OF PRIMITIVE TIMES RESPECTING THE STATE OF THE FAITHFUL DEAD, AND THEIR RELATIONSHIP TO THE LIVING

BY

HERBERT MORTIMER LUCKOCK, D.D.

CANON OF ELY, PRINCIPAL OF THE THEOLOGICAL COLLEGE, AND SOMETIME FELLOW OF JESUS COLLEGE, CAMBRIDGE

τὰ ἀρχαῖα ἔθη κρατείτω.—NIC. CONCIL. CAN. VI

SIXTH EDITION

RIVINGTONS
WATERLOO PLACE, LONDON
MDCCCLXXXVII

VIRO : ADMODUM : REVERENDO :

JACOBO : RUSSELL :

EPISCOPO : ELIENSI :

S : T : P :

BENEFICIORUM :

CONSILII : HORTATIONIS : AMICITIÆ :

HAUD : IMMEMOR :

HOC : OPUS : QUANTULUMCUNQUE :

E : PIETATE : DEDICO :

Preface.

THE following treatise is in the main an examination of evidence, which is to be found by searching in early Christian documents of divers kinds. Not a few investigators have traversed some portions of the ground before me, and I feel conscious of having profited by their labours, but to what extent I find it difficult to say. Excepting in the chapter on the Catacombs, I have not taken anything of importance directly from them, but have endeavoured, however imperfectly, to work the matter out for myself. In this one instance

I could not have done otherwise; and I wish to acknowledge in the fullest manner my obligations to De-Rossi for his truly magnificent work, entitled *Inscriptiones Christianæ urbis Romæ septimo sæculo antiquiores*. Some few of the epitaphs have been copied from the last book of Dr. Northcote, who deserves the thanks of English readers for placing within their reach so much of the substance of De-Rossi's writings.

With Archbishop Usher's *Answers to a Jesuit*, and Bishop Forbes' *Considerationes Modestæ*, I have long been familiar, and feel that at some time or other their works have been very helpful in directing me to Patristic Treatises where the subject is treated of.

Dr. Lee in his *Christian Doctrine of Prayer for the Departed* has dealt with one part of the subject, and in a somewhat similar manner, but I have not availed myself, except in some unimportant particulars, of the fruit of his labours.

I have received valuable aid from Dr. Schiller-Szinessy, by conversations with whom I have been enabled to enter in a measure into the real state of Jewish feeling respecting the dead. My thanks are due to the Rev. H. B. Swete for assistance in revising the proof-sheets, and for making many useful suggestions and criticisms. For the translations generally I am myself responsible.

It only remains now that I should send forth this book, upon gathering materials for which I have spent much thought and care, with the humble prayer that the Spirit of truth will regulate its influence upon the hearts of those who read it according as its teaching may be found agreeable to the mind of Christ.

And while to me belongs the reproach of failure or incompleteness, to Him be all the praise.

H. M. L.

The Feast of S. Michael and All Angels, 1879.
　　COLLEGE, ELY.

Preface to the Second Edition.

THE speedy demand for a second edition proves that the interest in all subjects connected with the state of the soul after death continues to be felt with unabated force. Numerous private communications received from friends and strangers have made me realise more and more the existence of a wide-spread longing for a fuller recognition in our Public Services of the doctrine of the Communion of Saints. As this edition is being issued before anything like a general criticism has been brought to bear on the arguments, I send it forth without any material change. I have, however, slightly supplemented the Jewish testimony, and endeavoured to vindicate the relevancy of certain Jewish inscriptions, which one reviewer deemed wholly beside the purpose.

H. M. L.

The Feast of the Purification, 1880,
COLLEGE, ELY.

TABLE OF CONTENTS.

PART I.

THE STATE OF THE FAITHFUL DEAD AND THE GOOD OFFICES OF THE LIVING IN THEIR BEHALF.

		PAGE
I.	The Test of Catholicity,	3
II.	The Value of the Testimony of the Primitive Fathers,	17
III.	The Intermediate State,	26
IV.	Change in the Intermediate State,	36
V.	Prayers for the Dead: Reasons for Our Lord's Silence on the Subject,	50
VI.	The Testimony of Holy Scripture,	67
VII.	The Testimony of the Catacombs,	81
VIII.	The Testimony of the Early Fathers,	98
IX.	The Testimony of the Primitive Liturgies,	103
X.	Prayers for the Pardon of Sins of Infirmity, and the Effacement of Sinful Stains,	117
XI.	The Inefficacy of Prayer for those who died in wilful unrepented sin,	127

PART II.

THE GOOD OFFICES OF THE FAITHFUL DEAD IN BEHALF OF THE LIVING.

	PAGE
I. Primitive Testimony to the Intercession of the Saints,	153
II. Primitive Testimony to the Invocation of the Saints,	174
III. The trustworthiness of the Patristic evidence for invocation tested,	185
IV. The Primitive Liturgies and the Roman Catacombs,	198
V. Patristic opinions on the extent of the knowledge possessed by the Saints,	204
VI. The Testimony of Holy Scripture upon the same Subject,	212
VII. The Beatific Vision not yet attained by any of the Saints,	219
VIII. Conclusions drawn from the foregoing Testimony,	228

SUPPLEMENTARY CHAPTERS.

	PAGE
A. Is a fuller recognition of the Practice of praying for the Dead desirable or not?	236
B. Is it lawful or desirable to practise Invocation of Saints in any form or not?	255
Table of Fathers, Councils, etc.,	261
Passages of Scriptures explained or quoted,	264
General Index,	265

PART I.

THE STATE OF THE FAITHFUL DEAD AND THE GOOD OFFICES OF THE LIVING IN THEIR BEHALF.

A

CHAPTER I.

The test of Catholicity.

CHURCHMEN in this generation are no longer satisfied with relegating the title of "Catholic" to the Creeds, and desire to vindicate their right to the use of it in common speech and conversation. It is quite time, they think, to put an end to that improper restriction of the term which the long Protestant ascendency not only tolerated but encouraged, which even the authority of the State did its best to stereotype, by designating a Bill for the abolition of disabilities affecting one section of the Church merely, "the Catholic Emancipation Act." "Catholic teaching," "Catholic opinion," "Catholic usages," bid fair soon to become familiar as household words amongst us; but in this praiseworthy endeavour to reclaim that of which the Church can disinherit herself only with positive harm and loss, there is need of caution lest the term be again misapplied, in some cases even so

The Catholic Revival.

narrowed as to be synonymous with what after all may turn out to be Occidental only.

The need of a recognised test. Some recognised test of Catholicity is urgently called for. Doctrines and usages, of which our forefathers for several generations were in many cases entirely ignorant, have obtained, or are likely to obtain, prominent places, both in public worship and in private devotion. For our guidance in their acceptance or rejection, especially in private, where so little restraint can be exercised from without, some guarantee that they bear the stamp of Catholic antiquity is absolutely indispensable.

Changes brought about by the Reformation. In that great revolution of Church teaching which the sixteenth century witnessed, the changes which took place were generally speaking of three kinds: some doctrines were openly and authoritatively condemned; others, together with the forms in which they found expression, were discarded from public worship on grounds of expediency; while a third class, though not formally forbidden, fell into disfavour and went out of use in the general neglect which ensued.

How far are we justified in revising the acts of the Church at that period in any or all of these cases?

Under the first head it may be possible to find

instances where in the heat of controversy the foreign Reformers transgressed the bounds of sober judgment; and in any revision of the Liturgy or Formularies of Faith hereafter to be taken in hand, such cases would very naturally be brought under consideration, and possibly some of their decisions may be reversed. But till that time arrive and the work be lawfully undertaken, it is obviously our wisdom, as well as our duty, to wait with patience. And the same may to a great extent be said also of the second kind. Nothing which has been removed with the full sanction of the Church, may be reintroduced without the approval of the same authority; but this holds good only for public worship. Under altered circumstances individuals are at perfect liberty, without any sacrifice of loyalty to the Church, to use forms for private edification, which were once proscribed as unsuited for public purposes, even though their discontinuance in the Church did lead to almost absolute disuse in the closet.

With regard to the third class of changes, a return to Pre-Reformation rule and practice is in many things "much to be wished," but, if the restoration is to deserve our confidence, nothing will be restored till it has been subjected to some rigid test and standard of Catholicity.

The term Catholicity we apply to the doctrines and constitution of the Church which were recognised by the Council of Nicæa and the three General Councils which followed. The criterion which has commended itself to the leaders of the Church in almost every age of her history is the Vincentian Canon. Everything must be brought to the test of acceptance in the undivided Church, because the power of interpreting and defining can only be exercised by a church at unity in itself. Divided and rent into portions she loses authority as she loses universality. Henceforward each Church has doctrines of its own; as Jeremy Taylor quaintly writes, "The Catholic Church hath been used as the man upon a hill used his heap of heads in a basket; when he threw them down the hill, every head ran his own way, *quot capita tot sententiæ*."[1]

For this reason in the following pages we confine ourselves to the testimony of the Church up to the Council of Chalcedon, the last occasion upon which her united voice was uttered with authority. Vincentius maintained that in judging of heresy the best exponent of the Church's views was an Œcumenical Council, but in cases where the controverted doctrine had not come under the cognisance of such

[1] Serm. xi. : "The Minister's Duty in Life and Doctrine."

an Assembly, recourse must be had to the concordant testimonies of many and great doctors; and the exact test which he proposed for acceptance he describes in these words: "Within the Catholic Church itself we must take great care, that we hold that which has been believed everywhere, always, and by all men. For that is truly and properly Catholic. And this we shall do if we follow universality, antiquity, consent. Now we shall follow universality in this way, if we profess that one faith to be true which the whole Church acknowledges throughout the world: so also antiquity, if we do not depart in any wise from those views which it is plain that our holy elders and fathers held; consent again, if in this very antiquity we follow the definitions and opinions of all or at least almost all the priests and doctors together."[1]

Vincentius' exposition of his Canon.

How far are we prepared to admit the validity

[1] "In ipsa autem Catholica Ecclesia magnopere curandum est, ut id teneamus quod ubique quod semper quod ab omnibus creditum est. Hoc est etenim vere proprieque catholicum. Sed hoc ita demum fiet si sequamur universitatem, antiquitatem, consensionem. Sequemur autem universitatem hoc modo, si hanc unam fidem veram esse fateamur, quam tota, per orbem terrarum confitetur Ecclesia: antiquitatem vero ita, si ab his sensibus nullatenus recedamus quos sanctos majores ac fratres nostros celebrasse manifestum est: consensionem quoque itidem, si in ipsa vetustate omnium vel certe pœne omnium sacerdotum pariter et magistrorum definitiones sententiasque sectemur."
  VINC. *Commonit.* ii. *ad fin.*

The value of the test.

of the Vincentian test? Its value, it is well known, has been disputed in our own as in past generations. Beautiful as it seems in theory, it has been found in application beset with difficulty; some have gone so far as to maintain that for all practical purposes it is little more than useless. It has been disparaged

Its supposed encroachment on the authority of Scripture.

chiefly on the ground that it is superfluous, because there can be only one true test of Catholic doctrine, that is, the authority of Holy Scripture. It is expressly said that the sum of that which Christians were called upon to believe was revealed once for all. "𝕮𝖔𝖓𝖙𝖊𝖓𝖉," said S. Jude, "𝖋𝖔𝖗 𝖙𝖍𝖊 𝖋𝖆𝖎𝖙𝖍 𝖔𝖓𝖈𝖊 𝖉𝖊𝖑𝖎𝖛𝖊𝖗𝖊𝖉 𝖚𝖓𝖙𝖔 𝖙𝖍𝖊 𝖘𝖆𝖎𝖓𝖙𝖘."[1] That implied that nothing could be added to that which the Holy Spirit had made known to the Apostles and Evangelists and holy men of that and former generations. To attempt, therefore, as Vincentius did, to set up, as a joint standard of orthodoxy, the authority of the Doctors and Fathers of a later age, is necessarily to detract from the sufficiency of the complete and final revelation of Holy Writ. But the author of the Canon was no less jealous for the supreme honour and authority of God's Word: "it is perfect," he says, "and most abundantly sufficient of itself for all things;" but with all its rich stores of information

---

[1] Ep. of S. Jude, 3.

and resources for every emergency of doubt and difficulty, something was needed from without to render them available. Experience had taught him that its language was so far from being self-interpreting, that it was confessedly hard to be understood, and in the absence of authoritative explanation the word of truth might be, too often had been, wrested and appealed to in support of heresy and falsehood.

The revelation of God's will to man, if complete, contained within its pages all that he would ever want to enable him to live well and believe rightly, there was no undeveloped need ever after to be felt by the soul of the faithful, which might not be supplied out of its fulness; there was no possible assault ever to be made upon the Truth, for which weapons of defence would not be found stored somewhere in the armoury of Scripture; but it was left to time and circumstance to draw out the consolatory teaching, and to formulate the principles of the Faith. Had the construction of the Creeds followed immediately upon the gift of Revelation, and had the inspired writers themselves, who indited the Scriptures, defined also the articles of faith, such a rule as that which we are considering could have had no part in the settlement. But their growth was gradual; and as each new definition was called for, some test of general application for the right interpretation of the grounds of belief was found absolutely necessary.

From the beginning the Church was the keeper of Holy Writ, and therefore the rightful exponent of its teaching. Christ had promised that the powers of evil would be ineffectual for its destruction, "the gates of hell shall not prevail against it." But after the Church became scattered throughout the world, there being no one recognised episcopal see or central government to appeal to, the voices of the separate individual communities had to be collected together to constitute "the majestic evidence" of the universal voice of the Church Catholic, to which the Holy Spirit had been vouchsafed to "guide" it "into all truth."

Methods of ascertaining the voice of the Church.

There were two ways in which this *vox universa* made itself heard: either authoritatively and formally by the Church assembled in Council, and passing decrees after full deliberation and open discussion; or else failing this, its utterances might be gathered, less convincingly perhaps, but yet in a manner worthy of confidence, out of the written opinions of the representatives of the Church at large. The results, however, of this twofold method of ascertaining the voice and mind of the Church are not exactly the same. In the one case the decisions arrived at are loyally accepted by the whole body as binding upon all: in the other, they deserve, though they may not always receive, the respect and assent of the individual to whom they have become known.

We may illustrate this by two articles of belief of different kinds, which have been formulated and accepted in the ways we have described. The first, the doctrine of the Trinity in Unity. The second, the existence of a bond of union between all the members of Christ's Church. *[Illustrations from the Creeds.]*

When in the second and third centuries heresies were broached touching the Godhead of Jesus Christ, and His consubstantiality with the Father, the great Doctors of the Church betook themselves to a thorough and exhaustive study of God's Word for the further confirmation of the belief, which had gained common acceptance without having been authoritatively enunciated, and imposed as necessary to salvation. It was nowhere in its fulness declared *totidem verbis*, and for such an investigation time and care were requisite; misunderstood passages had to be adjusted, contradictory statements to be reconciled, and it was only after these considerations had occupied the thoughts and labours *[The Godhead of Jesus Christ.]*

of the godly and learned of several generations, that the results were embodied in the Nicene and the so-called[1] Constantinopolitan Creeds.

The principles which guided the Councils in these deliberations, and directed their decisions, were strictly Vincentian.[2] They did not take the Holy Scriptures alone and unsupported, but had recourse to tradition. They asserted, without any hesitation, that the doctrines which they enforced were such as they had received from their predecessors, as they in their turn had received from theirs, and so on by unbroken tradition till they reached their fountainhead in the preaching of the Apostles. In short, the interpretations which they put forth under their official seal were such as could claim the support of universality, antiquity, and consent.

The Communion of Saints.

Take again the doctrine of the Communion of Saints; it was introduced into the Formulary, not to counteract evil tendencies, nor as an antidote to some acknowledged heresy,[3] but simply for the

---

[1] It is now believed that the Second Council did not put forth any Creed of its own.

[2] At Nicæa, for instance, they appealed to the ἐκκλησιαστικὴ πίστις, by which they meant the faith as interpreted by tradition. Cf. S. ATHANAS. *de Decr. Nic. Synod.* iii. 1, 210, ed. Bened.; cf. also *Conc. Chalced.* Act ii.

[3] "It was not," writes DR. LUMBY, "against heretical opinions that the clauses were enlarged. The only sentence in a Western Creed that was inserted as a safeguard against heresy soon died

comfort and encouragement of the faithful. There can be no question that it had no place in the original form[1] of the Apostles' Creed, or in fact in any of those forms which were extant before the middle of the fifth century. Few, however, would venture to deny that it was lodged in the hearts of men. They found the groundwork of it laid in Scripture, and many individuals professed their belief in it, but as nothing as yet had called for an explicit declaration, no distinct

away, even from the Creed of the Church which employed it. This was the 'invisible and impassible' of the Aquileian Symbol, which was never widely adopted, and which soon fell out of use in Aquileia. This is very strong testimony to the truth of those statements on which Western writers lay such stress, that the Western Church was free from the taint of heresy for a long period."—*Hist. of the Creeds*, cap. iii. p. 173.

[1] The form of the Western Creed in use for the first three centuries was much briefer than that now called the Apostles' Creed. Articles were added to it during the fourth and fifth, but it was not developed into its present form till the sixth or perhaps the seventh.

The article *communionem sanctorum* is absent from all the following Latin Creeds,—the Creeds of S. Irenæus, Tertullian, Cyprian, the Aquileian as expounded by Ruffinus, that of Northern Africa as expounded by S. Augustine, and that which is gathered out of the sermons of Chrysologus. Likewise it is wanting in the Greek Creeds of Eusebius, Arius, Epiphanius, Cyril, Chrysostom, and the Councils of Constantinople and Ephesus.

The first occurrence of the article is in a creed attributed to Eusebius Gallus in the middle of the sixth century, though it has been given by some to Faustus, of the province of Arles about 490 A.D. After this it is found again in the Gallican Sacramentary. Cf. Dr. Swainson, *The Nicene and Apostolic Creeds*, cap. xiv., and Dr. Lumby, *Hist. of the Creeds*, cap. iii. and Appendix

authoritative assertion of the principle was put forth; at last, though at what definite time, and under what special emergency, we are left in ignorance, the prevailing ideas and persuasions were consolidated, and the article, "I believe in the Communion of Saints," gained admission into the Creed. But how are we to ascertain exactly what is involved in the confession? The Church has, no doubt, for wise purposes, left it vague and indefinite; but if we would realise the nature and extent of the Communion, and determine how much may be legitimately held, we can only satisfy ourselves by the application of some such test as must have been brought into use when the formula itself was accepted and put forth. We cannot but suppose that there was something more definite than appears in the minds of those who authorised it; but what it was, and how much they comprehended under the general form, which they were satisfied to impose as binding, must be determined by such principles as Vincentius enforced.

Roman Catholic objections to it as opposed to their doctrine of development.

But while the Protestant disparages the Vincentian Canon as tending to lower the authority of Scripture, it is rejected by the Roman Catholic on grounds totally different. It is incompatible with his system of doctrinal development, and therefore must be discarded. Dr. Newman, in rejecting its validity, tries to prove that the gradual growth in the Creeds of primitive times was analogous to the development of dogma, which is still going on in the Roman Church. There is, however, a very essential difference between them. The development which led to the formation of the Catholic Creeds is of one kind; that which is still in process in the formation of the Roman is of another. Without entering at all fully upon such a wide field of discussion, it may be well to state briefly wherein the difference lies. On one side the revelation of doctrine delivered to the Apostles is held to be final: in substance nothing can ever be added to the "faith once delivered to the saints;" but by way of explanation and interpretation additions continued to be made till the articles of belief were authoritatively fixed and defined in the Primitive Creeds. In other words, the doctrine of the fourth and fifth centuries is identically the same with that of the first, and if circumstances had been such as to have led the earliest Christians to fathom the full meaning of Scripture, they would have found in it all that the Nicene or Ephesian Fathers declared to be there.[1]

The difference between development of interpretation and development of doctrine.

---

[1] This is very clearly brought out by Vincentius in a chapter on the growth of doctrine: "Let the religion of our souls imitate

On the other side it is claimed that the body of doctrine committed to the Apostles is capable of positive substantial augmentation, that in short it would have been quite impossible for the Church in its infancy, without the gift of præternatural foresight, to have discerned all that she would hold in her youth or maturity; a theory, which it is very difficult to reconcile with the practical teaching of S. Paul and S. Jude that the revelation given by God in the beginning was final and complete.

the nature of our bodies, which, although with process of time they develop and unfold their proportions, yet they remain the same that they were. There is great difference between the flower of youth and the ripeness of age, yet the same men become old, which before were young, so that although the stage and condition of one and the same man be altered, yet one and the same nature, one and the same person doth still remain. . . . This is the due and right rule of training."

And he concludes his observation thus: "What hath the Church at any time attempted by the decrees of Councils, but that what before was simply credited, the same afterwards should be more diligently believed: that what before was more lazily preached, should afterwards be preached more instantly. that what before was more securely reverenced, should afterward be more carefully cherished? This I say and nothing else, the Church, provoked by the novelties of heretics, hath effected by the decrees of her Councils, only to confirm to posterity in writing, and with her sign-manual, that which before she had received of her forefathers by tradition alone."—*Commonit.* xxiii.

CHAPTER II.

The Value of the Testimony of the Primitive Fathers.

IN the application of the standard proposed, recourse may be had to several kinds of evidence, but the great bulk of it must be drawn from the writings of the Primitive Fathers; it will be well, therefore, to consider briefly whether the objections, which have been raised on the ground of their liability to error, are sufficient to shake our confidence in the general trustworthiness of their testimony.

There are two ways in which they may be used; either simply as so many chroniclers of what was passing around them, each one of them contributing from the scattered Churches of Christendom his individual testimony to the state of opinion faith and practice prevalent at the time and place in which he lived, or else they may be treated as independent exponents of God's Word, and by

[marginal note: Independent Chroniclers of prevailing opinions.]

Contributors to the formation of doctrines. virtue of their position in the Church, as judges of dogma claiming respect, if not even more than this for their decisions. In either case anything like unanimity of expression, in regard to any particular article of belief, will carry conviction of its general acceptance; but in the latter, its validity cannot but be affected by the character for trustworthiness, which they may have gained by their life and labours: for they had no such promise of divine guidance as was vouchsafed to the Apostles, and there is no question that individually some of them held erroneous views.

Instances of erroneous teaching in the works of the Fathers. Justin Martyr, for example, was a Millenarian; he held that before the final resurrection and judgment, Jerusalem should be rebuilt, and that certain saints should dwell in it for a thousand years.

Tertullian was a Montanist, and lost all power of discriminating between true and false prophecy.

Origen broached opinions both on discipline and doctrine, which have met with universal condemnation; he tried to blend Platonism with Christianity, and advocated a belief in the præ-existence of souls, while in his interpretation of some parts of Scripture he ran riot in all the extravagancies of allegory.

Eusebius was denounced for Arianising. S. Jerome

drew upon himself the censures of S. Augustine, and S. Augustine in his Retractations confesses with sorrow to having written some things that were false.

How then will the knowledge of all this fallibility influence us in our estimate of their authority in matters of faith? We must be careful not to depreciate all antiquity because of the errors of a few, and involve all in a sweeping charge of untrustworthiness, because in some instances our confidence has been shaken. *The influence of their errors upon our estimate.*

Those whose views were erroneous are well known, as well as the exact points where they went astray. Here none will wish to follow them; but upon matters wholly independent of and unconcerned with these, there is nothing to prevent their evidence being taken. Even here, however, it must be expected that the arguments which they may have used will lose something of their cogency from the admitted failure of their judgment elsewhere.

But when we read the works of those whose orthodoxy is above suspicion, we shall not merely welcome them for the testimony which they bear to the prevalence of the doctrines upon which they treat, but we shall esteem them also for the part which they took in helping to develop and enunciate the same.

As witnesses then testifying to the state of feeling and belief when they lived, all are valuable, and whenever a *consensus* of opinion is found, their united testimony is irresistible as far as general acceptance is concerned.

As authoritative exponents of the Faith, their claims must rest in each individual case upon the estimate which they have won for themselves in the judgment of the Church. What this is, in by far the majority of cases, is made sufficiently clear in her public formularies, and by the utterances of her chief ministers.

In reviewing these we pass over the testimony of the General Councils, which is unquestionable, and turn to the records of the Reformed Church.

The weight of their authority recognised in the Prayer-Book. In the explanatory introduction to the Prayer-Book "Concerning the Service of the Church," we read at the beginning the first distinct avowal of the respect in which the Reformers held the authority of the Fathers: "The first original and ground whereof [*i.e.* of Divine Service], if a man would search out by the ancient Fathers, he shall find, that the same was not ordained but of a good purpose, and for a great advancement of godliness." A little later it describes how "this godly and decent order of the ancient Fathers hath been altered, broken, and neglected," and it concludes by commending the new rules for prayer and the reading of the Holy Scripture, not only on the ground of profit and convenience, but as "much agreeable to the mind and purpose of the old Fathers."

Here then the Church has clearly laid down, in the forefront of her Reformed Service, the principle by which she determined to be guided; and a few years later, in her Canons of 1571, she expressly enjoined her clergy to follow on the same lines: that they should "never teach aught in a sermon to be religiously held and believed by the people, but what is agreeable to the doctrine of the Old and New Testaments, and which the Catholic Fathers and ancient Bishops have collected from that very doctrine."[1]

In the Ecclesiastical Canons.

And not only here, but also in the Canons of 1604, the principle is recognised, and that repeatedly. In Canon xxx., touching the use of the sign of the Cross, it is asserted to have been "held by the Primitive Church, as well by the Greeks as the Latins," and certain rules of doctrine concerning things indifferent are pronounced true, "which are consonant to the Word of God and the judgment of the ancient

---

[1] WILKINS, *Concilia*, iv. 267, "De concionatoribus." These Canons are not held to be binding, as not having received the formal sanction of the Queen, but they were approved by Convocation, and may be held to express the mind of the Church.

Fathers." In Canon XXXI. the Fasts of Embertide are enjoined as a following of "their holy and religious example." And the next Canon forbids any one to be admitted to Holy Orders who has not a definite sphere for the exercise of his functions, on the ground that it had been so "provided by many decrees of the ancient Fathers."

Book of Homilies.

To mention one more authority,—the Book of Homilies, prepared for the instruction of the people, and recommended in the Articles for the excellence of its teaching: if it bears one characteristic more strongly marked than another, it is the oft-recurring appeal to "the learned and godly doctors" of the Primitive Church.[1]

And we find corroborative evidence in the private utterances of the leading Bishops and divines.

In the works and confessions of the Reformers.

Cranmer protests that he had never any other intention "but purely and simply to imitate and teach those things only which he had learned of the sacred Scriptures and of the holy Catholic Church of Christ from the beginning, and also according to the exposition of the most holy and learned Fathers and Martyrs of the Church," and that it was his earnest

---

[1] The Homilies contain numerous quotations from almost every Father, and the greatest deference is claimed for their authority. Expressions of respect and admiration for the voice of antiquity meet us wherever we turn.

wish to "use the same words that they used, and not use any other words, but to set his hand to all and singular their speeches phrases ways and forms of speech, which they do use in their treatises upon the Sacrament, and to keep still their interpretation."[1]

Many illustrations of the same kind might be drawn from the writings of Jewel; let one suffice.

In his Defence of the Apology which had been called forth by the strictures of Harding, he writes: "In like sort do we also this day allege against you the manifest and undoubted and agreeable judgments of the most ancient learned holy Fathers, and thereby, as by approved and faithful witnesses, we disclose the infinite follies and errors of your doctrine."[2]

In most of the seventeenth-century divines the same high appreciation of Patristic authority is manifest. Beveridge says, "We may rightly conclude that all, both separate works of individual Fathers and acts and monuments of Synods, as well provincial as universal, which exist at this day, are in the first place of this very great and remarkable use to us: that from them we may consider it made out with certainty what the universal Church hath

In leading Anglican Divines since the Reformation.

[1] CRANMER's *Works*, vol. iv. pp. 126-7: "Appeal and Confession of his Faith at S. Mary's."
[2] i. ix.

ever believed and openly taught as necessary articles of faith and rites ecclesiastical, and therefore what is to be ever believed and taught in the Church." [1]

Bramhall in his Replication to the Bishop of Chalcedon's Survey writes: "I submit myself and my poor endeavours first to the judgment of the Catholic Œcumenical essential Church, which if of late days some have endeavoured to hiss out of the schools as a fancy, I cannot help it. From the beginning it was not so. . . . I do implicitly, and in the preparation of my mind, submit myself to the true Catholic Church, the spouse of Christ, the mother of saints, the pillar of truth. My adherence is firmer to the infallible rule of faith, that is the Holy Scriptures interpreted by the Catholic Church, than to mine own judgment or opinions." [2]

The last quotation which we make is from one whose profound studies made him familiar with the literature of preceding ages, and enabled him to form a sound judgment upon the value of what he read. And this is his verdict on the authority of Patristic teaching:—"We allege not Fathers as

---

[1] Preface to *Codex Canonum Ecclesiæ Universalis vindicatus*, COTEL. vol. ii.

[2] Preface to Replication. To the above names might be added Ussher, Hall, Cosin, Bull, and others.

grounds or principles or foundations of our faith, but as witnesses, and as interpreters, and faithful conveyers."[1]

Having now established the claim of the Fathers to be heard, before we proceed to the direct application of the Vincentian test to the doctrines with which we are dealing, it will be well to consider some questions connected with the intermediate state in which the soul remains between death and the resurrection.

[1] *On the Use and Value of Ecclesiastical Antiquity.*—WATERLAND, vol. iii. p. 653; ed. Oxford, 1856.

CHAPTER III.

The Intermediate State.

The teaching of the parable of Dives and Lazarus based on substantial truth.

IT has long been a matter of dispute how far we are justified in using the passage of Scripture familiarly known as the parable of Dives and Lazarus to establish or illustrate the doctrine of the Intermediate State.

"Parables," it is said, "may not be made primary sources and seats of doctrine," and we should hesitate to construct a belief out of parabolical teaching, if it derived no support from other quarters.

But we must not overlook the fact that in the case before us there are points in the story which distinguish it from the ordinary parable. Indeed they were felt in the early Church[1] to be so marked, that there was a general concurrence of opinion in favour of its historical character. The etymological

---

[1] "Plenissime autem Dominus docuit . . . in ea enarratione quae scribitur de Divite et Lazaro."—IREN. *adv. Haer.* ii. 62.

"Quid illic Lazari nomen, si non in veritate res est? sed etsi imago credenda est, testimonium erit veritatis."—TERTULL. *de Anima*, vii.

τοῦ πλουσίου καὶ τοῦ Λαζάρου καὶ τῶν ἑκατέροις συμβάντων

meaning of the name Lazarus[1] has been regarded as an obvious impediment to imagining it to be a true history; but though its peculiar appropriateness does create some suspicion in the mind, it is rather bold to speak positively in the face of the well-known fact that, in one or other of its forms, it was one of the commonest[2] names in vogue at the time. It is worthy also of note that one[3] of the Fathers seems to have drawn the very opposite

ἱστορία.—CHRYS., De Laz. i., vol. v. ἀπόβλεπε πρὸς τὸν Λάζαρον τὸν λαμπρότατον.—De Lazaro et Divite Tract. vol. vi. ed. Paris.

But in several places he also designates it παραβολή.

ἐστὶ τοίνυν παραβολῆς τρόπος ἀστείως ἐσχηματισμένος, τά τε ἐπὶ τῷ πλουσίῳ καὶ τῷ Λαζάρῳ εἰρημένα παρὰ Χριστοῦ. ἔχει δὲ ὁ λόγος ὡς τῶν Ἑβραίων ἔφη παράδοσις, Λάζαρον εἶναί τινα κατ' ἐκείνου καιροῦ ἐν τοῖς Ἱεροσολύμοις.—S. CYRIL, adv. Anthropomorph. xvi.

It is not clear what opinion Augustine held, but the following passages may be consulted:—*Euodio Epist.* xcix. ; *De Civitate Dei*, xxi. 10 ; *Quæst. Evang.* xxxviii. ; *De Verbis Dom.* Serm. xxiv.

[1] In Dindorf's Index to the works of Josephus there are no less than twenty-three Eleazars enumerated. Mentioned by Trench *in loc.*

[2] Its etymology has been held to be doubtful. It has been regarded by some as an abbreviated form of אֱלִיעֶזֶר "my GOD is (my) help," but the punctuation is against this, cf. Exod. xviii. 4. Others have maintained that it is from לֹא עֵזֶר, ἀβοήθητος, helpless. But it is simply the equivalent of the Palestinian לְעָזָר, which is for אֶלְעָזָר, cf. MISHNAH, *Berach.* i. 8.

[3] "Narratio magis quam parabola videtur quando etiam nomen exprimitur."—S. AMBROSE, *Expos. Luc.*, lib. viii. 13.

And so Tertullian, at least as an alternative, cf. p. 26.

conclusion from the introduction of a name at all, and several of them call attention to the circumstance as unsuited to a parable.

But even admitting its parabolical character, and knowing that parables do frequently contain unrealities, are we compelled to allow the same of this?

Was there any necessity, was there any likelihood, that He, Who knew perfectly "the fitness of things and their correspondencies," would fall back upon pure fiction for the inculcation of truth? In our weakness and want of experience we can hardly do otherwise when we speak parables; but there is no evidence that anything which He taught, Who was Himself the Truth, in doctrine or in illustration of doctrine, was other than absolutely true.[1]

How much of the language is figurative. There are parts of the narrative which must be interpreted figuratively.[2] All that is said, for instance, of the tongue of the rich man, the finger of the beggar, the tormenting thirst, the cooling water, and the colloquies between the lost and the

---

[1] This is worked out at length in a chapter on "The spirit world" in *Out of the Body*, by J. S. POLLOCK, to whom I am indebted for the reference to Stier's *Reden Jesu* on this subject.

[2] "Quomodo intelligenda sit illa flamma inferni, ille sinus Abrahæ, illa lingua divitis, ille digitus pauperis, illa sitis tormenti, illa stilla refrigerii vix fortasse a mansuete quærentibus, a contentioso autem certantibus nunquam, invenitur."—S. AUGUST. *de Gen. ad Lit.* viii. 6.

saved,—such modes of expression find an exact parallel in those numerous passages in which God, Who is a Spirit, in condescension to finite intelligences, applies to Himself the parts and passions of a man.

While, then, admitting that the literal interpretation of details must be rejected, we hold that its whole teaching is based on substantial truth, and that the following deductions are of the very essence of Christ's doctrine :—That the souls of the departed, in the intermediate state, are possessed of consciousness, memory, and sensibility to pain and pleasure; that the life of all men, whether good or bad, is continued without interruption after the separation of soul and body; and that retribution commences between death and the judgment. And all of these conclusions are in direct antagonism to the theory that the soul falls asleep when the body dies, and will not awake again till the resurrection of the dead at the last day.[1]

We pass to the familiar prayer of the thief upon the cross, and our Lord's reply. By perhaps the highest act of faith recorded in the Bible the dying

The thief upon the cross.

---

[1] "The souls of them that depart this life do neither die with the bodies nor sleep idly. They which say that the souls of such as depart hence do sleep, being without all sense, feeling, or perceiving, until the day of judgment . . . . do utterly dissent from the right belief declared to us in Holy Scripture."—Cf. *Art. XL. of the Forty-two Articles put forth in the reign of Edward VI*

thief is carried in thought away from the scene of shame and dishonour, in which he was taking part, and he sees in the Crucified One some convincing signs of His real Messiahship, and with a far-reaching prayer asks that, as he had shared His misery upon earth, he may not be forgotten in the midst of His coming glory. And what is the answer? His petition is for a reward in the future; but that good confession deserves even a better boon than he sought to obtain, and immediate happiness is promised, even a foretaste of the fruition on that very day—to be with Him, in short, in the Paradise of joy and delight, where He was about to join the souls of the righteous, who were awaiting their perfect consummation and bliss. Would it be at all consistent with right reason,—would it not rather have been a simple evasion of the thief's request,—to have replied as He did, had our Lord known that Paradise was a land of forgetfulness or unconscious sleep? We have only to observe the expedients which they[1] have been driven to adopt, who hold

---

[1] The conversation between Saul and Samuel, whom the witch had called up from the dead, expresses very clearly the Jewish belief in the consciousness of the soul in the Intermediate State. Cf. BAB. TALM. *Berach.*, 1 SAM. xxviii.

The following are examples selected from a representative writer:—

i. σήμερον is to be connected with the words which precede it,

the opposite theory of the soul's sleep in the intermediate state, to satisfy ourselves that the ordinary interpretation alone is to be relied upon.

We have further confirmation, in the language in which S. Paul[1] expresses his ardent longings for that which was to follow. What bright hope was it which cheered him as this earthly vision was fading from his sight? It was the confidence,[2] the unwavering conviction, that so soon as his spirit had shuffled off this mortal coil, he should be "with Christ." But could he have derived consolation from the thought that he should be with

S. Paul's hopes in the prospect of approaching death.

"I say unto you to-day." There is little to determine the proper punctuation of MSS. but the context. This presents no possible reason why our Lord should lay stress upon the time at which He was speaking. The thief had asked for a blessing to take effect at some particular time. The reply states at what time, albeit nearer than was expected, the prayer should be granted.

ii. Our Lord adhered to the time, to which the petition looked, and by σήμερον, or, as it means, τῇδε τῇ ἡμέρᾳ, signified the day of which the thief spoke,—on this you shall be with Me in the Paradise to which you hope to go.

iii. He used the expression in the ordinary acceptation of the word, but as the thief was at the point of death, and seeing that when he died he would fall asleep till the resurrection, he would take up time where he had left it, and the day of Christ's coming would be to him the day of his death, the hand of the dial pointing, as it were, to the hour of his departure,—the end of that old Jewish day, the beginning of that which he would spend with Christ in His kingdom.—CONSTABLE, *Hades*, chap. xxii.

[1] 2 COR. v. 6-8.; PHIL. i. 21-23.
[2] θαρροῦντες πάντοτε καὶ εἰδότες—θαρροῦμεν δὲ καὶ εὐδοκοῦμεν.

Him if he knew at the same time that being with Christ meant nothing more than going where He was, with no hope of realising His presence and communing with His Spirit, which would be an impossibility if, from the very moment of his departure, his soul was bound over to a state of unconscious sleep?

Or again, what possible "gain" could it have been for him "to die," if death were to be but the passing from a realisation of the Divine fellowship, which he already felt and enjoyed so keenly, into an union of place and habitation with the object of his love, in which, no matter how close and immediate, the sleeping spirit could find no satisfaction?

It has been said[1] that the Apostle overleapt the bounds of intervening time and space; that in the intensity of his longing he reached forward to the Resurrection and to his final home with Christ in heaven. This is to suppose that he was forgetful of the fact that he could not enter heaven until his soul should have been united with his risen and glorified body, for he speaks, and that with an emphasised repetition, of absence from the body as a prerequisite for that presence with Christ for which he yearned.

[1] CONSTABLE, *Hades*, chap. xxiii.

The Intermediate State.

The conclusion is forced upon us that it was the conviction of an intermediate state of conscious spiritual fellowship with Christ in paradise which filled him with hope and consolation in the prospect of approaching death.

Additional support is to be found in the well-known passage from S. Peter on the spirits in prison: "For Christ also hath once suffered for sins, the just for the unjust, that He might bring us to God, being put to death in the flesh, but quickened by the spirit: by which also He went and preached unto the spirits in prison."[1]

The descent of Christ's spirit into Hades.

The Apostle here testifies not only to the continuance of the life of Christ's human spirit after death, but to its receiving fresh-added vigour and activity for its disembodied existence.

The authorised version is obviously in error in destroying the reference to Christ's human spirit. It was the spirit of the Man Christ Jesus which went and held converse with the spirits of the men of a former generation in that place of detention and waiting which is common to all during their separation from the body.

Furthermore, it seems to be almost necessary to attach something beyond the common meaning to

[1] 1 S. Peter iii. 18, 19; for further explanation, see page 47.

the "quickening" here spoken of, in order to justify the antithesis "**put to death in the flesh, quickened in the spirit.**" Both are changed: the body from life to death; the spirit from the life which it lived in the flesh to the new powers of vitality and energy which it acquired by its liberation. And in the power of this "quickening," His spirit went down to Hades, not to pass its three days' sojourn in unconscious torpor, but in active intercourse with the spirits which had preceded Him there.

The great difficulty, no doubt, which is felt in accepting these conclusions arises out of man's inability to conceive of the soul existing in a conscious sentient condition independently of bodily organs of sense. The following quotations may lessen the difficulty. Bishop Bull[1] has suggested how the disembodied soul may be able to perceive "by the help of some new subtler organs and instruments fitted to its present state, which either by its own native power given in its creation it forms to itself, or by a special act of the Divine power it is supplied with." Stier[2] also, speaking of a tongue and finger in Hades, says that this is not said "in the sense of perfect corporeity, for that has been put off; it is

---

[1] Serm. iii., Concerning the Middle State of Happiness or Misery.—*Works*, vol. i. p. 52, ed. Burton.

[2] Stier's *Reden Jesu, in loco*, vol. iv. pp. 227, 228, Pope's transl.

not on that account, however, a mere figure, but indicates a certain corresponsive corporeity of the soul with which it is already and essentially invested;" and he explains further on, by a quotation from another writer, how, "in our corporeal life, it is not the eye of the body, properly speaking, which sees, but the soul sees through the eye. It is not the bodily tongue, which speaks and so forth. Thus there exists a spiritual capacity of seeing, hearing, speaking, which may find its operation and act without the organs of the earthly corporeal body."

We may conclude this subject by an appeal to the opinion of S. Paul when he wrote, "I knew a man in Christ above fourteen years ago, (whether in the body, I cannot tell; or whether out of the body, I cannot tell: God knoweth;) such an one caught up to the third heaven. And I knew such a man, (whether in the body, or out of the body, I cannot tell: God knoweth;) how that he was caught up into paradise, and heard unspeakable words, which it is not lawful for a man to utter."[1] It is evident that he believed in the possibility of a disembodied soul possessing faculties of perception, otherwise he could have had no doubts whether it was while in the body or in the spirit that those unearthly sounds had made themselves heard.

[1] 2 Cor. xii. 2-4.

CHAPTER IV.

Change in the Intermediate State.

The progress of sanctification in the disembodied state.

IF it be admitted that the soul exists after death, and is conscious, it seems almost impossible to believe that it remains altogether unchanged.

Conscious life by all analogy involves progress or retrogression, growth or decay.

Now if the soul has not been made perfect in this world, on the supposition that no change passes over it in its disembodied condition, then there is a long period in which the operations of God's Spirit upon it are suspended, and an imperfect soul is left to stagnate in its imperfection.

But is not progress, steadily advancing progress, a very law of God's kingdom? Is it not the principle upon which He has been working from the beginning of the creation in the world around us, and if the God of nature and the God of grace are one, may we not expect a corresponding mode of operation upon the moral character of man?

Look at the long ages which the Almighty spent in perfecting the material world for the use and habitation of the human race. In the light of such a consideration, does it not seem almost a contradiction to suppose that threescore years and ten may suffice for the perfecting of the soul for the Divine Presence? *An analogy from the material world.*

It is quite conceivable that the soul might continue in a state of lethargy without undergoing any change. As it happens sometimes in a long trance that the physical functions are suspended, so it would be with the spiritual. Time would, moreover, to all intents and purposes, be annihilated, and the intermediate state have no apparent duration. It would be, it is said, with the soul as it was in the fable with the seven sleepers at Ephesus.[1] They awoke from a sleep of two hundred years and resumed the thread of being where they had left it suspended. While they had lain wrapt in that mysterious slumber, the earth had changed in all its features, physical and moral, but no change had passed over them, and they were wholly unconscious of the lapse of time. But the comparison fails, because, as we have shown, the soul

---

[1] For a full account of this legend and its wide-spread adoption reference may be made to GIBBON's *Decline and Fall*, chap. xxxiii., and to numerous works on the subject mentioned in the notes.

is not unconscious between death and judgment. It has been said, however, that when the soul leaves the body and passes into the spiritual world, whether sleeping or waking, it knows nothing of time. There is no inspired sanction for the belief that such a condition of things exists in the intermediate state.

The expectation of the souls under the altar. There can be little doubt that it will be set free from all those limits of time which are measured by human calculations, by the numbering of days and weeks, of months and years; indeed it could not be otherwise, but Scripture hints at least at something of a corresponding nature, when it reveals the souls beneath the altar crying "How long!"[1]

So long as the condition of souls is not finally fixed, but some change is contemplated, there must be something of the nature of time. When that for which all creation is groaning, for which the souls in paradise are waiting, for which the souls of martyrs are passionately crying, when all this is come, we can conceive of the ending of time, and we can understand the meaning of the Apocalyptic vision, in which the "angel sware by Him that liveth for ever and ever, who created heaven, and the things that therein are, and the earth, and the things that therein are, and the sea, and the

[1] Rev. vi. 10.

things which are therein, that there should be time no longer."[1]

Let us look at the matter from a slightly different point of view. We are told, on the authority of God's Word, that "anything that defileth"[2] will not be suffered to enter heaven. Now, take the case of a man whose whole life up to his last illness, or it may be till he was actually at the point of death, has been spent in sin, in constant association with evil, in accustoming himself to all that is the very opposite of heaven and heavenly things; suppose that with his dying breath he has sought and obtained pardon, does he require no time to form new habits of holiness, and attune the spiritual life to the harmonies of heaven, so that there shall be no discord or jarring sounds? or does the pardon which he receives wipe out the stain of guilt and infuse

---

[1] REV. x. 6.—This has been interpreted by Corn. a Lapide, Ewald, De Wette, and others, as implying that the appointed delay is at an end (καὶ ἐρρέθη αὐτοῖς ἵνα ἀναπαύσωνται ἔτι χρόνον μικρόν), that there should be no longer any postponement of judgment, except that brief respite in the days of the last angel when he is about to sound his trumpet. If we accept this in place of the ordinary interpretation, as I think we are bound to do, it affords additional evidence that the departed souls are expecting "the fulfilment of the mystery of God," and expectation involves a consciousness of the lapse of time.

[2] REV. xxi. 27.—The reading of the best MSS. is κοινόν, instead of κοινοῦν, but whether it is that which maketh unclean or which is itself unclean, it is equally pertinent.

perfect holiness, as well as release him from punishment? May there not be something here analogous to the remission of sins in Baptism, in which we are taught that pardon is granted when the rite is administered, but the infection of the corrupt nature remains, and is only eradicated by the after-sanctification of the Holy Spirit? Such a question brings us face to face with a theological dispute which has at divers times perplexed and bewildered the Church respecting the proper relationship of justification and sanctification.

The distinction between justification and sanctification.

Anglican Divines[1] hold that the latter differs from the former in that it is a progressive work,—a

---

[1] "Ye are made free from sin and made servants to God; this is the righteousness of justification. Ye have your fruit unto holiness; this is the righteousness of sanctification."—HOOKER, Serm. ii. 6.

"In the progress of a Christian man from his original justification to his final salvation, these several states or conditions of righteousness successively appertain to him.

"First in order comes the forensic righteousness of justification; a righteousness reputatively his through faith, and on account of the perfect meritoriousness of Christ.

"Next in order comes the inherent righteousness of sanctification; a righteousness infused into him by the Holy Spirit after he has been justified.

"And last in order comes the complete righteousness of glorification; a righteousness acquired by him when this corruptible puts on incorruption, and this mortal puts on immortality.

"The first . . . is perfect but not inherent. The second . . . is inherent but not perfect. The third . . . is both perfect and inherent."—FABER, cited in HOOK's *Church Dict.*, Art. "Sanctification."

process begun, it is true, coincidently with it, but requiring to be continued afterwards.

If, then, by reason of death immediately supervening, there is no time allowed after the forgiveness of sins, it follows, either that absolute holiness is not a *sine qua non* for admission to heaven, which is contrary to Scripture, or else that justification is not only remission of sins but sanctification also, which is the doctrine of the Roman Church,[1] and in effect of Calvinists also.[2]

It has been thought[3] that, though sanctification be normally progressive, yet that in some cases it may be instantaneous, as for example with those "which are alive and remain unto the coming of the Lord."[4] When no time has been allowed for the completion of the work in life, God will effect it at the moment of the resurrection. The following passage seems to bear upon the argument: "We shall not all sleep, but we shall all be changed, in a moment,

---

[1] "Justificatio ipsa consequitur quæ non est sola peccatorum remissio sed et sanctificatio et renovatio interioris hominis."— *Concil. Trid.*, Sess. vi. cap. 3.

[2] "Though black as hell, polluted with guilt, defiled with sin, yet in Christ all fair, without spot, fully reconciled to God, and without trespasses before Him."—MASON, *Spiritual Treasury for the Children of God*, vol. i. p. 141 (1779).

[3] This was the view of S. MACARIUS, *Hom.* xxvi. ; *Bibl. Patr. Gallandii*, 7. 29.

[4] 1 THESS. iv. 15.

in the twinkling of an eye, at the last trump."[1] The Apostle is arguing about the resurrection of the body, in which there will certainly be an instantaneous change from death to life, from the death of corruption in which it had lain, to a life of incorruption which will then begin. He says nothing here about any change, instantaneous or other, passing over the soul.

There is, no doubt, a difficulty which suggests itself touching sanctification after death, in cases where the sins have been essentially carnal, in which the body has shared the contamination of the consenting spirit. Is it possible that the sanctification of the soul in its separate state can suffice for both? It may be that an answer is to be found in something of a kindred nature which is constantly going on.

Different sins, we know, are incidental to different stages of life. When a man has passed into the second stage, is it impossible for him to wipe out by repentance[2] the stain of guilt incurred in the first? May not the sorrows of the man atone for the errors of the child, or the tears of old age wash away the impurities of youth and manhood? To put an extreme case of this kind, let us imagine one who

[1] 1 Cor. xv. 51.
[2] "Repentance" here, of course, is spoken of as the "*conditio sine qua non*," not the "*causa efficiens*" of the cleansing.

has spent his early days in unrestrained indulgence, in making his body an instrument of sensual gratification, and then lingers on into decrepit age, till the very ashes of fleshly lust have ceased to smoulder in his veins, till he is practically dead to his former temptations. Should we not hesitate to pronounce his past irretrievable, or to deny the possibility of his wiping out the old stains of defilement by the purification of his soul? It is not easy to draw much distinction between such a case and that of the man whose body, with all the material organs of sense, has been laid in the grave.

There are some well-known texts of Scripture which are often quoted in opposition to the idea of any change in Hades, and as a proof that virtually the day of death rather than the day of judgment is "the last line of things." Most of them, on investigation, will be found to be wholly irrelevant.

The misapplication of texts of Scripture to support the opposite theory.

That most frequently urged is, "𝔴𝔥𝔢𝔯𝔢 𝔱𝔥𝔢 𝔱𝔯𝔢𝔢 𝔣𝔞𝔩𝔩𝔢𝔱𝔥, 𝔱𝔥𝔢𝔯𝔢 𝔦𝔱 𝔰𝔥𝔞𝔩𝔩 𝔟𝔢."[1] The Preacher is describing certain natural phenomena, and pointing out how the powers of nature are regulated by God, and he takes as illustrations the direction of the wind, or the inclination of a falling tree, both of which he implies are beyond the control of man.

[1] ECCLES. xi. 3.

There is not the least hint given, or anything whatever to suggest the likelihood that he employed such figures to teach the unalterable condition of the soul after death.

We cannot but regard with satisfaction the alteration of a verse in a familiar hymn which contributed so much to fix the common application of the words on the popular mind:—

> "As the tree falls, so must it lie:
> As the man lives, so will he die;
> As the man dies, such must he be,
> All through the days of Eternity."[1]

"𝔚hatsoever thy hand findeth to do, do it with thy might; for there is no work, nor device, nor knowledge, nor wisdom, in the grave, whither thou goest."[2]

The writer confines his observations to what he sees in this life, to the works which are carried on "under the sun," and there is no reason to suppose that he referred at all to the mode of existence of the soul in another world. Indeed, considering the general tone of his writing, it would be a manifest over-straining of the meaning of his words to adopt

---

[1] "O by Thy power grant, Lord, that we
At our last hour fall not from Thee;
Saved by Thy grace, Thine may we be
All through the days of eternity."
Hymns Ancient and Modern, 289.

[2] ECCLES. ix. 10.

such a reference. We should hesitate, moreover, under any circumstances, knowing how imperfect the conception of the future was in his age, to consider the inactivity of the disembodied soul proved by any words which he might use.

"The night cometh when no man can work."[1]

It was the reason which our Lord gave for doing works of mercy on the Sabbath-day, when most men rested from their labours. The day was the period of His earthly ministry, the space allotted to Him by the Father for the fulfilment of a special mission; the night was the time when that mission would close. It receives a fuller illustration in a later chapter, when He likens Himself to a traveller walking during those hours of the day in which he has the light to enable him to see the path.

The idea that His words, beyond their immediate application to His own case, had a further reference to the ordinary life-work of each individual, has been imported into them, in all probability, from a false conception that the soul is asleep in the night of death.

"We must all appear before the judgment-seat of Christ; that every one may receive the things done in his body, according to that he hath done, whether it be good or bad."[2]

[1] S. JOHN ix. 4.   [2] 2 COR. v. 10.

If the view set forth in these pages be rightly understood, it will be seen that such a declaration as this in no way militates against the idea of a progressive sanctification of the soul continuing after death. It is not held that the work done by it in the disembodied state will affect the final judgment. That, according to the teaching of Holy Scripture, will depend entirely upon the conduct of the body and soul during the probation of the earthly life, and have no concern with the state in which the after-preparation of the soul for the presence of God is carried to completion.

<small>Passages of Scripture which appear to countenance the theory of a change taking place in Hades.</small>

There are a few passages which, though of uncertain significance, may be set in the opposite scale, and have some counteracting influence.

"And these all, having obtained a good report through faith, received not the promise: God having provided some better thing for us, that they without us should not be made perfect."[1]

It would seem from this that those old saints and martyrs who had died in faith before the Advent, were benefited by something which took place after their death. Their perfection was made dependent upon a later generation. If, therefore, they were capable of such an improvement in their condition

[1] Heb. xi. 39, 40.

as is here indicated, and if, moreover, as the following passage shows, they were conscious of the change, we can hardly apply to them the image of the fallen tree, and if not to them, why to any departed souls?

"𝕮𝖍𝖗𝖎𝖘𝖙 𝖆𝖑𝖘𝖔 𝖍𝖆𝖙𝖍 𝖔𝖓𝖈𝖊 𝖘𝖚𝖋𝖋𝖊𝖗𝖊𝖉 𝖋𝖔𝖗 𝖘𝖎𝖓𝖘, 𝖙𝖍𝖊 𝖏𝖚𝖘𝖙 𝖋𝖔𝖗 𝖙𝖍𝖊 𝖚𝖓𝖏𝖚𝖘𝖙, 𝖙𝖍𝖆𝖙 𝕳𝖊 𝖒𝖎𝖌𝖍𝖙 𝖇𝖗𝖎𝖓𝖌 𝖚𝖘 𝖙𝖔 𝕲𝖔𝖉, 𝖇𝖊𝖎𝖓𝖌 𝖕𝖚𝖙 𝖙𝖔 𝖉𝖊𝖆𝖙𝖍 𝖎𝖓 𝖙𝖍𝖊 𝖋𝖑𝖊𝖘𝖍 𝖇𝖚𝖙 𝖖𝖚𝖎𝖈𝖐𝖊𝖓𝖊𝖉 𝖇𝖞 𝖙𝖍𝖊 𝕾𝖕𝖎𝖗𝖎𝖙, 𝖇𝖞 𝖜𝖍𝖎𝖈𝖍 𝖆𝖑𝖘𝖔 𝕳𝖊 𝖜𝖊𝖓𝖙 𝖆𝖓𝖉 𝖕𝖗𝖊𝖆𝖈𝖍𝖊𝖉 𝖚𝖓𝖙𝖔 𝖙𝖍𝖊 𝖘𝖕𝖎𝖗𝖎𝖙𝖘 𝖎𝖓 𝖕𝖗𝖎𝖘𝖔𝖓."[1]

Whatever disputes have gathered round the interpretation of these words in past times, an unprejudiced reader, aided by the light which modern criticism has thrown upon them, would hardly fail to draw the conclusion[2] that our Lord, in His human spirit, during the time that His body lay in the grave, visited certain disembodied spirits detained somewhere in ward or custody, and that He bore to them intelligence, which they were capable of receiving, and by which their existing condition was ameliorated.[3]

---

[1] 1 S. PETER iii. 18, 19.

[2] That this is the natural *prima facie* interpretation we conclude from the shifts and subterfuges to which men have had recourse in order to avoid it.

[3] "Solvit vincula inferni et piorum animas elevavit."—S. AMBROSE, *de Fid. ad Grat.* iv. 1.

"Ad Tartara ima descendens seras inferni januasque confrin-

"I saw under the altar the souls of them that were slain for the word of God, and for the testimony which they held: and they cried with a loud voice, saying, How long, O Lord, holy and true, dost thou not judge and avenge our blood on them that dwell on the earth?"[1]

Admitting that the language is highly mystical, it nevertheless must be in some way "a figure of the true." Is, then, such looking forward, such ardent longing for the fulfilment of their hopes, compatible with the idea of standing still? Is this cry one long monotonous moan, relieved by no rise and fall, no relaxing energy or intensified eagerness? Such changelessness is contradicted by what follows, for "white robes were given unto every one of them; and it was said unto them, that they should rest yet for a little season."

Again, an argument against the cessation of progress at death may be drawn from the fact that the Apostles set before Christians the coming[2] of the Lord, not the end of life, as the goal towards which they are bidden to strive.

gens vinctas peccato animas mortis damnatione destructa e diaboli faucibus revocavit ad vitam."—S. AMBROSE, *de Myst. Pasch.* 4.

"Descendit ad inferos et destructis clausis Tartari, suos quos ibi reperit eruens, victor ad superos ascendit."—S. HIERON., *In Lamen.* lib. II. c. iii.

[1] REV. vi. 9, 10, 11.   [2] PHIL. i. 6; 1 COR. i. 7, 8.

Change in the Intermediate State. 49

S. Paul[1] writes to his Philippian converts in full confidence that God, Who has inaugurated a good work in their hearts, will carry it on from one stage to another till it arrives at perfect maturity, not in the hour of death, but on the day of Jesus Christ.[2] And to the Corinthians he expresses a thankful assurance that they will be kept firm unto the end, and that such keeping will insure their being found irreproachable at the final test.

[1] It has often been confidently asserted that the Apostle expected the Second Advent in his own lifetime; an admission of which would of course weaken in some degree what has been urged above, because the conviction of the imminence of that day would leave less room for thoughts of an intermediate state between death and judgment. Some of the passages adduced in support of the belief contain casual expressions, such as would not unnaturally fall from the lips of one who had been told that it would come suddenly and unexpectedly. Others admit, perhaps, of the explanation that he spoke in the first person only by $\mu\epsilon\tau\alpha\sigma\chi\eta\mu\alpha\tau\iota\sigma\mu\acute{o}s$ (1 COR. xv. 51; 1 THESS. iv. 17). When called upon to give his deliberative judgment in consequence of opinions held by the Thessalonians, he speaks as though he did not believe the day to be immediately impending (2 THESS. ii. 1-2). It may here be observed on this disputed question, that if it were absolutely certain that the Apostle was mistaken, no argument adverse to the inspiration of his writings generally ought to be drawn from it. Our Lord expressly said that the Father had kept the knowledge of this to Himself (S. MATT. xxiv. 36). This then is an exceptional case, and one in which the claim for inspired knowledge in the Apostle ought not to be set up.

[2] Dr. Newman writes, "It will be found on the whole that death is not the object put forward in Scripture for hope to rest upon, but the coming of Christ, as if the interval between death and His coming was by no means to be omitted in the process of our preparation."—Vol. iii. *Serm.* xxv. ed. 1875.

D

CHAPTER V.

Prayers for the Dead: Reasons for our Lord's Silence on the Subject.

How the principle of intercession runs through the whole Bible.

IF we are justified in the conclusion which we have drawn from the foregoing evidence, that the soul is capable of change after its separation from the body by death, it becomes a deeply interesting question how far, or whether at all, such change may be aided or affected by the intercessions of the living.

There is a recognised principle running through Holy Scripture, and illustrated by the common experience of God's dealings with us, that He has chosen that the destiny of man, for weal or woe, shall be influenced by the conduct of his fellow-men.

We see abundant proofs of this principle in the lives of the most eminent characters of Bible history. Look at its exercise in the intercessory prayers of the Patriarchs: Abraham pleading with God for Sodom; Moses, with his uplifted arms, winning victory for Israel; Job interceding successfully for his friends; and we gather from the prophet

Ezekiel[1] that it is only when wickedness has passed all bounds that the prayers of the faithful prove ineffectual.

The principle is seen in its fullest development in the life of our Lord, when He spent whole nights in prayer, not only communing for Himself with God, but seeking deliverance for those in distress, or when He said to His Apostle, "Simon, Simon, behold, Satan hath desired to have you, that he may sift you as wheat: but I have prayed for thee, that thy faith fail not: and when thou art converted, strengthen thy brethren;"[2] or yet once more when He interceded with His dying breath for the forgiveness of His murderers.

And we hear the echo of His teaching in the manifold injunctions of His Apostles, in S. Paul's appeal to his converts to offer supplication for himself and for all saints, and in his oft-expressed intercessions for them,[3] and in S. James' declaration that to recover the sick, and to obtain forgiveness of his sins, "the effectual fervent prayer of a righteous man availeth much."[4]

[1] Ezek. xiv. 24. [2] S. Luke xxii. 31.
[3] Ephes. vi. 18; Phil. i. 3, 4; Col. i. 3; 1 Thess. i. 2.
[4] S. James, v. 14, 15. ἐνεργουμένη should be rendered "in its working;" to make it equal ἐνεργὴς as the A. V. does, and consider it as an attribute of δέησις, is opposed to N. T. usage, and weakens the force of the Apostle's assertion.

It will be said that all this is not to the point, that it only concerns the living; but our object in recalling such familiar examples is to press home the fact that we are all brethren, and by the bonds of human sympathy and the ties of Christian brotherhood are bound to help one another by prayer. And if the whole body of Christians, both those in the flesh and those out of the flesh, are but one family, then it seems hard to believe that separation by death can interpose a barrier to our intercessions.

But here, if anywhere, of ourselves "we know not what we should pray for as we ought," and we gladly fall back upon the teaching of the Primitive Church, in the confidence that in the freshness of the faith she was better able to understand the mind of Christ than we can be, seeing that the mists of prejudice and error have obscured our vision.

It will be our endeavour, then, to find out, from the writings of antiquity, how far the souls of the departed were considered to come within the range of the prayers of the Church on earth.

Objections to prayers for the dead grounded   Before considering those passages of Holy Scripture which appear to have any bearing upon this question, it will be well to notice briefly the oft-repeated objection that the Great Teacher Himself was silent upon the subject. Assuming for the moment that the statement is correct, how is His silence to be accounted for? Was He silent because, the custom of praying for the dead being unknown, there was nothing to call forth an expression of opinion, or was it that, being known, He gave it His tacit approval? *on the supposed silence of Christ.*

Now, if the practice existed, it could not have been of very long standing, for before the Captivity little was revealed to the ancient people touching the state of the soul after death; and from that time onward their interest in the subject could have been only of slow growth and gradual development. We may not, therefore, draw any adverse conclusions from the absence of reference to it in the Old Testament writings, which for the most part antecede the rise of the doctrine. By the nature of things it could hardly have been otherwise. But in the Apocryphal Books, which to some extent fill up the gap between the close of prophecy, about a century after the return from Captivity, and the beginning of the Christian Era, we have a right to expect some evidence of the belief, if it had taken any hold upon the minds of men. Of course they will not be "applied to establish doctrine," but they may fairly be used as helping to confirm the historical fact of the existence of the belief, without affecting its orthodoxy one way or the other.

<small>The evidence of the second century before Christ.</small>

In this collection of writings there is one mention of the subject, and though it stands alone, it is so emphatic, and is introduced so naturally, that the conclusion is almost forced upon us that, at the period referred to, the habit of praying for the dead had become wide-spread and general.

In the latter part of the Second Book of Maccabees[1] the historian describes some special events in the life of Judas, and, in connection with one of these, we have a positive declaration that prayers were offered for the dead.

"So Judas gathered his host and came into the city of Odollam. And when the seventh day came, they purified themselves, as the custom was, and kept the Sabbath in the same place. And upon the day following, as the use had been, Judas and his company came to take up the bodies of them that were slain, and to bury them with their kinsmen in their fathers' graves.

"Now, under the coats of every one that was slain they found things consecrated to the idols of the Jamnites which is forbidden the Jews by the

---

[1] 2 Macc. xii. 39-end.

law. Then every man saw that this was the cause wherefore they were slain.

"All men therefore praising the Lord, the righteous Judge,

"Who had opened the things that were hid,

"Betook themselves unto prayer, and besought Him that the sin committed might wholly be put out of remembrance. Besides, that noble Judas exhorted the people to keep themselves from sin, forasmuch as they saw before their eyes the things that came to pass for the sins of those that were slain.

"And when he had made a gathering throughout the company to the sum of two thousand drachms of silver, he sent it to Jerusalem to offer a sin-offering, doing therein very well and honestly, in that he was mindful of the resurrection:

"For if he had not hoped that they that were slain should have risen again, it had been superfluous and vain to pray for the dead.

"And also in that he perceived that there was great favour laid up for those that died godly, it was an holy and good thought.

"Whereupon he made a reconciliation for the dead, that they might be delivered from sin."

We shall consider, at a later stage of the inquiry,

whether in this particular case there was not an undue extension of the legitimate purpose of such prayers. Here we only observe that there is nothing in the narrative to lead us to suppose that, in ordering that prayer should be made for his dead countrymen, Judas was doing anything out of the ordinary course; on the contrary, the readiness with which the money for the sin-offering was contributed points to a belief that what he proposed was thought likely to be advantageous to the dead.

The evidence of the Jewish services in commemoration of the dead. There is no more definite evidence which can be appealed to, but it is well known that such prayers are found in many old Jewish services and commemorations. That which is called KADDISH is universally allowed to be of great antiquity. It is composed of several parts, of which the oldest, unquestionably pre-Christian, varies by amplification according to the countries in which it is used and other circumstances. Now although in its original form this contains no direct prayers for the dead, indirect reference to their use is traceable in several portions of it. When the existing prayers were composed and engrafted upon the public service, it is impossible to decide, but there is no doubt that it was at a very early date; and when we reflect that they have been used unhesitatingly by Jewish communities differing from each other as widely as German, French, Italian, Provençal, Spanish, Babylonian, and those of Jemen, the conclusion is forced upon us that the principle had been acted upon in the private devotions of the people not only for some time previously but also to a very wide extent.

In the HASKARATH NESHAMOTH, or "Commemoration of Souls," which is appointed to be said on the Day of Atonement, and the last days of the three chief Festivals, there are distinct prayers for the dead. In his introduction to that used on the former, a learned Jew[1] of our own day throws much light upon the spirit of the Commemoration, addressing the assembled congregation in these words: "Children of the house of Israel! in this life of frailty, where all that is united to us by the strongest bonds to-day, is to-morrow relentlessly torn away—where nothing is permanent except change, nothing constant except instability—it is the greatest comfort to us to have one steadfast pillar—Remembrance. . . . The ancient heathens adorned the graves of their beloved with flowers and wreaths, for they thought that the souls of their beloved were laid in the tomb; they materialised the soul, they were

The intense reality of the Jewish prayers for the dead.

---

[1] *Occasional Prayers, Addresses*, etc., Manchester, 2d ed., 1852, intended as a Manual for young Rabbis, by Dr. S. M. SCHILLER-SZINESSY.

only heathens. But the Jewish religion, which also makes use of symbols, yet not to materialise the spiritual but to spiritualise the material, teaches us to seek the souls of the departed, not in the grave, but in heaven, in the bosom of God the Father of love. Therefore, on the recurrence of such commemorations, Israelites do not strew earthly flowers on the grave, but offer spiritual wreaths to heaven: *they offer prayers to God for the blessedness of the departed.*"

Again, in that for the principal festivals, after dwelling on the beauties and advantages of such services, he bears witness to the intensity of their belief in the words, "look around you and see how bitterly they weep *who are about to pray for the blessedness of their departed ones,*" and calls upon them to join in "the heart-affecting prayer,"[1] "May God remember the soul of my father, my lord, N. the son of M., who is gone to his everlasting home, because that I offer here a charity for him; for the reward of this may his soul be bound up in the bundle of life together with the soul of Abraham, Isaac, and Jacob, Sarah, Rebekah, Rachel, and Leah, and with other saints, male and female, who are in Paradise."

---

[1] יזכר אלהים נשמת אבא מורי פ׳ ב׳ פ׳ שהלך לעולמו בעבור שאני נודר צדקה בעדו בשכר זה תנצלה וג׳:

It may be observed, as a very striking proof of the reality of their prayers for the dead, that at this point of the service those worshippers who happen not to have lost parents or near and dear friends are in the habit of withdrawing from the assembly.

The above prayer is deserving of careful notice, because it is by no means improbable that our blessed Lord had it, or something similar, in His mind in that part of His Sermon on the Mount which touches upon the subject of charity and alms-giving.

Jewish alms and charity commonly offered in behalf of the dead.

It was especially provided by the law of Moses,[1] that every person who took part in the great festivals should offer unto the Lord "the free-will offering of his hand according as God had blessed him," that they should "not appear before the Lord empty." This gift was usually made at the "Commemoration," either with a view to relief from sickness or any other trouble, or as an atonement[2] for some dead relation or friend, under the firm con-

[1] DEUT. xvi. 10, 16.

[2] The Jews admit four means of procuring atonement:—1. repentance; 2. the Day of Atonement; 3. sufferings; 4. death, of which the last, death, *i.e.* the dying, possesses the greatest power. During the first year after a parent's death, a child, in commemorating the deceased, says or writes after his name, ה׳ כ׳ ל׳, *i.e.* הריני כפרת משכבו I am ready to serve as atonement for his couch, I am ready to suffer for his transgressions, provided only that his rest may be peace. This explanation is borne out by Rashi, whose commentary *in loco* runs thus:—

עלי יבא כל רע הראוי לבא על נפשו:

viction that they would be benefited in whose behalf the offering was presented.

Light is thrown upon this by the SIPHRÈ, the oldest continuous Midrash on the fourth and fifth books of Moses, which, though only committed to writing in the second and third centuries (180-220 A.D.) contains the record of customs generally supposed to have prevailed for hundreds of years. In its commentary upon the passage,[1] "**Be merciful, O Lord, unto Thy people Israel, whom Thou hast redeemed, and lay not innocent blood unto Thy people of Israel's charge. And the blood shall be forgiven them,**" we find the following explanation:[2] "'Forgive thy people,' that is, 'the living:' 'whom thou hast redeemed,' that is, 'the dead,' which shows that the dead also want an atonement."

Indirect reference

It has been thought that it was the ostentatious

When the first year had expired, by which time it was supposed that the deceased would be purged from his sins, the language changed, and the child said,

זכרונו לברכה לחיי העולם הבא:

"may his memory be for a blessing for the life of the world to come."—TALM. BAB., *Kiddushin*, xxxi. B.

[1] The close of the section שופטים, on DEUT. xxi. 8.

It ought to be noticed that the Siphrè is older even than the Palestinian Talmud. It is a Baraitha, *i.e.*, a Mishnah taught outside the Lecture Room. It testifies therefore to a generally admitted doctrine.

[2] כפר לעמך אלו החיים אשר פדית אלו המתים מלמד שהמתים צריכים כפרה:

Cf. TALM. BAB., *Horayoth*, 6 a.

offering of this "atonement" or free-will offering, which was made in the Temple or in the Synagogues, as well as the parade of their benevolence abroad, which our Lord alluded to when He gave His admonition, "𝕎hen thou doest thine alms, do not sound a trumpet before thee, as the hypocrites do in the synagogues and in the streets, that they may have glory of men."[1] *to the custom in the Sermon on the Mount.*

Before passing from the consideration of Jewish services and commemorations, we must briefly refer to certain Jewish formulas in common use to express distinct prayers for the dead, taken from the language of Holy Writ.[2] We turn to the testimony, which is appealed to, on Jewish tombstones and in other inscriptions. If the age of some of these could be decisively fixed, as early as at first sight would appear, we should not be left in any uncertainty, but the subjoined notes will show that their great antiquity is not unreasonably disputed. *The evidence of old Jewish inscriptions in different countries.*

The first to be noticed are those which have been discovered by R. Jacob Saphir, a distinguished Jew who has travelled through Egypt, Arabia, Jemen,

---

[1] S. Matt. vi. 2.

[2] יִשְׁעֲךָ, נַחֲלוּאָ, יַחֲבִיעָם, from Is. lvii. 2, Ps. xxv. 13, and cxlix. 5.

In all these cases the A. V. translates as promises: the Jews use them as prayers. For confirmation of this, cf. Palest. Talm. Leyden MS. p. 11 in Dr. Schiller-Szinessy's Occasional Notices of Hebrew MSS. No. 1.

and other countries, with the special object of collecting records of his nation among extant monuments of antiquity and traditional stories. Several of the inscriptions deciphered by him bear on their face dates which carry us back beyond the present era.[1] Some of the tombstones are inscribed with different formulas of prayers for the dead; for the most part they are abbreviated by the use of initial letters only, precisely the same as in the custom of writing R. I. P. on the graves of Christians. The commonest are the following:—

   MAY HIS REST BE GLORY.[2]
   MAY HIS MEMORY BE FOR A BLESSING.[3]
   MAY HIS MEMORY BE FOR THE RESURRECTION.[4]
   MAY THE SPIRIT OF THE LORD LEAD HIM TO REST.[5]

[1] They are all dated according to the era of Contracts, which begins 311 years and 4 months before Christ. It is identical with the Grecian era, or the era of the Seleucides. In 1 MACC. i. 10, of Antiochus it is said that "he reigned in the hundred and thirty and seventh year of the kingdom of the Greeks," which corresponds to 175 B.C. The above method of dating was used frequently by the Jews down to the fifteenth century, and in some places is still used. On the tombstones the dates of the above inscriptions are 28, 29, 1. The last date does create some suspicion, because it is hardly likely that people would begin to employ the dates of an era at its very commencement. Dr. Schiller-Szinessy suggests that in each case 1000 has been omitted for the sake of brevity, as we might write 78 for 1878, and as western Jews do occasionally omit the thousands in dating from the Creation of the world.

[2] In allusion to ISAI. xi. 10. : תָּמֹכ׳ : תהי מנוחתו כבוד
[3] זָלָב׳ : זכרונו לברכה :
[4] זָלָת׳ : זכרונו לתחיה :
[5] רֹיֹת׳ : רוח יהוה תניחנו : ISAI. xiii. 14.

The English word "memory" is far from indicating the full idea of that which the original conveys to the mind of the Jew. This may be seen from the writings of Maimonides.[1] He says, for instance, "May his memory be for a blessing and for the resurrection," meaning, as the reference to the resurrection clearly implies, much more than remembrance, even the principal essence of existence, or, as we should say, the soul. In much the same way "the memorial" of the meat-offering is used in Leviticus. According to the Jewish idea it signifies the essence, the savour, or, so to say, the soul of the material offering.

The next inscription of the kind to be considered is an epitaph[2] discovered at Aden, and now deposited in the British Museum, bearing date 12th of Ab, era of Contracts, 29. (B.C. 282.)

It commemorates Mashta, a daughter of David, who died at Aden in South Arabia. The following is the portion of it which calls for our notice :— *An epitaph from Aden.*

---

[1] In his autograph on a disciple's copy of the "Mishneh Torah" (Bodleian Lib., Oxford. Cod. Hunt. 40), the formula occurs, זִלֹלֹח *i.e.*, זכרו לברכה ולתחיה, which shows that the inscriptions signify much more than "may his memory be blessed."

[2] החסידה משתא תמב בת הזקן החסיד העניו הטוב הירא
שמים דויד ר'ח יום יב לחודש אב שנת כט לשטרות

For a full description of the epitaph by Dr. Schiller-Szinessy, see Plate XXIV. of Facsimiles of Ancient MSS., Oriental Series, of the Palæographic Society, part ii.

THE PIOUS MASHTA (MAY HER REST BE GLORY!) DAUGHTER OF THE AGED, THE PIOUS, THE HUMBLE, THE GOOD, THE GOD-FEARING DAVID (MAY THE SPIRIT OF GOD LEAD HIM TO REST!)

Inscriptions on gravestones discovered in the Crimea.

The last inscriptions to which we call attention are from some tombstones recently discovered in the Crimea,[1] containing the oft-recurring formula, "may his soul be bound up," etc. The discoverer claims for them different dates from A.D. 6 downwards, but though he is very confident of their authenticity, they will require further investigation than they have yet undergone before we can accept them as trustworthy evidence.

We have put forward all the evidence which we have been able to meet with from Jewish sources. A considerable amount of doubt must exist as to the value of a portion of it, but however much it may be shaken by closer examination, the great fact still remains in the history of the Maccabees, that the custom of praying for the dead was known in the second century before Christ. We know, moreover, that unprejudiced Jews, who of course understand the habits and mind of their own nation far better than we can do, do not hesitate for a moment

[1] Dr. Chwolson has translated and described them. It is to be noticed that the mode of dating is not by the era of Contracts, as in the previously cited cases, but either from the Creation of the world or after the Exile; in some instances both are combined.

to pronounce in favour of its great antiquity, and feel assured that, when it found expression in their public services, it must have been widely practised for a considerable time.

We may then fairly accept this testimony as sufficient indication that our Lord's silence upon the practice is not attributable to its non-existence; and when all things are considered, there seems to be no alternative but to interpret it as a sign of the Divine acquiescence. Opportunities must have presented themselves in His teaching had He desired to denounce the practice as erroneous, or to discourage it as liable to misconstruction. It is true that but little fell from His lips touching the state of the dead, but amidst all the stern denunciations which the Jews drew down upon themselves for their perversion of the Law, it is almost impossible to believe that He could have ignored and winked at the prevalence of any habit of which He disapproved. We may interpret His conduct in this matter very much as is usually done in the case of Infant Baptism, though of course we are far from attaching the same importance to a pious practice, which is what we hold praying for the dead to have been, as we do to the Initiatory Rite for the remission of sins. It is said that this receives no direct

Our Lord's silence not attributable to the non-existence of the doctrine.

The close connection

between the Old and the New Dispensations.

countenance from Christ Himself, but if there is that close connection between the Jewish and Christian religions, which He admitted when He said that He came "𝖓𝖔𝖙 𝖙𝖔 𝖉𝖊𝖘𝖙𝖗𝖔𝖞, 𝖇𝖚𝖙 𝖙𝖔 𝖋𝖚𝖑𝖋𝖎𝖑,"[1] it follows that anything which formed part of the Old system, unless the contrary were distinctly expressed, ought to be regarded as stamped with His sanction for continuance in the New. If by Divine appointment infants were considered eligible for admission into covenant with God in the one, they would certainly not, in the absence of any direction to the contrary, be excluded from the other. So in a somewhat similar manner if, side by side with an increasing realisation of the certainty of the resurrection and judgment, and of the intermediate state of disembodied souls, there had grown up the comforting belief that after death they might be benefited by the prayers of the living—a belief which seems to be the natural outcome of the conviction of a trial for which they were waiting—unless we are prepared to accuse our Lord of allowing His creatures to be buoyed up with empty hopes and barren comfort, we must perforce accept the conclusion that He did give His approval to the doctrine, and that it was hardly less distinct because given in silence.

[1] S. MATT. v. 17, $\pi\lambda\eta\rho\tilde{\omega}\sigma\alpha\iota$, rather, to develop, to expand, to fill up.

CHAPTER VI.

The Testimony of Holy Scripture.

NOW although there is no positive and direct teaching on the subject in the recorded utterances of our Lord, there are indications which are not without importance in estimating the probability of His disapproval or sanction. Indirect reference in Christ's teaching.

To the Pharisees, who had accused Him of casting out devils by the power of Beelzebub, He said:—

"All manner of sin and blasphemy shall be forgiven unto men: but the blasphemy against the Holy Ghost shall not be forgiven unto men. And whosoever speaketh a word against the Son of Man, it shall be forgiven him: but whosoever speaketh against the Holy Ghost, it shall not be forgiven him, neither in this world, neither in the world to come."[1]

If we could read this statement of our Lord without prejudice we should naturally conclude that it furnishes the highest authority for believing that, while some sins are forgiven during the lifetime of the sinner, there are others which admit of forgive-

[1] S. MATT. xii. 31, 32.

ness also after his death. If, then, death is found to interpose no barrier to the forgiveness of these latter, we may either continue to pray for it in behalf of the dead, or else our cherished belief in the all-prevailing efficacy of prayer and intercession must be abandoned, and a limit placed to the promise, "𝔚𝔥𝔞𝔱𝔰𝔬𝔢𝔳𝔢𝔯 𝔶𝔢 𝔰𝔥𝔞𝔩𝔩 𝔞𝔰𝔨 𝔦𝔫 𝔭𝔯𝔞𝔶𝔢𝔯, 𝔟𝔢𝔩𝔦𝔢𝔳𝔦𝔫𝔤, 𝔶𝔢 𝔰𝔥𝔞𝔩𝔩 𝔯𝔢𝔠𝔢𝔦𝔳𝔢."[1]

Attempts to explain away the obvious meaning.

But the supposed dangerous tendency of such teaching has induced some of our leading commentators to seek for another explanation. It is said "this world" and "the world to come" were familiar expressions amongst the Jews to express respectively the ages before and after the advent of the Messiah in the flesh, and consequently there is no necessary reference in Christ's words to the times subsequent to man's death. But the old controversy,[2] carried on with such vehemence in the seventeenth century, bears witness to the uncertainty which hangs over the Jewish meaning[3] of "the coming age," or "the world to come." In order, however,

---

[1] S. MATT. xxi. 22.

[2] Between Witsius, the eminent Calvinistic divine, and Rhenferd, the celebrated Oriental scholar, both professors of Franeker.

[3] "The world to come, עוֹלָם הבא, hints two things especially. 1. The times of the Messias: 'Be mindful of the day wherein thou camest out of Egypt all the days of thy life. The wise men say, by "the days of thy life" is intimated "this world;" by "all the days of thy life," the days of the Messias are superinduced.' In this

to show that the explanation which we have adopted is not in violation of the Jewish usage of familiar terms, we have carefully examined the writings of a very distinguished Rabbi, whose learning was such that it was said of him, "from Moses to Moses there has arisen none like Moses;" and we are contented to shelter ourselves in this matter at least under his interpretation.

Moses Maimonides, in his Mishneh Torah on the *Precepts of Repentance*, writes thus: "The good which is laid up for the righteous is the life of 'the world to come,' that is, a life in which there is no death, and a good in which there is no evil."[1] And again, "In the world to come there is no bodily frame, but the souls of the righteous are alone without the body as the angels which minister."[2] He explains too how the patriarchal expression "the bundle of life," is only a synonymous term, and after

The testimony of a learned Rabbi to the meaning of disputed terms.

---

sense the Apostle seems to speak, HEB. ii. 5, and vi. 5. 2. The state after death, עולם הבא לאחד שיצא האדם מעולם הזה, 'The world to come is, when a man is departed out of this world.'"—LIGHTFOOT, *Exercit.* S. MATT. *in loc.*

[1] הטובה הצפונה לצדיקים היא חיי העולם הבא והיא החיים שאין מות עמהן והטובה שאין עמה רעה Chap. viii. 1.

[2] העולם הבא אין בו גוף וגניה אלא נפשות הצדיקים בלבד כלא גוף כמלאכי השרת ed. BERNARD, viii. 3.

enumerating a variety of others, all of which are employed allegorically to convey the same meaning, he concludes, "the good which is prepared for the righteous is however more generally called the world to come."[1] Indeed, this Jewish sage is so far from accepting the interpretation, which some modern writers think the only justifiable one, that he runs directly counter to it, for he says that the future blessings foretold by the prophets referred only to those which Israel should enjoy in the flesh in the days of King Messiah, when sovereignty should be restored to the nation, but those which were laid up in "the world to come" baffled description, because there is no correspondency between the happiness of the body and that of the soul. This is why Isaiah said, "Neither hath the eye seen, O God, beside Thee, what He hath prepared for him that waiteth for Him."[2]

Nothing can show more clearly than these quotations that it is by no means so certain as some have maintained, that, in accordance with Jewish phraseology, our Lord intended "the Messianic Age" when He spoke of "the world to come." When, moreover, we take into consideration the parallel passage from

[1] וקורין לה בכל מקום העולם הבא: viii. 6.
[2] ISAIAH lxiv. 4.

S. Mark's Gospel,¹ we seem almost forced to adopt the wider application.

"𝔙𝔢 𝔱𝔥𝔞𝔱 𝔰𝔥𝔞𝔩𝔩 𝔟𝔩𝔞𝔰𝔭𝔥𝔢𝔪𝔢 𝔞𝔤𝔞𝔦𝔫𝔰𝔱 𝔱𝔥𝔢 𝔥𝔬𝔩𝔶 𝔊𝔥𝔬𝔰𝔱 𝔥𝔞𝔱𝔥 𝔫𝔢𝔳𝔢𝔯 𝔣𝔬𝔯𝔤𝔦𝔳𝔢𝔫𝔢𝔰𝔰, 𝔟𝔲𝔱 𝔦𝔰 𝔤𝔲𝔦𝔩𝔱𝔶 𝔬𝔣 𝔞𝔫 𝔢𝔱𝔢𝔯𝔫𝔞𝔩 𝔰𝔦𝔫."

If forgiveness were limited entirely to the present life, a period of threescore years and ten, would there not be something unnecessarily strong in such a deep-reaching expression as this, something almost unnatural in the accumulation of the "never" and the "eternal"? It would surely have sufficed to have pronounced the sin to be simply unpardonable.

But another method of escape from the obvious teaching of the passage has been found in understanding the expression "neither in this world nor in the world to come" as merely a periphrastic way of expressing "never," which is said to be found in the Talmud² *Further attempts to explain it away.*

We may take it for granted that such an interpretation is quite admissible, but whether it is that which is most natural, and in accordance with the usage elsewhere in the New Testament, is another matter. It is only found once besides: "𝔥𝔢 𝔯𝔞𝔦𝔰𝔢𝔡

¹ S. MARK, iii. 29, ἔνοχός ἐστιν αἰωνίου ἁμαρτήματος. κρίσεως of the Textus Receptus has clearly been adopted to simplify a difficult expression.

² Cf. Bishop WORDSWORTH *in loco*, who refers to Vorstius de synedriis Hebræorum.

𝔥im from the dead, and set him at 𝔥is own right hand in the heavenly places, far above all principality, and power, and might, and dominion, and every name that is named, not only in this world, but also in that which is to come."[1] This last expression, by analogy with the above, is said to be a Hebraism for "always." But it is far better not to refer this to the clause immediately preceding it, viz., "above every name that is named," but more generally to the statement that Christ has been set above all things, not only in the present earthly state but in the future heavenly, so that it brings out distinctly His Headship of the Church, in its twofold division, the Visible and the Invisible.

If Christ did not admit the possibility of forgiveness for some kind of sin after death,[2] it is difficult to believe that He would have run the risk of using an expression so calculated to mislead, and so certain to be laid hold of by those who held the

---

[1] Ephes. i. 20, 21.

[2] In support of the above interpretation we quote the testimony of S. Augustine, and S. Isidore "the oracle of Spain:" "Nam pro defunctis quibusdam, vel ipsius Ecclesiæ, vel quorundam piorum exauditur oratio. . . . Neque enim de quibusdam veraciter diceretur, quod non eis remittatur neque in hoc sæculo, neque in futuro, nisi essent quibus, etsi non in isto, tamen remittetur in futuro."—*De Civ. Dei.* xxi. 24. 2.

"Quum Dominus dicit, neque in hoc sæculo neque in futuro demonstrat quibusdam illic dimittenda peccata."—*De Off. Eccles.* 18.

erroneous doctrine, and to be employed in a manner destructive of the truth.

Of course, even if interpreted as we believe the passage should be, it is no proof of our Lord's acquiescence in the legitimacy of praying for the dead; but indirectly it lends considerable weight to the supposition, for if there are sins whose stains may be wiped out in another world, so long as the efficacy of prayer and intercession is held to be as potent as it is, those who survive their friends can hardly fail to pray for such a result.

There are one or two passages in the Epistles of S. Paul which bear more or less distinctly upon our subject. Touching the resurrection, he writes to the Corinthians, "𝕰𝖑𝖘𝖊 𝖜𝖍𝖆𝖙 𝖘𝖍𝖆𝖑𝖑 𝖙𝖍𝖊𝖞 𝖉𝖔 𝖜𝖍𝖎𝖈𝖍 𝖆𝖗𝖊 𝖇𝖆𝖕𝖙𝖎𝖟𝖊𝖉 𝖋𝖔𝖗 𝖙𝖍𝖊 𝖉𝖊𝖆𝖉, 𝖎𝖋 𝖙𝖍𝖊 𝖉𝖊𝖆𝖉 𝖗𝖎𝖘𝖊 𝖓𝖔𝖙 𝖆𝖙 𝖆𝖑𝖑? 𝖜𝖍𝖞 𝖆𝖗𝖊 𝖙𝖍𝖊𝖞 𝖙𝖍𝖊𝖓 𝖇𝖆𝖕𝖙𝖎𝖟𝖊𝖉 𝖋𝖔𝖗 𝖙𝖍𝖊 𝖉𝖊𝖆𝖉?"[1] The words certainly seem to indicate the existence at the time of a custom which we know from the censures of some of the Fathers[2] was practised by

The evidence of a superstitious practice prevailing at Corinth in S. Paul's time.

---

[1] 1 Cor. xv. 29.

[2] τί οὖν ἐστιν ὅ φησιν; τί βούλεσθε πρῶτον εἴπω, πῶς παραποιοῦσι τὴν ῥῆσιν ταύτην οἱ τὰ Μαρκίωνος νοσοῦντες; καὶ οἶδα μὲν ὅτι πολὺν κινήσω γέλωτα, κ.τ.λ.—S. CHRYSOST. *Hom.* xl.; 1 Cor. xv.

ἐν οἷς καί τι παραδόσεως πρᾶγμα ἦλθεν εἰς ἡμᾶς· ὡς τινων μὲν παρ' αὐτοῖς προφθανόντων τελευτῆσαι ἄνευ βαπτίσματος ἄλλους δὲ ἀντὶ αὐτῶν εἰς ὄνομα ἐκείνων βαπτίζεσθαι.—EPIPHAN. *adv. Hær.* Lib. i. xxviii. 6.

certain heretical sects at a later period. The Cerinthians and Marcionites administered vicarious baptism in behalf of persons who had died without receiving the rite.

<small>Erroneous interpretations suggested to avoid a difficulty.</small>

Many strange and untenable interpretations[1] have been put forward with the view of avoiding all allusion to the practice, and getting rid of a difficulty which is created by the supposition that an inspired apostle could have had anything to say to such a superstitious custom. Most of them are self-condemned. One, however, calls for consideration, because it commended itself to some of the Catholic Fathers,[2] and has been urged with considerable earnestness in a popular commentary[3] of our own time. It is that whenever the rite of Baptism is administered, a profession is made by the baptized person of his belief in the resurrection. Every baptismal creed contains this article of our Faith. Therefore all who are baptized may well be said to be baptized for or on behalf of the dead.

But whatever candidates for Baptism were required to believe in later times, there is no reason for supposing that at the beginning the doctrine of the

---

[1] Dean STANLEY has collected together twelve of these.—See Com. *in loco.*
[2] S. CHRYS. *Hom.* xl.
[3] Bishop WORDSWORTH *in loco.*

resurrection was submitted as a test of fitness, but it is far more likely that a simple confession of Jesus Christ was deemed sufficient qualification.

As regards the difficulty suggested by the improbability of an Apostle running the risk of damaging his argument by an appeal to a superstition, which, if mentioned at all, ought to have received from his lips the severest reprehension, we have only to observe S. Paul's practice[1] under somewhat similar circumstances. A careful examination would no doubt afford sufficient evidence that he did not hesitate to use an *argumentum ad hominem*, and accommodate himself to the views of his hearers, and that without any expression of approval or condemnation. There is an interesting solution proposed by the distinguished leader of the Old Catholics.[2] After speaking of the practice as a common one, he says, "Probably it was done for those who had shown an intention of being baptized, but had died without fulfilling it. A surviving relative would then be baptized for the dead, in order to give a public testimony to the Church that

The views of two distinguished men, both characterised by independence of thought.

---

[1] Dean Stanley mentions as examples, Gal. iv. 21-31; Acts xvii. 23; xvii. 18, 21; xxi. 26. See his Commentary for the second quotation.

[2] Dr. Döllinger, *The First Age of Christianity and the Church*, tr. Oxenham, iii. 2.

he had died a member of it in mind and desire, and so to obtain for him the prayers of the Church, which else were not offered for those who died unbaptized." One of the most popular writers in our own Church sets his seal to the natural interpretation as follows: "There was then, as always, the natural longing of the survivors to complete the work which untimely death had broken off; and in that early age, when the self-devotion of a Christian's life was concentrated in the one act of baptism, it might have seemed fitting that where the conversion either had not been completed, or had not taken place (for there is nothing in the passage which necessarily confines it to the case of catechumens), the friends of the dead should step, as it were, into his place, and in his name themselves undertake the dangers and responsibilities of baptism, so that after all the good work would not have been cut off by death, but would continue, in the words of the Apostle, 'confirmed to the end, blameless in the day of Jesus Christ.'"[1]

But though we feel that there is no escape from the conclusion that the Apostle did draw an argument from an existing practice of such a kind, and that without at the same time expressing any dis-

---

[1] Dean STANLEY'S Commentary on the Epp. ad COR. *in loco.*

approbation, we cannot suppose for a moment that he intended to lend his sanction to the principle of vicarious baptism for the dead. There is a very wide difference between praying for the dead who died in faith and in covenant with God, and undergoing the sacred rite of initiation for those who had not received it in life, and were consequently "aliens from the commonwealth of Israel," and without the pale of God's promises.

Nevertheless, it appears to us to be just such an extreme development of the belief in the power of the living to aid the dead as might naturally arise, in the absence of safeguards, when the belief became general or widely accepted; and we are content to use it in our investigation simply as historical evidence, that in the earliest times death was not supposed to place an impassable barrier between the good offices of the living in behalf of the souls of the dead. *The extreme development of a praiseworthy custom.*

The case of Onesiphorus next calls for our consideration. *S. Paul's prayer for Onesiphorus.*

The passages which bear upon it are from the first and fourth chapters of S. Paul's Second Epistle to Timothy.

"The Lord give mercy unto the house of Onesiphorus; for he oft refreshed me, and was not ashamed of my chain: but when he was in Rome, he sought me out very diligently, and found me.

"The Lord grant unto him that he may find mercy of the Lord in that day."

"Salute Prisca and Aquila, and the household of Onesiphorus."[1]

Was Onesiphorus alive or dead when the Apostle wrote these words? We can obtain no direct evidence from Scripture, and beyond a solitary tradition derived from an unknown source, and like so many traditions touching the later labours of early Christians of note, little worthy of credit, we can learn nothing about him. Fabricius,[2] the voluminous biographer of the last century, in his catalogue of Christian Bishoprics, places the seat of Onesiphorus' Episcopal labours at an obscure town in Messenia. Now if he ever occupied such a see, it must of necessity have been at a time subsequent to the writing of the above Epistle. But as an unsupported statement, we cannot consider what Fabricius says as sufficient to outweigh the extreme probability, arising out of the language which we have quoted, that he was dead at the time when S. Paul wrote.

The whole tone of the passage seems to indicate

[1] 2 Tim. . 16, 18, and iv. 19.   [2] *Salutaris Lux Evangelii*, p. 117.

this. When the Apostle thinks of the household of Onesiphorus, he prays that God will bestow upon them the blessings of His mercy; the time for its bestowal is not expressed, but if, as we suppose, the family was in bereavement, it would be for immediate comfort, and the absence of any specified time points rather to the present. But when his thoughts were carried on to his benefactor, knowing that he had no longer need of it in this world, as his survivors had, the vision of the future judgment rises up before the writer's mind, and he adds, "The Lord grant to him," not to the household, "to find mercy in that day."

But very few attempts[1] have been made to evade this, which it must be allowed is the most natural inference; it has however been maintained that, granting that Onesiphorus was dead, the language used is not expressive of prayer, but only of a pious hope or aspiration.

The slightest acquaintance with the forms of prayer for the dead in the Primitive Liturgies will be enough to identify it with the expressions in common. use; this petition for mercy, and rest through mercy, being one of most frequent recurrence. We cannot better conclude the consideration of this case

The similarity of the Apostle's prayer to those most commonly found in primitive Liturgies.

---

[1] S. Chrysostom says that Onesiphorus was then in Rome, but it is only a conjecture, which is ill suited to the tenor of the passage.

than by quoting the opinion of one of the most eminent divines of the seventeenth century. In speaking of the communion of saints, he exhorts his hearers thus: "We should do well to remember that in this world we are something besides flesh and blood; that we may not, without violent necessities, run into new relations, but preserve the affections we bore to our dead when they were alive. We must not so live as if they were perished, but so as pressing forward to the most intimate participation of the communion of saints. And we also have some ways to express this relation, and to bear a part in this communion, by actions of intercourse with them, and yet proper to our state: such as are —strictly performing the will of the dead, providing for and tenderly and wisely educating their children, paying their debts, imitating their good example, preserving their memories, privately and publicly keeping their memorials, and desiring of God, with hearty and constant prayer, that God would give them a joyful resurrection and a merciful judgment, for so S. Paul prayed in behalf of Onesiphorus, that 'God would show him mercy in that day,' that fearful and yet much to be desired day, in which the most righteous person hath need of much mercy and pity, and shall find it."[1]

[1] JER. TAYLOR, *Works*, viii. 436, ed. Eden.

CHAPTER VII

The Testimony of the Catacombs.

NO little controversy has gathered round the origin and date of the Catacombs at Rome. It will be well briefly to indicate the conclusions which have been arrived at by the latest investigation, that we may be in a position rightly to estimate the importance of the evidence which they furnish of the primitive belief respecting the condition of the faithful dead and their connection with the living.

<small>The original construction and use of the Catacombs strictly Christian.</small>

They were constructed by Christians in the earliest ages of Christianity for the burial of their own dead exclusively;[1] they may neither, therefore, be identified with the ancient *arenariæ*[2] or exhausted

---

[1] This is established by the investigations of Padre Marchi and the two De-Rossi, his pupils, who have done perhaps more than any others to throw light upon the whole subject of the Catacombs. See their works, *I monumenti delle arti Christiane primitive nella metropoli del Christianesimo*, and *Inscriptiones Christianæ*, and *Roma Sotteranea*. Mr. J. H. Parker, however, dissents from this view in his last work on the Archæology of Rome,—Part xii., The Catacombs.

[2] The soil in which nearly all the Catacombs have been constructed is the *tufa granolare*, which is easily worked, and of suffi-

sand-pits of pre-Christian times, nor may they be considered, as was once so vigorously maintained, as common cemeteries for Pagans and Christians alike.

The intermixture of heathen symbols not contradictory of this view. The presence of heathen symbols and inscriptions, which gave rise to the latter theory, antecedently so improbable when we take into consideration the relationship in which Christianity and Paganism stood to each other during the greater part of the first three centuries, may be satisfactorily explained upon other grounds. Pagan burial-places differed in their construction from Christian just as the disposal of the bodies of the dead differed. Though inhumation was the original mode of burying adopted by the Romans, it was almost entirely superseded by burning during a large portion of the time which is covered by the use of the Catacombs, and the cells of the *Columbaria*, in which the ashes of the dead were preserved, are of the smallest dimen-

cient solidity to bear excavation. That in which the old sand-pits are found, *pozzolana*, is of a looser and more friable character, and without the addition of solid masonry could not have been utilised as burial-places. The *arena* might well have been dug by the ancients as a valuable ingredient in their cement: the *pozzolana* could not have been. The plan of the sand-pits, again, is arranged so that its roads are curved to allow of the easy passage of carts; while the galleries of the Catacombs are narrow, and frequently intersect one another at right angles.

The above-quoted writers have explained how the *arenariæ* came to be identified with the Catacombs.

sions compared with the *cubicula* or *loculi* of the Catacombs.

It has been observed too that in by far the majority of instances the Pagan inscriptions are found in unnatural positions, inverted or sideways, and not unfrequently on the inner surface of the stone, from which it is thought probable that the Christians had removed from Pagan cemeteries and other places such slabs as came conveniently to hand, and utilised them without troubling themselves to erase the marks which indicated their original use.[1] But it cannot be denied that there are instances where the stones show no signs of such adaptation, but were deliberately set up over Christian graves and inscribed with heathen symbols.[2] The explanation of this,

Pagan Inscriptions, how to be accounted for.

---

[1] Cf. MABILLON, *Iter Italicum Litterarium*, p. 136.

[2] The most frequent of these are the initials D.M. or D.M.S., which are said to occur about forty times among 15,000 inscriptions. On Pagan monuments their usage is almost universal—ninety-five per cent. at least—and the meaning is obvious, *Dis Manibus* or *Dis Manibus sacrum*. Besides the theory of explanation given above, it is quite possible that Christians, finding stones so inscribed, justified themselves in the use of them by giving to the initials an altered significance, *Deo Maximo, Deo Maximo Salvatori*, and the addition in some cases of the sacred monogram of Christ does certainly give an air of probability to the supposition.

Mr. Parker explains the presence of Pagan symbols by supposing that the claims of family were considered stronger than those of religion, and relations who differed in creed were laid in one and the same burial-place.

84   *The Testimony of the Catacombs.*

which may well seem strange to us, who are apt at this distance of time to draw a strong line of demarcation between the new faith and the old, is to be sought in the difficulty which in all ages individuals[1] have experienced in cutting themselves off entirely and at once from the associations of their ancestors.

The period of time covered by the Catacombs. But not only is it proved that the Catacombs were distinctively the work of Christians, it is equally clear also, and even more interesting in connection with our present subject, that they belong to the very earliest period of Christian history, ranging in all probability from the sub-apostolic age to the close of the fourth century, when from the public recogni-

---

[1] Dean STANLEY, in his Life of Constantine, *East. Ch. Lect.* vi., has illustrated this principle by a variety of examples which are very pertinent to the subject. It is quite true that figures resembling in a great measure the heathen representation of Orpheus and Pan are found engraven on Christian tombs. The Good Shepherd was one of the favourite representations on the early monuments, but because He is accompanied by a goat, or is playing upon a lyre or a rustic pipe, it by no means follows necessarily that He is to be identified with Orpheus or Pan. We can find another explanation in the idea that the goat was emblematical of the sinners whom He came to save, and the musical instrument of the voice which His sheep knew so well ; as S. Greg. Naz. writes :—" The Good Shepherd will at one time give His sheep rest, and at another drive and direct them—with his staff seldom, but more generally with his pipe ;" cf. NORTHCOTE, *Rom. Cat.* p. 51. But the probability is that the early Christians had learned to look upon Orpheus as a sort of type and precursor of Christ, just as they saw in the old heathen religions foreshadowings of the Gospel.

tion of Christianity by the State the concealment which led to burial in subterranean cemeteries had quite ceased to be necessary. The first dated[1] inscription hitherto discovered is of 71 A.D., and no underground interment is believed to have taken place after the capture of Rome by the Goths in 410 A.D.

Now although the allusions to the state of the dead found in the monumental inscriptions of this early period are necessarily brief and simple, the value of them is by no means insignificant. *The brevity and simplicity of the inscriptions enhances the value of their testimony.*

All that has come to light reveals a Church steadfast in the faith, calm in temper and without exaggeration in its expressions of bereavement, and this, be it borne in mind, in the midst of unexampled provocation, when men's belief in the providence of God must have been sorely tried, and we should have expected to see at least some signs of wavering and impatience. But none are to be found. It is the record of an age to which we may turn with confidence for guidance in difficulty, for on no period of the Church's history has the true spirit of her

[1] The dated inscriptions hitherto discovered are upwards of 110 ; one only in the first century, two in the second, twenty-three in the third, about five hundred each in the fourth and fifth, but the dates of many of the others, by a comparison of style and various other indications, may be approximately fixed. About 6000 altogether are extant, and considerably more than half of these are assigned to the Ante-Nicene period.

Founder left so clear an impress. We accept, therefore, whatever illustrations it may give of primitive usage or doctrine with feelings of satisfaction, assured that we shall find nothing but the calm deliberate belief of the generations for which it speaks.

Before attempting to extract from the sculpture and inscriptions of these early tombs the prevailing sentiments of the times touching the condition of the faithful dead and their relationship to those who survived, it may be well to prepare the way by a brief illustration of the value of their testimony in reference to matters of faith generally accepted. Nothing could be ruder[1] or less imaginative than their symbolical representations of the two great Sacraments, but they manifest a complete grasp of the doctrines involved.

Their witness to the full teaching of the two Sacraments predisposes us to follow them in other matters.

The emblem of the first Sacrament is that which has become so familiar to us from the language of our Baptismal Service, in which the ark is made to prefigure the Church into which the baptized child is received. Now in the Catacombs this is represented in a manner almost grotesque; but we can hardly fail to be struck by the way in which the sculptor or painter, out of the whole circumstance of the Mosaic

[1] Such monuments best express the contemporary belief; those of later times generally lose in value in proportion as they gain in beauty and ornament.

narrative, seized upon those features which bore directly upon the doctrine to be enforced. The gigantic ship, the eight souls, the concourse of animals, all are forgotten, and we see on those underground monuments four things, and four only, viz., water, a vessel, frequently in the shape of a box or tub, one human being, and a bird[1] with a branch in its beak. What more is required to exhibit the full teaching of baptismal grace?

Of the other Sacrament there are numerous symbols, and they recur very frequently; the commonest are the vine, ears of corn, loaves of bread, and a fish and bread. It may seem that these have no necessary connection with the Holy Eucharist, and are nothing more than "pictorial representations" of some of our Lord's miracles, but a careful study of the subject proves that such an idea runs counter to the principle which governs all the monumental imagery of the Catacombs. Nothing is

[1] The connection of this emblem, though no longer familiar, was quite intelligible in the earliest times, as the following quotation testifies:—"Quemadmodum enim post aquas diluvii quibus iniquitas antiqua purgata est, post baptismum (ut ita dixerim) mundi pacem cælestis iræ præco columba terras annunciavit dimissa ex arca et cum olea reversa . . . eadem dispositione spiritalis effectus terræ, id est carni nostræ emergenti de lavacro post vetera delicta columba Sancti Spiritus advolat pacem Dei afferens emissa de cælis ubi ecclesia est arca figurata."—TERTULL. de Bapt. c. viii.

portrayed in a simply historical way. All, whether paintings or sculptures, are what has been called "ideographical," and bear a distinct symbolical interpretation. But we have selected two which deserve especial note. In the one[1] a priest is represented clothed in a *pallium*, extending his hand in the attitude of benediction over a tripod, upon which a fish and some loaves marked with a cross are laid; while a woman, as typifying the Church, kneels before him. In the other a fish is swimming in the water and carrying on its back a basket containing bread and a small vessel of wine. When we keep in mind the significance of the fish,[2] we have vividly depicted

---

[1] "The priest is clothed only in the pallium; now we know that Tertullian defends the pallium, that Justin Martyr wore it, whilst Cyprian denounced it. This painting, then, would lead us to conclude that at the beginning of the third century the Eucharist was looked upon as a sacrifice celebrated by the priest, and in the offering of which the congregation had its part."—DRAKE, *On the Teaching of the Church*, etc., p. 7.

[2] The symbol ἰχθύς, which probably owed its origin to the *disciplina arcani*, has been found on monuments of every kind in he primitive Church. "Sint autem nobis signacula columba, vel piscis, vel navis," etc.—CLEMENS ALEX. *Pædag.* iii. p. 246 (ed. Græc. Lat. *Heinsii*). Its anagrammatic use is commented upon or alluded to by many of the Fathers. "ἰχθύς quod est Latinum Iesus Christus Dei Filius Salvator."—OPTATUS MILEV. *de Schism. Donat.* iii. 2. "Nos pisciculi secundum ἰχθύν nostrum in aqua nascimur nec nisi in aquis permanendo salvi sumus."—TERTULL. *de Bapt.* i. Augustine inserts the acrostic verses supposed to have been written by the Erythræan Sibyl, *de Civ. Dei*, xviii. 23. See also Marriott's Essay on the *Autun Inscrip.* in the Testimony of the Catacombs.

the true doctrine of the Holy Eucharist as taught in the Church Catechism, "the outward and visible sign, and the inward and spiritual grace," the consecrated elements and that which underlies them, the Body and Blood of Christ.

Now, to turn directly to the subject immediately before us, we propose to select from the vast collection of inscriptions which have been gathered out of the subterranean cemeteries several specimens of three different classes. *On what points their testimony will be used.*

The first will be brought forward to show that the doctrine of the Church, which teaches that the faithful dead are not detained in a state of suffering or purgatorial pain, but pass at once to a place of rest, is the same which was held by the Roman Christians of the first four centuries.

The second will witness to the belief that death does not separate interests, but that the preservation of the souls of the righteous in union with God and Christ in the world of spirits, and in consequent rest, was held to be a legitimate subject of prayer for the surviving friends and members of the same Church.

The third class exhibits traces of the practice of appealing to the dead for their prayers and intercessions; but these will be more fitly introduced in the Second Part.

On the present state of the faithful dead.

Under the first head all those inscriptions will naturally fall which bear the familiar formulæ of *pax, in pace, in pacem,* and the like. An attempt has been made to prove that such expressions merely indicated that the deceased had died in communion with the Catholic Church, but one argument will suffice for the refutation of such a theory.

It is not probable that among the early Christians the number of those who had been cut off and excommunicated could have been so great as to call for a distinguishing mark in behalf of those who had not.

Again, the expression has been interpreted of the rest or peace of the body in the tomb, or to separate confessors from martyrs, those who died a natural death from those who perished by the hand of the executioner, as the prophet[1] says, "Thou shalt not die by the sword, but thou shalt die in peace." No doubt there may be cases where such explanations are possible, but the frequent expression, "he lives in peace," altogether excludes any such limitation. Moreover, a full and unbiassed consideration of the following inscriptions will satisfy most candid people that all such limited and restricted interpretations are wholly inadequate. The language can be satisfied by no less a meaning

[1] JER. xxxiv. 4-5.

than is obtained by referring it to the peace of the pardoned soul, which it enjoys, when, set free from the encumbrances of the body with all its sinful desires and restless passions, it realises the prospect of a joyful resurrection and an eternity of bliss already begun.

There are a large number of inscriptions which give merely the name of the deceased and the date of his death, followed by the formula—IN PACE.

A few examples are given, but they are so numerous that it is hardly necessary to recall them; indeed the occurrence of the formula is so frequent that, after the middle of the fourth century, it is rarely absent:—

IRENEO—LAURENTIUS—FELICITAS—SABINA—
AGRIPPINA—TURBANTIA—IN PACE.

One or two may be quoted which contain other expressions indicative of the same state of peace :—

No. 243.[1]

BENEMERENTI IN PACE LIBERA QUE BIXIT A. XI.
NEOFITA. DEP. DIE., ETC.

To the well-deserving Libera in peace, who lived eleven years. A neophyte. Committed to the grave, etc.

[1] Wherever the inscriptions are numbered, it is in accordance with DE-ROSSI, *Christianæ Inscriptiones*, 243.—Taken from the Kircherian Museum, dated 374 A.D. The dates actually found on the Inscriptions are according to *consulship*, but we have given the more convenient corresponding forms.

We have made no attempt at correcting the grammar, which is so frequently at fault, but have printed the inscriptions as they are found.

No. 31.

ARCESSITUS AB ANGELIS QUI VIXIT
ANN. XXII. MESIS VIII. DIEB. VIIL, IN PACE
DEP. IDIBUS DEC. MAXENT. III. COSS.[1]

Fetched by angels, who lived twenty-two years, eight months, and eight days, in peace committed to the grave on the Ides of December in the third consulship of Maxentius.

The expression "fetched by the angels" is indicative of peace and rest, and "committed to the grave," as has been frequently noticed, was fitly chosen to represent Christian burial, because the idea it suggests witnesses to the resurrection; the body is not so much placed or laid in the grave, but intrusted to it as a sacred "deposit," to be reclaimed hereafter.

A very considerable number of the epigraphs are composed of a mixture of Greek and Latin; many too exhibit the words of one language in the characters of another. An example of these is quoted only because they have an additional interest as being, in the judgment of De-Rossi, before the middle of the third century :—

ΦΟΡΤΟΥΝΑΤΟΥC ΕΥΜΕΝ. . . . ΚΟΙΟΤΕΙ ΙΝ ΠΑΚΕ.
Fortunatus Eumenes lieth in peace.

---

[1] 31 said to have been taken from the Crypts of S. Sebastian, dated 310 A.D.

We turn from these, which are of the simplest kind, and are cited only to show the belief of the early Christians that the faithful dead were in a condition of rest, to those which express the wishes and prayers of the survivors for their continuance in peace, or for light, or for refreshment, three things which we shall see hereafter were the special objects of prayer in the Primitive Liturgies :—

ΕΙΡΗΝΗ COY TH ΨΥΧΗ ΖΩCΙΜΗ.

Peace to thy soul, O Zosima.

ΕΙΡΗΝΗ ΤΕ ΦΟΡΤΥΝΑΤΕ ΘΥΓΑΤΡΙ ΓΛΥΚΥΤΑΤΗ.

And peace be to Fortunata my sweetest daughter.

No. 17.

EX VIRGINIO TUO BENE MECO VIXISTI LIBENT CONJUGA INNOCENTISSIMA CERVONIA SILVANA REFRIGERA CUM SPIRITA SANCTA, DEP.

Cervonia Silvana, thou didst live well and happily with me, from thy virginity, as a most innocent wife. Refresh (thy soul) with the holy spirits.[1] *Committed to the grave.*

---

[1] The preposition *cum* is frequently found governing an accusative case in these inscriptions. The neuter form is not stranger than many other anomalies with which they abound. In fact, grammatical errors and peculiarities of many kinds meet us at every turn, as the following pages testify.

94 *The Testimony of the Catacombs.*

The following express prayers for the refreshment of the soul :—

HILARIS VIVAS CUM TUIS FELICITER SEMPER REFRIGERIS IN PACE DEI.[1]

Hilaris, may you live happily with your friends, may you be refreshed in the peace of God.

KALEMERE DEUS REFRIGERET SPIRITUM TUUM UNA CUM SORORIS TUAE HILARE.[2]

Kalemeros, may God refresh thy spirit together with that of thy sister Hilara.

BOLOSA DEUS TIBI REFRIGERET QUAE VIX : ANN : XXXI.

Bolosa, may God refresh you, who lived, etc.

REFRIGERA DEUS ANIMA

God refresh the soul of . . . .

ΗΡΑΚΛΙΑ ΡΩΜΗ IC ΑΝΑΠΑΥCΙΝ COY Η ΨΥΧΗ.

Heraclea Roma, may thy soul (go) into refreshment.

---

[1] This is taken from one of the Gilded Glasses, upon the early date of which, however, Mr. Parker has thrown doubt.
Refrigeris is apparently an abbreviated form for *refrigereris*.
[2] From the Kircherian Museum, found in the Catacomb of S. Ermetes. It is marked 124 in BURGON's *Letters from Rome*.

The next two are for light:—

DOMINE NE QUANDO ADUMBRETUR SPIRITUS VENERES DE FILIUS IPSEIUS QUI SUPERSTITIS SUNT BENIROSUS PROJECTUS.[1]

O Lord, let not the spirit of Venus be overshadowed. Of her sons who survive Benirosus (and) Projectus.

ETERNA LUX TIBI TIMOTHEA IN XP.

Timothea, mayest thou have eternal light in Christ.

Then there are many which pray for eternal life or union with **God** and Christ and life with the saints:—

ΥΓΕΙΑ ΖΗCΕC ΜΕΤΑ ΙCΤΕΡΚΟΡΙΟΥ ΤΟΥ ΛΕΓΟΜΕΝΟΥ ΥΓΕΙΝΟΥ ΕΝ ΤΕΩ.

Hygeia, mayest thou live with Stercorius, who is called Hyginus, in God.

ERENEA VIVAS IN DEO. A. Ω.

O Irenea, mayest thou live in God. The Alpha and Omega.

[1] From the Cemetery of S. Callixtus. Preserved in Column xvii. at the Lateran.

CHRESIME DULCISSIMA ET MIHI PI
ENTISSIMA FILIA VIVAS IN DEO QUE
REDDEDIT ANN. V. M. VII. D. V. CHRESIMUS ET
VICTORINA PARENTES VICTORIA
VIVAS IN DEO.[1]

My sweetest Chresime and most affectionate daughter, mayest thou live in God, who gave back (thy soul) at the age of five years, seven months, and five days. Chresimus and Victorina her parents. Victoria, mayest thou live in God.

MARIUS VITELLIANUS PRIMITIVÆ CONJUGI
FIDELISSIMAE. AAIKCBBIN.[2]

Marius Vitellianus to his most faithful wife Primitiva. Hail, innocent soul, dear wife, mayest thou live in Christ.

---

[1] This is interesting from the repetition of the prayer. It has been conjectured that the first part was dictated by the father addressing his daughter by the name she had received from him; the latter part was inscribed perhaps later by the mother, who wished her daughter to be commemorated also by the name she had received from her.—See NORTHCOTE, *Christian Epigraphs*, p. 82.

[2] This is from a Sarcophagus preserved in the Lateran. De Rossi considers the mysterious combination of letters at the end to be an acrostic: Ave anima innocens kara conjux bibas in Christo.

No. 10.

PASTO . . . VIBAS INTER SANCTIS IHA.

Mayest thou live among the saints in peace.

Many more illustrations of a similar kind might be brought forward, but the preceding exhibit ample proof that the early Christians believed not only that the faithful dead entered at once into a state of rest and peace, where "no torment could touch them," but also that death interposed no barrier to the prayers of those who survived.

Taken by themselves the inscriptions may appear meagre and unimportant, but when we remember that the character of the times is often "most accurately reflected in Christian epigraphy," we learn to value their testimony.

It may be said again that the expressions referred to are nothing more than "pious acclamations," but the same might be alleged of the *requiescat in pace*, and yet Catholics who inscribe the words on their tombs would never consent to the restriction. They may be, and often have been, used simply as such, but far more frequently they set forth the language of direct prayer.

---

[1] This inscription in the earlier part is much mutilated and almost beyond recall. The last letters are considered a corruption of *inpa*. The date of it is given by De-R. as 268 or 279 A.D.

CHAPTER VIII.

The Testimony of the Early Fathers.

THE writings of the Early Fathers supply abundant evidence of the practice of praying for the dead. It will suffice here to quote a few passages almost without comment, leaving for later consideration the extent to which prayer in such cases was regarded by them as efficacious.

Tracing backwards from the middle of the fifth century, where our investigations cease, we meet in the Acts of the Council of Chalcedon with a discussion which intimately concerns the question.

The Council of Chalcedon, 451 A.D.

Dioscurus was delated to the Council for a breach of trust. A saintly woman[1] of blessed memory had provided in her will for large grants of money to be made to the monasteries, hospitals, almshouses, and

---

[1] τὸ γὰρ κατὰ τὸν τῆς λαμπρᾶς μνήμης Περιστερίαν πρᾶγμα οὐδεὶς ἠγνόησε. ἐκείνης γὰρ ὑπὲρ τῆς ἑαυτῆς ψυχῆς ἐν τῷ διατίθεσθαι παρακελευσαμένης ποσότητα χρυσίου παρασχεθῆναι τοῖς Μοναστηρίοις, οὐ μὴν ἀλλὰ καὶ τοῖς ξενεῶσι καὶ πτωχείοις καὶ ἑτέροις πένησι τῆς Αἰγυπτιακῆς χώρας. ὥστε μηδὲ τὴν εὐωδίαν ἣν ἀπὸ τῆς θυσίας τῆς λαμπρᾶς τὴν μνήμην Περιστερίας ἀνενεχθῆναι πρὸς τὸν Θεόν, τὸ ὅσον ἐπ' αὐτῷ.—*Conc. Lab.* p. 401, Act. 3.

the poor generally, in Egypt, in the belief that her soul would be benefited by the prayers of the faithful, to whose necessities she thus ministered. She appointed Dioscurus trustee for the execution of her will. An accusation was brought against him for failure of trust; that he had not done the very least that was required of him,—he had not even offered incense or a sweet-smelling savour to God to commemorate the illustrious dead.

It is obvious that such a matter as this could not have been brought within the cognisance of a General Ecclesiastical Council, or at any rate passed over without some marks of disapprobation, if the crime laid against Dioscurus were one of refusing to perform an act which the Church disallowed as contrary to Catholic practice.

S. Augustine says, "It has come down to us from the Fathers, and is universally held in the Church, that we should pray for those who died in the Communion of the Body and Blood of Christ, when they are commemorated in their proper place at the Sacrifice."[1] *S. Augustine.*

S. Ambrose, apostrophising Gratian and Valen- *S. Ambrose.*

---

[1] "Hoc enim a patribus traditum universa observat Ecclesia, ut pro eis qui in corporis et sanguinis Christi communione defuncti sunt cum ad ipsum sacrificium loco suo commemorantur, oretur."
—Sermo clxxii., *de Verbi Apostoli*, vol. v. p. 1196; ed. Paris.

tinian, thus speaks: "Blessed are ye both, if my prayers shall be of any avail! No day shall pass by you in silence, no prayer of mine pass over you unhonoured, no night shall fly past you without your receiving the boon of some earnest prayer; I will attend you with all my oblations."[1]

Epiphanius. Epiphanius argues that the Church has no alternative but to perform this duty, because she has received it as a traditionary custom from the hands of the Fathers.[2]

S. Chrysostom. S. Chrysostom goes so far as to say that the custom had received Apostolic sanction,—"not in vain was this law laid down by the Apostles."[3]

Eusebius. Eusebius narrates how at the tomb of Constantine "a vast crowd of people, in company with the priests of God, with tears and great lamentation

---

[1] "Beati ambo, si quid meæ orationes valebunt! nulla dies vos silentio præteribit, nulla inhonoratos vos mea transibit oratio, nulla nox non donatos aliqua precum mearum contestione transcurret: omnibus vos oblationibus frequentabo."—*De obitu Valentiani Consolatio*, 78.

This mode of address seems to have been suggested to him by the lines of Virgil—

"Fortunati ambo! si quid mea carmina possunt,
Nulla dies unquam memori vos eximet ævo."

[2] ἀναγκαίως ἡ ἐκκλησία τοῦτο ἐπιτελεῖ παράδοσιν λαβοῦσα παρὰ πατέρων· τίς δὲ δυνήσεται θεσμὸν μητρὸς καταλύειν ἢ νόμον πατρός;—EPIPH. *adv. Hær.* lib. iii. lxxv.

[3] οὐκ εἰκῇ ταῦτα ἐνομοθετήθη ὑπὸ τῶν ἀποστόλων.—*Hom.* iii. *ad Philipp.* cap. i.

offered their prayers to God for the Emperor's soul."[1]

Arnobius, writing of the persecution at the close of Diocletian's reign, when the Sacred Scriptures were ordered to be burnt, and the churches razed to the ground, asks, "What have our places of assembly done that they should be cruelly destroyed, in which we pray to the Most High God, and seek peace and pardon for all men; for magistrates, armies, kings, friends, and foes; for those still living, and for those who have been set free from the bondage of the flesh?"[2] *Arnobius.*

Tertullian closes the testimony of the Early Fathers by frequent reference to the prevalence of the custom. "We offer the oblations for the dead on the anniversary of their birth."[3] And again, speaking of a widow, he says, "She prays for his (her husband's) soul, and requests refreshment for him meanwhile, and fellowship in the *Tertullian.*

---

[1] λεὼς δὲ παμπληθὴς σὺν τοῖς τῷ Θεῷ ἱερωμένοις οὐ δακρύων ἐκτὸς σὺν κλαυθμῷ δὲ πλείονι τὰς εὐχὰς ὑπὲρ τῆς βασιλέως ψυχῆς ἀπεδίδοσαν τῷ Θεῷ.—*Vita Const.* lib. iv. c. 71.

[2] "Cur immaniter conventicula dirui meruerunt, in quibus summus oratur Deus, pax cunctis et venia postulatur, magistratibus, exercitibus, regibus, familiaribus, inimicis, adhuc vitam degentibus et resolutis corporum vinctione?"—*Adv. Gen.* iv. 36.

[3] "Oblationes pro defunctis, pro natalitiis annua die facimus."
—*De Cor. Mil.* c. 3.

first resurrection; and she offers sacrifice on the anniversaries of his falling asleep."[1]

Here, then, we have a chain of Patristic evidence which carries us back into the second century; and when we take into consideration the fact that it is fully corroborated by the Service-books of the Church, in which the religious opinions and feelings of a people are sure to find their outward expression, we can hardly do otherwise than accept the oft-repeated assertion that the Primitive Christians did not consider the interposition of death sufficient to silence the voice of prayer and intercession.

---

[1] "Pro anima ejus orat et refrigerium interim adpostulat ei et in prima resurrectione consortium," etc.—*De Monogam.* c. 10.

Tertullian was one of those who interpreted Rev. xx. 1-7 literally, and held that there will be a first resurrection of martyrs, and those saints who are worthy to share their honours, sooner or later according to their deserts, to live with Christ on earth for a thousand years, at the expiration of which period there will be a general resurrection of all the dead. He treated of the subject fully in a lost work, *de Spe Fidelium*, and more briefly in *adv. Marc.* iii. xxiv., and *de Monogam.* p. 682, and *de Resurr. Carnis*, p. 397, ed. Rig.

CHAPTER IX.

The Testimony of the Primitive Liturgies.

THERE can be little doubt that the Apostles attached great importance to the most sacred ordinance of "the Breaking of Bread," and it seems natural to suppose that, before they separated for their different spheres of missionary work, they would agree upon some definite form, or at least lay down some fixed general principles of Liturgical service,[1] according to which they would continue to celebrate the Holy Eucharist in the several Churches which they founded. But the principles being settled, and the central portion or nucleus, so to speak, being formed, the details of prayers and ceremonies which gathered round it would be suf-

The primal form of Liturgical service.

---

[1] Traces of these have been discovered in the Apostles' writings, *e.g.* the Act of Consecration, 1 Cor. x. 16; the Kiss of Peace, 1 Cor. xvi. 20, 2 Cor. xiii. 12, 1 S. Peter v. 14; the Amen of the Eucharist, 1 Cor. xiv. 15, compared with Just. Mart. *Apol.* lxvii. It has been noticed too that certain passages introduced by the Apostle with the formula "as it is written," are nowhere found in Scripture, but occur in the Liturgies; *e.g.* 1 Cor. ii. 9 may be seen in the quotation from S. Mark's Liturgy, p. 111. This is commonly regarded as an adaptation of Isaiah lxiv. 4.

fered to vary both in extent and character according to circumstances.

<small>The various groups into which it branched out.</small> Attempts have been made to classify the local and other varieties which existed in early times, and most Liturgiologists have decided to arrange all the Eucharistic Services used in different countries and by different communities, in four[1] or five groups or families, each one of which bears the name of the Apostle who is said to have laboured in the particular country where it was used.[2]

These are the Liturgies of S. James, S. Mark, S. John or S. Paul, and S. Peter, to which is added, by those who make five groups, another entitled the Liturgy of SS. Adæus and Maris, which is regarded as the parent of a vast class of Eucharistic Offices used by the Nestorians.

Accepting without controversy this mode of classification, we shall in the following investigation extract illustrations of the point under review from each of the parental forms, and also from some few of those which have been derived from them, merely giving, for the convenience of those who are un-

---

[1] Palmer in the *Origines Liturgicæ* reduces all forms to four, which he entitles the Great Oriental Liturgy, the Alexandrian, the Roman, and the Gallican.

[2] Cf. *Liturgies Eastern and Western*, ed. C. E. HAMMOND, Introd. p. xvi.

acquainted with the subject, as brief an account as possible of the several Liturgies cited.

Before, however, appealing to the evidence which lies in these Primitive Liturgies, it will be well to state distinctly how far these may be considered available for the purpose.

Some degree of hesitation must necessarily be felt by reason of the uncertain state of the text which has come down to us. In the absence of early manuscripts [1] we have no authentic evidence of their contents in their original form.

The uncertainty of the text.

If we accept the conclusions of those Liturgiologists [2]

---

[1] No doubt one great cause for the non-existence of early MSS. was the extreme reverence which was felt for the mysteries of the Faith, and the fear lest, if committed to writing, the books might be given up in times of persecution.

[2] It may be well to state briefly an outline of the arguments upon which the early date of some of the great Liturgies is said to rest. We take that of S. James as an illustration. This was originally used in the Patriarchate of Antioch. This Patriarchate is at this time occupied by two classes, the Monophysites and the Orthodox. Now the former retain a Liturgy, which they have used uninterruptedly, called after S. James. The latter have adopted that of Constantinople, but once a year, on the Apostle's Festival, they use that which bears his name. Here then we see the orthodox and the heretics ascribing a Liturgy in their possession to S. James, and they must have done so from a very remote period, clearly for more than fourteen centuries; for they separated from each other after the condemnation of Monophysitism at the Council of Chalcedon, 451 A.D., and it is not likely that either would borrow from the other after the separation. A Liturgy then bearing the title of S. James is proved to have been in use in the fifth century; and many portions of this are to be traced in the writings of certain Fathers, from Theodoret, 420 A.D., to Justin Martyr, 150 A.D., who lived at Samaria, in the Patriar-

who assign the origin of some of them to the beginning of the third century, or even to an earlier date, we are compelled to admit that they have since been greatly developed and added to under the influence of various circumstances. But apart from any legitimate development and additions, which are conformable to Catholic doctrine, there are also numerous undoubted interpolations of a totally different character. Are these sufficient to shake our confidence in the general trustworthiness of the documents? Or can we so far separate the later introduction as to leave the substantial parts free to be accepted as satisfactory evidence of the opinion of primitive times? We think it possible to do this. In some cases[1] there is no difficulty in recognising the interpolation, and frequently even the date of its insertion may be approximately determined.

chate of Antioch. He describes the celebration of the Eucharist, and, as far as it goes, his description corresponds almost precisely to that which is found in this Liturgy. And this carries back its existence to within a century of the Apostle whose name it bears.

[1] "Grant, Lord, we beseech Thee, that this oblation may benefit us by the intercession of the Blessed Leo."—*Miss. Fest. Leonis*, Jun. xxviii. Bingham gives the history of the change from the form, "Grant that this oblation may benefit the soul of Leo, Thy servant," as it appeared in the old Roman Missal.—*Op.* vol. v. xv. iii. 16, p. 312.

In HICKES' *Treatise on the Priesthood* he enumerates some of the additions which "any man, who is conversant in the history of the Councils, may see," such as ὁμοούσιος, τὸ Κύριον τὸ ζωόποιον, ἐκπορευόμενος, ἀτρέπτως, ἐνανθρωπήσας.—i. 143, ed. 1711.

Testimony of the Primitive Liturgies.

For instance, it would be useless to appeal to these Liturgies in support of the worship of the Blessed Virgin in the second or third or fourth centuries. After that her worship became an integral part of Christianity, as it did in the East during the fifth century, and not much later in the West, it was inevitable that it should find its expression in the Services[1] of the Church; and while we may avail ourselves of these as witnessing to the general acceptance of the doctrine after its introduction, it is obvious that documents which were confessedly open to interpolation, and the original forms of which are past recovery, could have no weight beyond this in the scale of evidence. The only condition under which their testimony is of value is, when that to which they witness is supported by the concurrence of contemporary history.

How far later additions detract from the value of their evidence.

To illustrate this we revert to the case above mentioned. Accepting, for the sake of the argument, the middle of the second century as the date of the Liturgies bearing the names of S. James and S. Mark, no discovery of allusions to the worship of the

---

[1] We find in the Liturgy of S. James the following:—"Let us commemorate our all-holy, pure, most glorious, blessed Lady, God-mother, and ever-Virgin Mary, and all the holy and just, that we may all find mercy through their prayers and intercessions."

Blessed Virgin in their existing forms would be of the slightest value, because it is wholly unsupported by contemporary writers. But if Justin Martyr or Origen or Tertullian, or any Father of that age, had left anything to indicate the prevalence of the *cultus* in their times, then, without being able to prove the absolute integrity of the Liturgies, we might appeal to their contents as corroborative evidence.

The Liturgy of S. James. In the first group that which holds the chief place is the Liturgy of S. James or of Jerusalem. Whether it was written in Syriac or Greek in its original form is a disputed point, but the arguments seem to incline rather in favour of the Syriac.

Since the separation of the Orthodox and the Monophysites at the Council of Chalcedon, the former have used the Greek, the latter the Syriac. In consequence however of their oppression by the Mohammedans, the Orthodox adopted the Liturgy of Constantinople, and only use that of S. James on one day in the year, the Feast of the Apostle.

In early times this Liturgy was adopted throughout the wide Patriarchate of Antioch, reaching from the Euphrates to the Hellespont, and from the Hellespont to the south of Greece.

In the Greek form, after the reading of the Diptychs of the dead the priest proceeds :—

"Remember, O Lord God, the spirits of all flesh, of whom we have made mention, and of whom we have not made mention, who are of the true faith, from righteous Abel unto this day; do Thou Thyself give them rest there in the land of the living, in Thy kingdom, in the delight of Paradise, in the bosom of Abraham and Isaac and Jacob, our holy fathers; whence pain and grief and lamentation have fled away: there the light of Thy countenance looks upon them, and gives them light for evermore."[1]

The Clementine[2] Liturgy has this petition, "Let us pray for those who rest in faith,"[3] and "We further offer to Thee for all Thy saints who have pleased Thee from the beginning of the world, patriarchs, prophets, just men, apostles, martyrs, confessors, bishops, elders, deacons, subdeacons, singers,

The Liturgy of S. Clement

---

[1] μνήσθητι, Κύριε ὁ Θεός, τῶν πνευμάτων καὶ πάσης σαρκός, ὧν ἐμνήσθημεν, καὶ ὧν οὐκ ἐμνήσθημεν, ὀρθοδόξων, ἀπὸ Ἀβὲλ τοῦ δικαίου μέχρι τῆς σήμερον ἡμέρας. αὐτὸς ἐκεῖ αὐτοὺς ἀνάπαυσον ἐν χώρᾳ ζώντων, ἐν τῇ βασιλείᾳ σου, ἐν τῇ τρυφῇ τοῦ παραδείσου, ἐν τοῖς κόλποις Ἀβραὰμ καὶ Ἰσαὰκ καὶ Ἰακώβ, τῶν ἁγίων πατέρων ἡμῶν. ὅθεν ἀπέδρα ὀδύνη λύπη καὶ στεναγμός. ἔνθα ἐπισκοπεῖ τὸ φῶς τοῦ προσώπου σου καὶ καταλάμπει διὰ παντός.—*Lit. S. Jacobi Græcorum.*

[2] The title of "Clementine" originated no doubt in the fiction of S. Clement's authorship of the *Constitutiones.* Their probable date is not earlier than the end of the third century, but in many parts they embody materials which are much older.

[3] ὑπὲρ τῶν ἐν πίστει ἀναπαυσαμένων δεηθῶμεν.

virgins, widows, laymen, and all whose names Thou Thyself knowest."[1]

The value of their evidence.

The evidence of these is important, because S. Cyril, Bishop of Jerusalem, and a successor in the see of S. James, in his Lectures on the Mysteries, bears distinct witness to the text of a Liturgy in use in his time containing a list of the saints for whom prayers were offered; and he gives a description of the Service, which corresponds minutely to that of S. James.

While the Clementine Liturgy, from the fact of its having been embodied in a literary work, has in all probability been left free from additions, which from time to time have been largely introduced into the forms of Eucharistic worship.

The Liturgy of S. Mark.

Of the second group the Greek Liturgy of S. Mark is the parental form. It was used in the Patriarchate of Alexandria, which extended over Egypt, Libya, and Ethiopia. The modern Christians of Egypt use three Coptic Liturgies, which have been derived from it, bearing the names of S. Cyril, S. Basil, and S. Gregory.

The following extract is from S. Mark:— "Give

[1] ἔτι προσφέρομέν σοι καὶ ὑπὲρ πάντων τῶν ἀπ' αἰῶνος εὐαρεστησάντων σοι ἁγίων πατριαρχῶν προφητῶν δικαίων ἀποστόλων μαρτύρων ὁμολογητῶν ἐπισκόπων πρεσβυτέρων διακόνων ὑποδιακόνων ἀναγνωστῶν ψαλτῶν παρθένων χηρῶν λαϊκῶν καὶ πάντων ὧν αὐτὸς ἐπίστασαι τὰ ὀνόματα.—*Apostol. Constit.* viii. 12.

rest, O Sovereign Lord, our God, to the souls of all those, who are in the tabernacle of Thy saints, in Thy kingdom, graciously bestowing upon them the blessing of Thy promises, which eye hath not seen, nor ear heard, nor have entered into the heart of man, which Thou hast prepared, O God, for them that love Thy holy Name."[1]

The next is from S. Cyril's:—"Be merciful, O Lord. Grant rest to our fathers and brothers, who have fallen asleep, and whose souls Thou hast received. Remember also all the saints who have pleased Thee since the world began."[2] *The Coptic Liturgy of S. Cyril.*

The parent form of the next group, which was used in the Patriarchate of Ephesus, is not extant, but portions of it are found in the Gallican and Mozarabic Liturgies. The first of these was used in the Churches of France, which were probably founded by missionaries from Asia Minor,[3] for several centuries, and only superseded by the Roman in the *The normal form, the Liturgy of S. Paul or S. John, not extant.*

---

[1] τούτων πάντων τὰς ψυχὰς ἀνάπαυσον, Δέσποτα Κύριε ὁ Θεὸς ἡμῶν ἐν ταῖς τῶν ἁγίων σου σκηναῖς, ἐν τῇ βασιλείᾳ σου, χαριζόμενος αὐτοῖς τὰ τῶν ἐπαγγελιῶν σου ἀγαθά, ἃ ὀφθαλμός, κ.τ.λ.—*Lit. of S. Mark.*

[2] "Domine miserere: patribus fratribusque nostris qui obdormierunt et quorum animas suscepisti quietem præsta. Memento etiam omnium sanctorum qui a sæculo tibi placuerunt."—*Lat. Transl. of the Anaphora of the Coptic Liturgy of S. Cyril.*

[3] As proof of the close connection between the Churches of Gaul and Asia, several early Bishops of the former are said to have been natives of Ephesus, and the well-known letter from the Christians at Lyons bears witness to the same.

reign of Charlemagne; and it has a special interest for us from the probability of its having been used by the British Church before the mission of S. Augustine.

The Gallican Liturgy.

In the Gallican Liturgy we read:—"At the same time we pray, beseeching Thee, O Lord, for the souls of Thy servants, our fathers and former teachers, . . . and for the souls of all our brothers, whom Thou didst deem worthy to call to Thyself from this place, and of strangers who died in the peace of the Church."[1]

The Mozarabic Liturgy.

The Mozarabic Liturgy[2] is the most complete of those which were derived from S. John and the Ephesian Church, and was used as the national Rite throughout Spain from the earliest times. In this there is less distinctness in the intercession, but the Apostles and others are commemorated, and "the spirits of many holy men, who are at rest."[3]

---

[1] "Simulque precantes oramus etiam, Domine, pro animabus famulorum tuorum, patrum atque institutorum quondam nostrorum . . . . vel omnium fratrum nostrorum, quos de hoc loco ad te vocare dignatus es; . . . ac peregrinorum in pace ecclesiæ defunctorum."—*Gallic. Lit.*

[2] Its use is generally supposed to have ceased when Gregory VII. prevailed upon Alphonso VI. to substitute the Roman Liturgy in its place. After having become practically a dead letter for many centuries it was re-introduced at Toledo by Cardinal Ximenes, and it is said regularly in the college of priests founded by him there at the present day.

[3] "Facientes commemorationem beatissimorum Apostolorum . . . item pro spiritibus pausantium."—*Mozar. Lit.*

Testimony of the Primitive Liturgies. 113

Much obscurity hangs over the original Liturgy of the fourth group. The oldest form now extant is probably the Ambrosian. Later developments of it are the Sacramentaries of Leo, Gelasius, and Gregory, from which so many of the Collects of the Anglican Liturgy have been taken. *The Liturgy of S. Peter.*

In the Liturgy which has been in use from time immemorial throughout the diocese of Milan the following prayer is found:—" Remember also, O Lord, Thy servants, men and women, who have gone before us with the seal of the faith, and are sleeping in the sleep of peace. To them, O Lord, and all who rest in Christ, we pray Thee to grant a place of refreshment light and peace."[1] *The Ambrosian Liturgy.*

In the Sacramentary of S. Gregory, which was derived from the Liturgy of S. Peter, we read the following prayers:—" Be favourable to the souls of Thy servants with an everlasting compassion, that they may be set free from the bonds of death, and kept in eternal light;" and "We pray that the souls of Thy servants, and all who rest in Christ, may attain to a participation in eternal light."[2] *The Sacramentary of S. Gregory.*

[1] "Memento etiam, Domine, famulorum famularumque tuarum qui nos præcesserunt cum signo fidei et dormiunt in somno pacis. Ipsis, Domine, et omnibus in Christo quiescentibus locum refrigerii lucis et pacis ut indulgeas deprecamur."—*Ambros. Lit.*

[2] "Propitiare animabus famulorum famularumque tuarum

The evidence derived from this is less trustworthy, because it is well known that Gregory made considerable alterations in the form which he revised, but they were chiefly by way of condensation rather than enlargement.

The Liturgy of SS. Adæus and Maris. The chief of the Nestorian group is that which bears the title of S. Adæus and S. Maris, of whom the former is to be identified with Thaddæus, who was sent on a mission to Abgarus, governor of Edessa, after the Ascension of the Lord; while of the latter little is known, except by tradition which makes him a founder of the Churches of Mesopotamia.

In the Great Intercession the following occurs:—

"O Lord, mighty God, receive this oblation for all the holy Catholic Church, and for all godly and righteous Fathers who have pleased Thee, . . . and for all the dead who have been separated and have departed from us."[1]

Quotations of a similar kind might have been largely multiplied, but we have abstained from

misericordia sempiterna, ut mortalibus nexibus expeditas lux eas æterna possideat."

"Inveniant quæsumus animæ famulorum famularumque tuarum omniumque in Christo quiescentium lucis æternæ consortium."— *Sacr. Greg.*, MURAT. ii. 221.

[1] "Domine Deus potens suscipe hanc oblationem pro omni Ecclesia sancta Catholica et pro Patribus piis et justis qui placiti fuerunt tibi . . . et pro omnibus defunctis qui a nobis separati migraverunt."—*Lit. SS. Adæi et Maris.*

introducing them, knowing that we should only see the features of the parent repeated again and again in the child, so closely in this matter do the derived Liturgies resemble those from which they originated.

We pass on to consider what value the early Christians could have attached to such petitions. This we estimate from two points of view. *The meaning and object of the petitions.*

Firstly, where the future is chiefly referred to, they felt that it was a "holy and pious thing to pray for the dead," because the Scriptures led them to believe that a man's final condition is not reached till the day of judgment; and though the Church in all her supplications breathes the spirit of a sure and certain hope, yet so long as judgment is delayed, the attitude of prayer is most in accordance with our Christian instincts. Whilst there is anything still future to be obtained (and the frequent reference to the resurrection and eternal happiness points distinctly to the future), it is certainly not unbecoming that a waiting Church, whether in the body or out of the body, should place itself upon its knees in prayer and supplication. It is this principle which has found such a happy expression in our own office at the Burial of the Dead,—"Beseeching Thee, that it may please Thee, of Thy gracious goodness, shortly to accomplish the number of Thine elect, and *The attitude of prayer most becoming till the judgment is passed.*

to hasten Thy kingdom; that we, with all those that are departed in the true faith of Thy holy Name, may have our perfect consummation and bliss, both in body and soul, in Thy eternal and everlasting glory."

Such prayers an acknowledgment of our dependence upon God.

Secondly, where the present condition is the prominent idea. Admitting that the day of death may be practically the day of judgment, that the sentence, though not yet delivered, is then determined and cannot be reversed, even under these circumstances it does not seem to be a violation of the principle of prayer to continue to pray for what we may feel confident that those for whom we pray already possess. God has willed that His creatures should live in continual acknowledged dependence on Him and His bounty; that at all times, and under all conditions of being, men should acknowledge that He is the Giver of all things; and this is the reason why all men, rich and poor, those in plenty no less than those in want, are taught to pray daily for the supply of their bodily needs, to ask for this day's bread, though all the time their garners may be "full and plenteous with all manner of store."

Upon these principles, apart from others which may be considered hereafter, the prayers of the Primitive Liturgies for the peace and refreshment of the dead receive their full justification.

CHAPTER X.

Prayers for the pardon of sins of infirmity, and the effacement of sinful stains.

THE preceding pages have afforded us an opportunity of judging how prevalent the habit of praying for the dead was in the early ages of Christianity, and at the same time have set forth the commonest forms in which prayers were expressed. So far no instance has been quoted in which any direct mention of sin is found in the petitions. The more perplexing consideration of those not infrequent cases in which it does find a place, when the language takes the form of a prayer either for the remission of sins, or for the effacing of the stains and defilements of sin, must now be entered upon. *Prayers in connection with sin.*

The evidence on this head does not carry us quite so far back as that produced above. There is much less in the great parent Liturgies, and, as far as we can discover, hardly anything worth recording in the Fathers before S. Jerome; but from his time onwards there was a general belief that those sins which were the inevitable consequence of a frail nature, common to the holy man as well as the wicked, might be done away after death; and that the defilements which the pardoned soul carried with it out of this life might be wiped out; and that in both cases entire remission and perfect purification could be furthered by the prayers of the faithful.

<small>Syriac Liturgy of S. James.</small>

Taking the Oriental Liturgies first, we read in the Syriac of S. James:—" We commemorate all the faithful dead who have died in the true faith, . . . and come to Thee, O God, the Lord of spirits and of all flesh: we ask, we entreat, we pray Christ our Lord, who took their souls and spirits to Himself, that by His own manifold compassions He will make them worthy of the pardon of their faults and the remission of their sins."[1]

The above is the prototype of a vast number of

---

[1] "Commemoramus omnes defunctos fideles, qui in fide vera defuncti sunt . . . et ad te Deum Dominum spirituum et omnis carnis pervenerunt. Rogamus imploramus et deprecamur Christum Deum nostrum, qui suscepit ad se animas et spiritus eorum, nt per miserationes suas multas præstet illos dignos venia delictorum et remissione peccatorum."—*Syr. Lit. S. Jacobi*, Latin trans., RENAUD., ed. Hammond, p. 75.

Liturgies which are used by that portion of the Syrian Church which professes Monophysite doctrine.

The titles which many of them bear are not authentic, but the Liturgies themselves are held to be very ancient.

The following extracts are taken from four of them:—

From that of S. John the Evangelist:—"Thou art the Creator of the souls and bodies, and they, who have lain down in the grave, wait for Thee, and look to Thy life-giving hope. Awake them, O Lord, in that last day, and may Thy look towards them be tranquil, and of Thy mercy forgive their faults and failings, for none of those who have lived on earth can be found clean from the stains of sin."[1] *Jacobite Liturgies.*

From that of S. Peter, chief of the Apostles:—

"Place in Abraham's bosom and bid them rest, who fulfilled their course of human life in the orthodox faith, . . . taking away and forgiving all their wrong deeds, . . . because it is impossible for those who have enjoyed the pleasures of the world,

---

[1] "Tu es enim Creator animarum et corporum et te expectant qui decubuerunt et spem tuam vivificantem respiciunt. Suscita illos, Domine, in die illo novissimo: tranquillusque sit erga illos vultus tuus: et dimitte per misericordiam tuam delicta et defectus eorum; quia eorum qui super terram fuerunt nullus reperitur mundus a sordibus peccati."—*Lit. S. Joannis Evang.*, RENAUD. i. 167.

even for a single moment, to be found other than guilty."¹

From that of S. James the Less:—"Load them with joy in the land which is lit by the brightness of Thy face, blotting out their prevarications, and not entering into judgment with them, for there is no one pure from sin in Thy sight."²

From that of S. Dionysius, Bishop of Athens:—"Remember, O Lord, all the dead, who died with Thy hope in the true faith; . . . write their names with the names of Thy saints in the blessed abode of those who keep holiday and rejoice in Thee; not calling back to them the recollection of their sins, or reminding them of their foolish deeds, because there is no one in the bonds of the flesh who is innocent in Thy sight."³

Before leaving the Eastern Liturgies we quote from one which belongs to a different family, and has

---

[1] "In sinu Abrahæ colloca et quiescere jube eos qui in fide orthodoxa humanæ vitæ periodum compleverunt . . . auferens et dimittens omnes iniquitates illorum . . . quia impossibile est illis qui vel unico momento aliquam temporalem voluptatem perceperunt, ut non rei inveniantur."—*Lit. S. Petri Princ. Apost.*, RENAUD. ii. 150.

[2] "Cumula eos lætitia in regione quam illuminat splendor vultus tui, delens prævaricationes eorum, nec intrans in judicium cum illis; neque enim quisquam purus est a peccato coram te."—*Lit. Minor S. Jacobi*, RENAUD. ii. 130.

[3] "Memento, Domine, omnium defunctorum qui decubuerunt cum spe tua in fide vera . . . adjunge nomina illorum cum nomi-

for its parent form the Liturgy of S. Adæus and S. Maris.

In the Liturgy of Theodore the Interpreter the priest prays God to accept the sacrifice of thanksgiving which he was offering in these terms:—"That the memory might be blessed of all the sons of the holy Catholic Church who passed out of the world in the true faith, that by Thy grace, O Lord, Thou wouldest grant to them pardon of all the sins and faults which they committed in their mortal bodies, with a soul ever subject to change, because there is none that sinneth not."[1]

Liturgy of Theodore the Interpreter.

Turning to the Western Liturgies it will suffice to quote from the three well-known Sacramentaries.

Western Liturgies.

In that of S. Leo we read:—"We pray that whatever stain he has contracted in his passage through the world may be wiped out by these sacrifices."

S. Leo.

nibus sanctorum tuorum in habitatione beata eorum qui festum agunt et lætantur in te : non revocans illis memoriam peccatorum suorum neque commemorans ipsis quæ insipienter egerunt; quia nullus est carni alligatus et innocens coram te."—*Lit. S. Dionysii Athenarum Episc.*, RENAUD. ii. 209.

[1] "Ut sit coram te memoria bona . . . omnium filiorum Ecclesiæ sanctæ Catholicæ, eorum qui in fide vera transierunt ex hoc mundo, ut per gratiam tuam, Domine, veniam illis concedas, omnium peccatorum et delictorum quæ in hoc mundo in corpore mortali et anima mutationi obnoxia peccaverunt aut offenderunt coram te, quia nemo est qui non peccet."—*Lit. Theodori Interpretis*, RENAUD. ii. 621.

And again: "Grant that the fact of his having ardently longed for repentance may suffice for the attainment of a perfect healing."[1]

S. Gelasius. In that of S. Gelasius:—"Let us make our commemorations beseeching the compassion of our God to forgive all the offences of a dangerous rashness, and having the pardon of full forgiveness granted, to atone by His own unspeakable goodness and mercy for all the mistakes into which he fell in this world."

And again: "Whatever stains the soul contracted from its sojourn in the flesh, do Thou, O God, of Thine innate mercy wipe them out."[2]

S. Gregory. In that of S. Gregory:—"We beseech Thee that the offering of this sacrifice may suffice for the soul of Thy servant, and that he may find the pardon which he sought, and reap in the reward of the longed-for repentance the fruit of that which the

---

[1] "Quæsumus, Domine, miserationum tuarum largitate concedas ut quicquid terrena conversatione contraxit, his sacrificiis emundetur."

"Ut devotio pænitentiæ quemgessit ejus affectus, perpetuæ salutis consequatur effectum."—*Sacr. Leon.*, MURAT. i. 451.

[2] "Commemorationem faciamus . . . obsecrantes misericordiam Dei nostri ut remittat omnes lubricæ temeritatis offensas, ut concessa venia plenæ indulgentiæ, quicquid in hoc sæculo proprius error adtulit totum ineffabili pietate ac benignitate sua compenset."

"Et si quas illa ex hac carnali commoratione contraxit maculas Tu Deus inoleta bonitate clementer deleas."—*Sacr. Gelas.*, Murat. p. 747.

labour of this life was unable fully to attain to."[1]

In what follows we give extracts from some of the Fathers who speak of prayers for the dead with reference to their sins. *Patristic writings.*

S. Jerome in commenting upon the words, "𝔚hen a wicked man dieth his expectation shall perish; and the hope of unjust men perisheth," says, "I would have you observe, that although there is no hope of pardon for the ungodly after death, there are nevertheless some who may be absolved after death from the lighter sins in which they were entangled when they died."[2] *S. Jerome.*

Theodoret in his History narrates, almost as though he had been an eye-witness, a scene in which the Emperor Theodosius offered prayers at the shrine of S. Chrysostom for his deceased parents. "He threw himself," he says, "on the coffin, and lifting *Theodoret.*

---

[1] "Satisfaciat tibi, Domine, quæsumus pro anima famuli tui sacrificii præsentis oblatio et peccatorum veniam, quam quæsivit, inveniat; et quod officio linguæ implere non potuit, desideratæ pœnitentiæ compensatione percipiat."—*Sacr. Greg.*, MURAT. ii. 220.

[2] "Notandum autem quod et si impiis post mortem spes veniæ non est: sunt tamen qui de levioribus peccatis, cum quibus obligati defuncti sunt, post mortem possunt absolvi."—*In Proverbia*, cap. xi. 7.

up his eyes and forehead offered supplication for those who had begotten him, entreating pardon for the sins which they had committed through ignorance."[1]

S. Augustine.

S. Augustine in his Confessions brings before us his own practice. After describing minutely his feelings at the burial of his mother, he gives the very words of the prayer which he offered in her behalf, after God had bound up the wounds of his broken heart. "I pour out unto Thee, our God, tears of a far different kind for Thy handmaid; ... although she, having been quickened in Christ even before she was released from the burden of the flesh, had so lived that Thy name should be praised by her faith and conversation, yet I dare not say that since Thou didst regenerate her in baptism, no word fell from her lips in violation of Thy commandment; ... I therefore, O God of my heart, my praise and my life, setting aside for a while her good deeds, for which I gladly give Thee thanks, do now entreat Thee for my mother's sins."[2]

---

[1] οὗτος ἐπιθεὶς τῇ λάρνακι καὶ τοὺς ὀφθαλμοὺς καὶ τὸ μέτωπον, ἱκετείαν ὑπὲρ τῶν γεγεννηκότων προσήνεγκε, συγγνῶναι τοῖς ἐξ ἀγνοίας ἠδικηκόσιν ἀντιβολήσας.—*Eccles. Hist.* Lib. v. c. xxxvi.

[2] "Ego autem fundo tibi pro illa famula tua longe aliud lacrymarum genus ... quamquam illa in Christo vivificata, etiam nondum a carne resoluta, sic vixerit ut laudetur nomen tuum in fide moribusque ejus: non tamen audeo dicere, ex quo eam per Baptismum regenerasti, nullum verbum exisse ab ore ejus contra

There can hardly be any question as to the character of the sins which he sought to aid in wiping out by his prayers, for in addition to the tone of reverence in which he speaks of her life, he says shortly after that she had continually sought the saving help of the Holy Sacrifice, and "waited on the altar without the intermission of a single day."

A careful examination of the whole context, and the general tone of the above passages, leaves upon the mind a distinct impression that those who were prayed for were held to be already saved, and to have had their pardon sealed. Nevertheless, even for these the intercessions of the Church still militant were not deemed to be misplaced or useless, inasmuch as all experience of human nature, even in its best estate as witnessed in the holiest life of the saint, excludes the possibility of any man continuing for any length of time wholly free from sin, or again, of his dying without some trace of defilement left upon his soul by its unavoidable contact with the evil that is in the world. *Conclusion.*

But it must be clearly laid down that this idea of purification during the intermediate state is quite

præceptum tuum . . . ego itaque, laus mea et vita mea, Deus cordis mei, sepositis paulisper bonis ejus actibus, pro quibus tibi gaudens gratias ago, nunc pro peccatis matris meæ deprecor te."—*Confess.* Lib. ix. c. xiii. 34, 35.

distinct from the doctrine of Purgatory as taught by the Roman Church. The Liturgies and the Fathers appealed to here deal with the dead who come within the range of our prayers, as being in a condition of peace and rest, of light and refreshment; whereas the Roman doctrine maintains that the faithful dead, as well as the sinful, are in a state of penal torment.

A Lutheran divine on a spiritual Purgatory.

In support of this distinction we may quote the opinion of a very distinguished Lutheran divine. "Since no soul," he writes, "leaves this state of being in a fully concluded and finished condition, the middle state must be considered as a realm of continued development, wherein souls may be prepared, and ripen for the last judgment. Although the Catholic doctrine of Purgatory is rejected, because it is mixed up with so much that is harsh and false, it contains nevertheless the truth that the intermediate state, in a purely spiritual sense, must be a purgatory determined for the purifying of the soul."[1]

[1] "Da keine Seele in einem völlig abgeschlossenen und fertigen Zustande dieses Dasein verläszt, musz der Mittelzustand als ein Reich fortgesetzter Entwickelung gedacht werden, wo die Seelen vorbereitet und reif werden sollen für das jüngste Gericht. Obgleich die katholische Lehre vom Fegefeuer verworfen ist, weil sie mit so vielen krassen und falschen Zusätzen vermischt ist, so enthält sie doch die Wahrheit, dasz der Mittelzustand in rein geistigem Sinne ein Purgatorium sein musz, bestimmt zur Läuterung der Seele."—*Die Christliche Dogmatik*, Dr. H. MARTENSEN, Bischof von Seeland; Der Mittelzustand im Todtenreich, § 276, p. 430, ed. 1870.

CHAPTER XI.

The inefficacy of prayer for those who died in wilful unrepented sin.

THERE remain to be noticed a few cases where prayers for the dead are spoken of not merely in connection with those who had the stains of sin to be effaced, or faults of human infirmity and imperfection to be forgiven, but who had died in wilful unrepented sin. Although they have little or nothing to do with "the faithful dead," of whom we are treating more particularly, they call for consideration on the following grounds:—Firstly, because they have been unduly pressed by those who seek to be supported by ancient authorities in the maintenance of their opinion that even grievous sins admit of remission after the sinner's death; Secondly, because, when men plead for a restoration of primitive usage, it is retorted, that if they appeal to the evidence of the Fathers, they must take it as it is—accept all their teaching or none—and this, they say, would bring the soul of the most wicked sinner within the range of the Church's prayers.

The necessity of extending the field of inquiry.

In order to arrive at a right estimation of the evidence, we shall not deem it sufficient to comment upon the several passages which are brought under notice; but, if it seem necessary, we shall place the writers themselves, as it were, in the witness-box, and by a searching examination endeavour to satisfy ourselves whether they speak with such uniform consistency that they may be regarded as reliable guides in this matter, or whether they are open to refutation out of their own works.

The example from the Apocrypha not to be followed. It will be well, however, before doing this, to revert to the earliest recorded instance of prayers for the dead, and see if it was an undue extension of the legitimate objects for which they may be offered.

Judas Maccabeus encouraged the people to make a propitiation and offer prayers for some whose death to all appearances had been inflicted by God as a direct punishment for an open and wilful transgression of His commands.

As we only used the example before as an historical proof, we are not called upon to defend the doctrine which it appears to involve; but it is just possible to find an explanation, though we should be very unwilling to accept it, which might bring it within the bounds of the Church's rule. It may have been that God, having visited His righteous anger upon them for the vindication of His law, which distinctly forbade what they had done, remitted their transgression in reward for their bravery and the patriotism which they showed in laying down their lives for their country. And it is almost certain that a patriot like Judas Maccabeus would wish to look at the brightest side of things; and while acknowledging the justice of God in visiting their offence with death, would persuade himself that their self-devotion had insured them a merciful judgment hereafter. There is perhaps just an indication of something of this kind in the expression, "They betook themselves unto prayer, and besought Him that the sin committed might *wholly* be put out of remembrance."[1]

Judas, however, was not acting under Divine inspiration, nor yet did he speak like some of the early Fathers of the Church, whom we have quoted, as it were under the influence of Christ's teaching and example, and we have no desire to defend his conduct; but whether any extenuating circumstances be found or not, its force, as an illustration of the prevailing belief that the dead might be benefited by the prayers of the living, is not weakened, because it exhibits a further development than we are prepared to accept.

[1] 2 Macc. xii. 42.

The Apostolical Constitutions.

In the Apostolical Constitutions, among the rules and regulations for services for the dead, we find these directions:—"Let us pray for our brethren that are at rest in Christ, that God, the lover of mankind, Who has received his soul, may forgive him every sin, voluntary and involuntary, and may be merciful and gracious to him, and give him his lot in the land of the pious, who are sent into the bosom of Abraham, and Isaac, and Jacob. . . . Do Thou now also look upon this Thy servant, whom Thou hast selected and received into another state, and forgive him, if voluntarily or involuntarily he has sinned."[1]

The language is very obscure, for it speaks of one who is "at rest in Christ," whom God "has selected and received,"—expressions which imply that his sins had at least been pardoned before he died, and which are wholly inconsistent with the idea that he still bears, not the defilements of sin merely, or even sins themselves of human imperfection, but volun-

---

[1] ὑπὲρ ἀναπαυσαμένων ἐν Χριστῷ ἀδελφῶν ἡμῶν δεηθῶμεν· ὅπως ὁ φιλάνθρωπος Θεὸς ὁ προσδεξάμενος αὐτοῦ τὴν ψυχήν, παρείδῃ αὐτῷ πᾶν ἁμάρτημα ἑκούσιον καὶ ἀκούσιον, καὶ ἵλεως καὶ εὐμενὴς γενόμενος, κατατάξῃ εἰς χώραν εὐσεβῶν, ἀνειμένων εἰς κόλπον Ἀβραὰμ καὶ Ἰσαὰκ καὶ Ἰακώβ . . αὐτὸς καὶ νῦν ἔπιδε ἐπὶ τὸν δοῦλόν σου τόνδε, ὃν ἐξελέξω καὶ προσελάβου εἰς ἑτέραν λῆξιν καὶ συγχώρησον αὐτῷ εἴ τι ἑκὼν καὶ ἄκων ἐξήμαρτε.—*Constitut. Apostol.* Lib. viii. c. xli.

tary wilful sins for which forgiveness needs to be sought.

But even supposing it were claimed in support of the Roman view, it must not be forgotten that a great deal of mystery hangs over the date of this whole document, particularly the seventh and eighth books, from which the above extract is taken: yet further, the very portion before us is altogether absent from one of the best manuscripts. *The uncertainty of the date of the work.*

On the whole, then, it does not seem that this quotation contributes anything trustworthy and important towards a real apprehension of the opinion prevalent on this subject in the early ages which we are investigating.

S. Cyril in his lecture on the words of S. Peter, "𝔚𝔥𝔢𝔯𝔢𝔣𝔬𝔯𝔢, 𝔩𝔞𝔶𝔦𝔫𝔤 𝔞𝔰𝔦𝔡𝔢 𝔞𝔩𝔩 𝔪𝔞𝔩𝔦𝔠𝔢 𝔞𝔫𝔡 𝔞𝔩𝔩 𝔤𝔲𝔦𝔩𝔢," etc., gives an explanation of the different parts of the office of "the Mysteries," and touching the commemoration of the dead writes thus: "We commemorate . . . the holy fathers and bishops, who have fallen asleep before us, in short, all who have fallen asleep amongst us, from the belief that it will be a very great advantage to those souls, for whom the prayer is offered, while the holy and most dread Sacrifice is laid on the altar." He then gives an illustration from a case where a king of a country *S. Cyril.*

had banished certain persons who had offended him, and was afterwards induced by the present of a crown, which their relations had woven and offered to him in their behalf, to grant a commutation of their sentence, and goes on to say, "In like manner we too, offering our prayers for those who have fallen asleep, even though they be sinners, do not, it is true, weave for them a crown, but we offer Christ, Who was slain for our sins, that we may obtain His favour both for them and for ourselves."[1]

This passage, by not defining the kind of sinners intended, leaves it to some extent in uncertainty what the writer's real views were; and he nowhere else, that we are aware of, expresses himself on the same subject. It has been urged, however, by those who hold that even grievous and mortal sin may be forgiven in the intermediate state, and it must be admitted that its general tenor, and especially the comparison of the exiled transgressors, favours such a theory.

[1] εἶτα καὶ ὑπὲρ τῶν προκεκοιμημένων ἁγίων πατέρων καὶ ἐπισκόπων καὶ πάντων ἁπλῶς τῶν ἐν ἡμῖν προκεκοιμημένων, μεγίστην ὄνησιν πιστεύοντες ἔσεσθαι ταῖς ψυχαῖς, ὑπὲρ ὧν ἡ δέησις ἀναφέρεται τῆς ἁγίας καὶ φρικωδεστάτης προκειμένης θυσίας . . . τὸν αὐτὸν τρόπον καὶ ἡμεῖς ὑπὲρ τῶν κεκοιμημένων τὰς δεήσεις προσφέροντες, κἂν ἁμαρτωλοὶ ὦσιν, οὐ στέφανον πλέκομεν, ἀλλὰ Χριστὸν ἐσφαγιασμένον ὑπὲρ τῶν ἡμετέρων ἁμαρτημάτων προσφέρομεν, ἐξιλεούμενοι ὑπὲρ αὐτῶν καὶ ἡμῶν τὸν φιλάνθρωπον.—*Catech. Mystag.* v. p. 242, ed. Lutet. Par. 1681.

The next testimony which we bring forward deserves careful notice; it is from Aerius of Sebasteia in Pontus, who flourished in the third quarter of the fourth century. We have his opinions only second-hand in the writings of Epiphanius and Augustine.

The objections of Aerius.

The latter merely says under this head, that "he held certain peculiar tenets, asserting that oblations ought not to be made in behalf of those who sleep."[1]

The former represents his views more explicitly in the following words:—"If the prayers of the living can in any way benefit the dead, then none need trouble himself to live a holy life or to be a benefactor to his race, but let him acquire friends by any means he pleases, winning them to his side by bribes, or claiming their friendship at his death, and let these pray that he may have no suffering in the other world, and that the heinous sins which he has committed may not be required at his hands."[2]

If this be a faithful representation of his language,

---

[1] "Dicens offerri pro dormientibus non oportere."—*De Hæresibus*, liii.

[2] εἰ δὲ ὅλως εὐχὴ τῶν ἐνταῦθα τοὺς ἐκεῖσε ὤνησεν, ἄρα γοῦν μηδεὶς εὐσεβείτω, μηδὲ ἀγαθοποιείτω, ἀλλὰ κτησάσθω φίλους τινας, δι' οὗ βούλεται τρόπου, ἤτοι χρήμασι πείσας, ἤτοι φίλους ἀξιώσας ἐν τῇ τελευτῇ, καὶ εὐχέσθωσαν περὶ αὐτῶν, ἵνα μή τι ἐκεῖ πάθῃ, μηδὲ τὰ ὑπ' αὐτοῦ γινόμενα τῶν ἀνηκέστων ἁμαρτημάτων ἐκζητηθῇ.—*Adv. Hær.* Lib. iii. lxxv.

and if he was a fair exponent of the prevailing belief in the extent to which such prayers were efficacious, his evidence of course must be allowed its full weight.

Reasons for distrusting his evidence. But there are reasons which dispose us to regard his views with suspicion. Disappointed in early life at the selection of his friend Eustathius for a vacant bishopric which he coveted for himself, he conceived a spirit of bitter dislike, which grew at last into active hostility to the Church in which his rival held office.

He was guilty of heresy and schism, denying the doctrine and setting at nought the discipline of the Church. His offences may be briefly summed up as follows:—

He held Arian views of the nature of Christ:—

He repudiated the grace of Orders, and depreciated the dignity of the Episcopal office:—

He condemned the appointed Fasts and Festivals, denouncing especially the keeping of Easter and the observance of Lent and Passion-tide as relics of Jewish bondage and superstition:—

Finally, he became the author of a schism, gathering around him a considerable body of followers, who formed many strange rules; and who, to judge from the hard treatment which they received at the hands of the orthodox, must have been considered dangerous to the Church.

The judicious Hooker gives a right estimate of his character, and by consequence also of the value to be attached to anything which he may have said affecting the principles of the Church, when he writes of him in these terms:—"Unable to rise to that greatness which his ambitious pride did affect, his way of revenge was to try what wit being sharpened with envy and malice could do in raising a new sedition."[1] *Hooker's estimate of his character.*

It is moreover clear, from the answer which Epiphanius made to the heretic's objections, that he had misunderstood the legitimate usage of intercessions for the dead:—"Touching the commemoration of the dead, what could be more advantageous? What more opportune or more advisable than that those who are still here should believe that those who have departed are alive, and not annihilated, but exist and live with the Lord?" Again, he says of the prayers which are offered for them, that "although they do not wipe away all their crimes, yet because men often trip knowingly and unknowingly, whilst they are in the world, they are advantageous for the manifestation of that *The answer which Epiphanius made.*

[1] *Eccles. Pol.* vii. ix. 1.

which is more perfect. For we commemorate
righteous men and sinners, sinners to pray for
God's mercy, but righteous men, fathers and
patriarchs, prophets, apostles, evangelists, martyrs,
confessors, bishops, anchorites, and all that class,
that we may separate the Lord Jesus Christ from
the order of men by the honour assigned to Him
and may pay to Him a holy worship."[1]

He is very far from accepting the interpretation
which his opponent had chosen to put upon the
practice; and there is no attempt to maintain the
efficacy of prayer for heinous sins. Indeed, he indirectly refutes the idea, when he says that there
were sins to cancel which it was powerless; and
the sins which he had in his mind were such, doubtless, as the heretic had spoken of; for we can hardly
conceive of anything more presumptuous than to sin
boldly in life—as long as sin were possible—and
run the risk of being forgiven through the interposition of surviving friends.

[1] ἔπειτα δὲ περὶ τοῦ ὀνόματα λέγειν τῶν τελευτησάντων, τί ἂν
εἴη τούτου προὐργιαίτερον; τί τούτου καιριώτερον καὶ θαυμαστώ-
τερον, πιστεύειν μὲν τοὺς παρόντας, ὅτι οἱ ἀπελθόντες ζῶσι καὶ ἐν
ἀνυπαρξίᾳ οὐκ εἰσὶν ἀλλὰ εἰσὶ καὶ ζῶσι παρὰ τῷ δεσπότῃ. . . .
εἰ καὶ τὰ ὅλα τῶν αἰτιαμάτων μὴ ἀποκόπτοι, ἀλλ' οὖν γε διὰ τὸ
πολλάκις ἐν κόσμῳ ἡμᾶς ὄντας σφάλλεσθαι ἀκουσίως τε καὶ
ἑκουσίως, ἵνα τὸ ἐντελέστερον σημανθῇ. καὶ γὰρ δικαίων ποιούμεθα
τὴν μνήμην καὶ ὑπὲρ ἁμαρτωλῶν· ὑπὲρ μὲν ἁμαρτωλῶν ὑπὲρ ἐλέους
Θεοῦ δεόμενοι, κ.τ.λ.—EPIPH. adv. Hær. Lib. iii. lxxv. sect. vii.

He speaks, it is true, of the benefit to be derived for our oft infirmities, for the "trippings" to which human nature is prone, but it is only to place them in contrast to the more grievous sins which nothing would obliterate.

Moreover, the brevity with which he dismisses the question for sinners, contrasted with the length to which he expands the class of the righteous, shows clearly for whom he considered prayers to be applicable.

S. Augustine, who has a much better claim to be heard as an authority, expresses himself without hesitation on several occasions.

S. Augustine.

In answering certain questions which one Dulcitius propounded to him, of which this was the second, "Whether the oblation, which is made for those at rest, confers any benefit upon their souls," he writes, "There are some souls whom such things help in no way, whether they be offered for those whose evil deeds made them unworthy of being helped, or for those whose good deeds render such help unnecessary."[1]

The effect produced by the prayers and oblations

---

[1] "Sunt enim quos omnino nihil adjuvant ista; sive pro eis fiant, quorum tam mala sunt merita, ut neque talibus digni sunt adjuvari; sive pro eis quorum tam bona ut talibus non indigeant adjumentis."—*De octo Dulcit. quæstion.* Lib. ii. 3.

offered for any particular person, he says, "will be regulated exactly by the kind of life which he led."[1]

"We must not deny that the souls of the departed are relieved by the piety of survivors, when the Sacrifice of the Mediator is offered for them; but it is efficacious only for those who in life earned the right of being benefited."[2]

Again, in his great treatise on the City of God:— "Prayer is not offered for the unbelieving and unholy dead;"[3] and he follows up the declaration with the arguments above quoted, that men must earn by their lives a participation in the prayers of the faithful to be offered for them in death.

Once more, in his sermon on the text, "I would not have you to be ignorant concerning them which are asleep, that ye sorrow not even as others, which have no hope." After reiterating this frequently expressed opinion, he adds that "for those who die without that faith which worketh by love, and without the Sacraments of the Church, it is

---

[1] "Ferat unusquisque secundum ea quæ gessit per corpus sive bonum sive malum."—*De octo Dulcit. quæstion.* Lib. ii. 3.

[2] "Neque negandum est defunctorum animas pietate suorum viventium relevari, cum pro illis sacrificium Mediatoris offertur, vel eleemosynæ in Ecclesia fiunt. Sed eis hæc prosunt, qui cum viverent, ut hæc sibi postea possent prodesse, meruerunt."—*Id.* ii. 4.

[3] "Quæ itidem causa est ut, quamvis pro hominibus, tamen jam nec nunc oretur pro infidelibus impiisque defunctis."—*De Civit. Dei*, Lib. xxi. cxxiv. 2.

vain that their friends should spend upon them duties which natural affection suggests."[1]

And lastly, to sum up his testimony, when he classifies the baptized dead in relation to the sacrifices and prayers of the living in their behalf, he says, "For the very wicked, although they bring no relief to the dead, they are yet some kind of consolation for the survivors."[2]

S. Chrysostom, in his comments upon the death and miraculous restoration to life of the disciple at Joppa, takes occasion to speak of the feelings and conduct of the survivors towards those who have died in sin:—"These men lived in vain: nay, not in vain merely, but to evil purpose, and of them one might fitly say, '𝔈𝔱 𝔴𝔢𝔯𝔢 𝔤𝔬𝔬𝔡 𝔣𝔬𝔯' them '𝔦𝔣' they '𝔥𝔞𝔡 𝔫𝔬𝔱 𝔟𝔢𝔢𝔫 𝔟𝔬𝔯𝔫.' For tell me what gain it is to have spent so much time to one's own injury? . . .

"And here is a man who wasted his whole life in vain, and never lived a single day even for his own good, but for luxury and wantonness and

S. Chrysostom.

---

[1] "Nam qui sine fide quæ per dilectionem operatur, ejusque Sacramentis, de corporibus exierunt, frustra illis a suis hujusmodi pietatis impenduntur officia."—*Sermo* clxxii. 1.

[2] "Pro valde bonis gratiarum actiones sunt: pro non valde malis propitiationes sunt; pro valde malis etiamsi nulla adjumenta mortuorum, qualescunque vivorum consolationes sunt."— *Enchirid. de fide, spe et charitate*, cx.

greed and sin and the devil. Shall we not then bewail him? Shall we not try to snatch him from his perils? For it is, it is possible, if we will have it so, that his punishment shall be lightened. If, then, we make constant prayers and offer alms in his behalf, even though he be unworthy, God will be importuned by us."[1]

Again, touching the legitimate use of mourning, he writes: "For if the dead man has been a sinner, and has ofttimes offended God, we must weep, or rather not weep merely, for this is of no use to him, but do what we can to procure for him some consolation,—offer alms and oblations."[2]

Again, in dealing with a kindred subject, he rebukes a mourner who said that he was bewailing

[1] Εἰκῆ ἔζησαν οὗτοι· μᾶλλον δὲ οὐκ εἰκῆ ἀλλὰ καὶ ἐπὶ κακῷ. καὶ ἐπὶ τούτων εὔκαιρον εἰπεῖν· σύμφερον ἦν αὐτοῖς, εἰ οὐκ ἐγεννήθησαν· τί γὰρ ὄφελος, εἰπέ μοι, τοσοῦτον ἀναλῶσαι χρόνον ἐπὶ κακῷ τῆς ἑαυτῶν κεφαλῆς; καὶ οὗτος πᾶσαν τὴν ζωὴν εἰκῆ κατεκόπη, οὐδὲ μίαν ἡμέραν ἔζησεν ἑαυτῷ, ἀλλὰ τῇ τρυφῇ, τῇ ἀσελγείᾳ, τῇ πλεονεξίᾳ, τῇ ἁμαρτίᾳ, τῷ διαβόλῳ. τοῦτον οὖν οὐ θρηνήσομεν; οὐ πειρασόμεθα τῶν κινδύνων ἐξαρπάσαι; ἔστι γὰρ, ἔστιν, ἐὰν θέλωμεν κούφην αὐτῷ γενέσθαι τὴν κόλασιν. ἂν οὖν εὐχὰς ὑπὲρ αὐτοῦ ποιῶμεν συνεχεῖς, ἂν ἐλεημοσύνην δίδωμεν, κἂν ἐκεῖνος ἀνάξιος ᾖ, ἡμᾶς ὁ Θεὸς δυσωπηθήσεται.—In Acta Apost. Homil. xxi. 3.

[2] εἰ μὲν γὰρ ἁμαρτωλὸς ὁ τεθνηκώς, καὶ πολλὰ τῷ Θεῷ προσκεκρουκώς, δεῖ δακρύειν· μᾶλλον δὲ οὐδὲ δακρύειν μόνον (τοῦτο γὰρ οὐδὲν ὄφελος ἐκείνῳ) ἀλλὰ ποιεῖν τὰ δυνάμενα τινὰ παραμυθίαν αὐτῷ περιποιῆσαι, ἐλεημοσύνας καὶ προσφοράς.—In Johann. Homil. lxii. al. lxi. 4.

his lost friend because he departed this life in his sins. "This," says S. Chrysostom, "is a mere excuse and pretext. For if this were the reason why you bewailed the departed, you ought to have reformed and corrected him while he was living. But the fact is, you look to your own interests not to his on every occasion. But even supposing that he did depart in his sins, we ought to rejoice on this account, because his sins were cut short, and he could not add to his wickedness; and we ought to help him, as far as it is possible, not by tears, but by prayers and supplications and alms and oblations."[1]

In estimating the value of the above passages, we cannot but notice, that in the first the meaning is not so clear as the words above quoted would lead us to suppose. It is possible, though by no means certain, that he is speaking of prayers for a dying sinner, not for one already dead.

The uncertainty of his views.

But the second passage is introduced with the qualifying admission that he made those statements,

[1] Σκῆψις ταῦτα καὶ πρόφασις. εἰ γὰρ διὰ τοῦτο ἀπελθόντα ἐθρήνεες, ζῶντα μεταπλάσαι ἐχρῆν καὶ ῥυθμίσαι. ἀλλὰ τὰ σαυτοῦ σὺ πανταχοῦ σκοπεῖς οὐ τὰ ἐκείνου. εἰ δὲ καὶ ἁμαρτωλὸς ἀπῆλθε, καὶ διὰ τοῦτο δεῖ χαίρειν, ὅτι ἐνεκόπη τὰ ἁμαρτήματα καὶ οὐ προσέθηκε τῇ κακίᾳ, καὶ βοηθεῖν, ὡς ἂν οἷόν τε ᾖ, οὐ δακρύειν, ἀλλὰ εὐχαῖς καὶ ἱκετηρίαις καὶ ἐλεημοσύναις καὶ προσφοραῖς.— *In Ep. 1 ad Cor. Homil.* xli. 4.

"not as giving commands, but in condescension to human infirmity."[1]

And in the third there is an expression indicative of doubt how far prayer would avail for one who died in his sins; and in what follows he says the object to be gained is some consolation, not remission; and finally he concludes with the declaration that the cry at the altar during the tremendous Mysteries is not in vain "for those who have fallen asleep in Christ."[2]

A close examination, then, of the context does modify in a measure the strong character of the quotations; but even had we found nothing in extenuation, we should have hesitated to accept them as conclusive, in the face of much that is said of a contradictory nature in other portions of his works. He has certainly laid himself open to a charge of inconsistency.

Here is a direct denial of the efficacy of prayer to obtain pardon for those who died in sin.

Contradictory views. In the moral which he draws from the text, "I am in a strait betwixt two, having a desire to depart, and to be with Christ, which is far better," he writes: "Sinners, wherever they may

---

[1] ταῦτα οὐ νομοθετῶν λέγω, ἀλλὰ συγκατιών.
[2] ὑπὲρ πάντων τῶν ἐν Χριστῷ κεκοιμημένων.

who died in wilful sin.

be, are far from the King. ... Let us not then wail for the dead simply, but for the dead in sins. These are worthy of wailing, of beating of the breast, and of tears. For what hope, tell me, is there in departing with sins upon them to that place where there is no putting off of sins? So long as they were here there was, it may be, great expectation that they would change and grow better, but if they have departed to Hades, where they can reap no fruits from repentance, for Scripture saith, '𝔌𝔫 𝔱𝔥𝔢 𝔤𝔯𝔞𝔟𝔢 𝔴𝔥𝔬 𝔰𝔥𝔞𝔩𝔩 𝔤𝔦𝔟𝔢 𝔗𝔥𝔢𝔢 𝔱𝔥𝔞𝔫𝔨𝔰?' how are they not worthy of lamentations? ... Weep for the unbelievers, weep for those who are in no way different from them, those who departed without baptism, without being sealed. Weep for those who died in riches and took no thought of consolation from their riches for their own souls, who had the opportunity of washing away their sins and would not do it."

It is true he goes on to speak as though even these could be benefited by the living: "Let us help them according to our ability, let us devise some help for them, small though it be, yet still a possible help. How and in what way? By praying for them ourselves, and encouraging others to offer prayers in their behalf, by constantly giving alms to the poor for them. Such an act has some consolation, for hear what God saith, '𝕴 𝖜𝖎𝖑𝖑 𝖉𝖊𝖋𝖊𝖓𝖉 𝖙𝖍𝖎𝖘 𝖈𝖎𝖙𝖞 𝖙𝖔 𝖘𝖆𝖇𝖊 𝖎𝖙 𝖋𝖔𝖗 𝖒𝖎𝖓𝖊 𝖔𝖜𝖓 𝖘𝖆𝖐𝖊, 𝖆𝖓𝖉 𝖋𝖔𝖗 𝖒𝖞 𝖘𝖊𝖗𝖛𝖆𝖓𝖙 𝕯𝖆𝖇𝖎𝖉'𝖘 𝖘𝖆𝖐𝖊.' If the remembrance merely of a just man availed so much, how shall it not avail when even deeds are done in his behalf? Not in vain was this law laid down by the Apostles, that we should commemorate the departed during the dreadful Mysteries. They know that much gain, much advantage, accrues to them."

Though there is a great deal that is ambiguous in the above, he concludes with a statement which brings his language into accord with what we believe to have been the prevailing opinion, excluding wilful sin from the operation of intercessory prayer after death,—"but this we do for those who passed away in faith."[1]

---

[1] οἱ ἁμαρτωλοί, ὅπου ἂν ὦσι, πόρρω τοῦ βασιλέως εἰσί. μὴ τοίνυν ἁπλῶς κλαίωμεν τοὺς ἀποθανόντας ἀλλὰ τοὺς ἐν ἁμαρτίᾳ. οὗτοι θρήνων ἄξιοι, οὗτοι κοπετῶν καὶ δακρύων. ποία γὰρ ἐλπίς, εἰπέ μοι, μετὰ ἁμαρτημάτων ἀπελθεῖν, ἔνθα οὐκ ἐστὶν ἁμαρτήματα ἀποδύσασθαι; ἕως μὲν γὰρ ἦσαν ἐνταῦθα, ἴσως ἦν προσδοκία πολλή, ὅτι μεταβαλοῦνται, ὅτι βελτίους ἔσονται. ἂν δὲ ἀπέλθωσιν εἰς τὸν ᾅδην, ἔνθα οὐκ ἔστιν ἀπὸ μετανοίας κερδᾶναί τι. ἐν γὰρ τῷ ᾅδῃ, φησί, τίς ἐξομολογήσεταί σοι; πῶς οὐ θρήνων ἄξιοι; . . . κλαύσων τοὺς ἀπίστους, κλαύσων τοὺς οὐδὲν ἐκείνων ἀπέχοντας, τοὺς χωρὶς φωτίσματος ἀπερχομένους, τοὺς χωρὶς σφραγῖδος· κλαῦσον τοὺς ἐν πλούτῳ τετελευτηκότας καὶ μηδεμίαν ἀπὸ τοῦ

Before drawing this subject to a close we turn to some evidence of a more definite nature.

S. Cyprian, in a letter which he wrote to the people of Furni, praises the wisdom of the Bishops for a decree, which they had made in Council, that no one who had been ordained to the priesthood for the constant service of the altar should ever suffer himself to be diverted from his Divine administration by the call of secular duties. The consequence of a breach of this Ecclesiastical order he illustrated by an example. One Geminius Victor had appointed Geminius Faustinus to be executor and guardian under his will. It was an act of deliberate disobedience to a rule of the Church, and as soon as it was discovered after his death, when the will was read, he was at once deprived of the good offices of

A special case noticed by S. Cyprian.

πλούτου παραμυθίαν ταῖς ἑαυτῶν ψυχαῖς ἐπινοήσαντας, τοὺς λαβόντας ἐξουσίαν ἀπολούσασθαι αὐτῶν τὰ ἁμαρτήματα καὶ μὴ βουληθέντας· . . . βοηθῶμεν αὐτοῖς κατὰ δύναμιν, ἐπινοήσωμεν αὐτοῖς τινὰ βοήθειαν. μικρὰν μέν, βοηθεῖν δὲ ὅμως δυναμένην. πῶς καὶ τίνι τρόπῳ; αὐτοί τε εὐχόμενοι καὶ ἑτέρους παρακαλοῦντες εὐχὰς ὑπὲρ αὐτῶν ποιεῖσθαι, πένησιν ὑπὲρ αὐτῶν διδόντες συνεχῶς. ἔχει τινὰ τὸ πρᾶγμα παραμυθίαν· ἄκουε γὰρ τοῦ Θεοῦ λέγοντος· ὑπερασπιῶ τῆς πόλεως ταύτης δι' ἐμέ, καὶ διὰ Δαυὶδ τὸν δοῦλόν μου. εἰ μνήμη μόνον δικαίου τοσοῦτον ἴσχυσεν, ὅταν καὶ ἔργα γένηται ὑπὲρ αὐτοῦ, πῶς οὐ ἰσχύσει; οὐκ εἰκῇ ταῦτα ἐνομοθετήθη ὑπὸ τῶν ἀποστόλων, τὸ ἐπὶ τῶν φρικτῶν μυστηρίων μνήμην γένεσθαι τῶν ἀπελθόντων. ἴσασιν αὐτοῖς πολὺ κέρδος γενόμενον πολλὴν τὴν ὠφέλειαν. . . . ἀλλὰ τοῦτο μὲν περὶ τῶν ἐν πίστει παρελθόντων.— *In Ep. ad Phil. c. 1, Hom. iii.*

his surviving friends, and a declaration was published to the effect that "no offering might be made for his repose, nor any prayer offered in the Church in his name."[1]

Of course this can hardly be urged as conclusive evidence that all wilful transgression cut the offender off *ipso facto* from the prayers of the faithful, but it may well be regarded, in the absence of anything to the contrary, as an illustration of a generally admitted principle which had gained acceptance at the time when he wrote.

Other special cases.

There were other cases of those who died in sin, where provision was expressly made to disqualify them from enjoying the benefit of the Church's prayers.

Those particularly mentioned are catechumens,[2] who died without baptism by neglect or their own default—suicides, who laid violent hands upon themselves—and those who for heinous offences paid the extreme penalty of the law; all were buried in silence without the religious rites of the

---

[1] "Si quis hoc fecisset, non offeretur pro eo, nec sacrificium pro dormitione ejus celebraretur."

"Et ideo Victor cum contra formam . . . ausus sit tutorem constituere, non est quod pro dormitione ejus apud vos fiat oblatio, aut deprecatio aliqua nomine ejus in Ecclesia frequentetur."—CYPR. *Epist.* i. *Presby. et Diacon. et plebi Furnis consistentibus.*

[2] BINGHAM, x. ii. 18.

Church, and had no place afterwards in her customary commemorations.

S. Chrysostom, when dealing with the sin of delaying Baptism, seems to place it in contrast with sin which may be forgiven after death, for he writes thus, "The man who has cast all upon God, and sins after baptism, as we should expect of one that is mortal, if he repent shall obtain mercy; but he who prevaricates as it were with God's mercy, if he die without partaking of the grace, shall not have his punishment begged off."[1]

This was in his eyes a wilful sin, and he expresses his conviction that there was no *locus pœnitentiæ* to be obtained for it after death; and if not for this, it is difficult to say that he believed there was ground for hope in the case of any other.

As an illustration from the class of suicides, we may recall the story which Cassian has told of the fate of the old hermit Hero, who under an incontrollable impulse, by the delusions of Satan, threw himself into a pit and was killed. Even in spite of the belief that he acted under some temporary

Cassian's story of one who committed suicide.

---

[1] ὁ μὲν γὰρ τὸ πᾶν ἐπὶ τὸν Θεὸν ῥίψας καὶ μετὰ τὸ βάπτισμα ἁμαρτάνων οἷα εἰκὸς ἄνθρωπον ὄντα μετανοῶν τεύξεται φιλανθρωπίας· ὁ δὲ ὥσπερ σοφιζόμενος τοῦ Θεοῦ τὴν φιλανθρωπίαν, ἀπελθὼν ἄμοιρος τῆς χάριτος, ἀπαραίτητον ἕξει τὴν τιμωρίαν.— *In Acta Apost. Homil.* i. 7.

hallucination, and not of set purpose, in destroying himself, it was with the greatest difficulty that he escaped being deprived of these Christian privileges. The head of the monastery to which he belonged, "could hardly be prevailed upon to let him be reckoned any other than a self-murderer, and unworthy of the memorial and oblation that was made for all those that were at rest in peace."[1]

The Council of Bracara. In the following century, perhaps in consequence of an undue relaxation of the rule, the matter was deliberated in an Ecclesiastical Council, and a most stringent decree passed to enforce its observance.[2]

Conclusions. To sum up then briefly the conclusions at which we have arrived by the investigations of this and the preceding chapter: The evidence of a few of the Fathers and the Primitive Liturgies is in favour of the view which admits of the effacement after death of the stain and defilement of sin, as also of the forgiveness of those lesser faults and failings which are due to human infirmity, and encourages the

---

[1] BINGHAM, xv. iii. 16, introduces the story, and also gives the decree of the Council of Bracara.

[2] "Placuit ut hi, qui sibi ipsis aut per ferrum, aut per venenum, aut per præcipitium, aut suspendium vel quolibet modo, violentam inferant mortem, nulla pro illis in oblatione commemoratio fiat, etc.—item placuit ut catechumenis, sine redemptione baptismi defunctis, simili modo neque oblationis commemoratio, neque psallendi impendatur officium."

prayers of survivors as helpful in the attainment of both these ends. While with regard to the extension of the field of the Church's prayers, so as to bring the man who dies in wilful sin within the range of their operation, though there are a few expressions in some of the Patristic writings which appear to sanction such a course, the general testimony is decidedly adverse. Our conclusions touching the general question of prayers for the dead will be combined with those to which the evidence of the following pages will lead us respecting the intercession of departed saints and the legitimacy of invoking their aid in prayer.

END OF PART I.

PART II.

*THE GOOD OFFICES OF THE FAITHFUL DEAD
IN BEHALF OF THE LIVING.*

CHAPTER I.

Primitive Testimony to the Intercession of the Saints.

IN the following pages we shall apply the test of Catholicity, first, to the belief that the saints in Paradise intercede for the well-being of those who are still in the flesh, and then to the practice of addressing or invoking them with a view to obtaining their assistance by intercession or otherwise. We begin with the evidence for their intercession.

It should be explained at the outset that we are only concerned in this inquiry with the souls of righteous men; we take no account of the angels, whose services in behalf of the heirs of salvation there can be no question that God has constituted in a wonderful order. Our special aim is to learn all that can be ascertained from the records of antiquity of the occupation after death, in connection with ourselves, of those who are related to us by the ties of a common faith and a common nature.

The ministry of the angels not entered upon here.

There is very little explicit revelation in Holy Scripture to help us; the belief grew naturally out of a special application of the general doctrine of the Communion of saints. If, therefore, but few passages can be adduced in direct support of this particular phase of it, it would be manifestly unfair to conclude that all the evidence has been brought forward. Here however we are content with the consideration of these alone.

The Apocalypse of S. John was written, partly at least, for the express purpose of disclosing the ministrations of the angels and of the spirits of just men made perfect.

<small>The witness of the Apocalypse.</small> There are two passages in it, where he describes the presentation of the prayers of the saints at the golden altar.

The first: "I beheld, and, lo, in the midst of the throne and of the four beasts, and in the midst of the elders, stood a Lamb as it had been slain, having seven horns and seven eyes, which are the seven Spirits of God sent forth into all the earth.

"And he came and took the book out of the right hand of him that sat upon the throne.

"And when he had taken the book, the four beasts and four and twenty elders fell down before the Lamb, having every one of them harps, and golden vials full of odours, which are the prayers of saints."[1]

The second. "And another angel came and stood at the altar, having a golden censer; and there was given unto him much incense, that he should offer it with the prayers of all saints upon the golden altar which was before the throne.

"And the smoke of the incense, which came with the prayers of the saints, ascended up before God out of the angel's hand."[2]

The following passage, though not containing a direct statement of the exact truth with which we are concerned, is sufficiently pertinent not to be passed over. At least it brings out the fact that the saints in the intermediate state so far interest themselves in the things of earth and in those who are alive, as to make them subjects of prayer to God.

"I saw under the altar the souls of them that were slain for the word of God, and for the testimony which they held: and they cried with a loud voice, saying, How long, O Lord, holy and true,

---

[1] Rev. v. 6-8.
[2] Rev. viii. 3, 4. The Authorised Version is not quite correct in its rendering, but the general sense of the passage is not affected by the inaccuracy.

𝔡𝔬𝔰𝔱 𝔱𝔥𝔬𝔲 𝔫𝔬𝔱 𝔧𝔲𝔡𝔤𝔢 𝔞𝔫𝔡 𝔞𝔳𝔢𝔫𝔤𝔢 𝔬𝔲𝔯 𝔟𝔩𝔬𝔬𝔡 𝔬𝔫 𝔱𝔥𝔢𝔪 𝔱𝔥𝔞𝔱 𝔡𝔴𝔢𝔩𝔩 𝔬𝔫 𝔱𝔥𝔢 𝔢𝔞𝔯𔱲𝔥 ?"[1]

The prayer, it is true, is not for an exhibition of Divine mercy, but of wrath; if, however, they concern themselves with the one it is quite inconceivable that they would not do so tenfold more with the other.

The witness of the Fathers. From Scripture we turn to the writings of the Primitive Fathers and Doctors, which, as will be seen, supply a large body of evidence in confirmation of the belief in the intercessory character of the occupation of the saints.

The first quotation is taken from a treatise of doubtful authority, but is by no means unworthy of consideration, inasmuch as the advocates of its genuineness are able to bring forward some forcible evidence in support of their view.[2]

---

[1] Rev. vi. 9-10.

[2] Its genuineness was first called in question by Daillé, but has been supported by numerous critics, such as Ussher, Grabe (in part only), Dodwell, Pearson, Cotelier, Moehler, and in later times Hefele; cf. his *Prolegomena*, pp. lx-lxiv.

One of the chief arguments against it is the fact that no quotation from or reference to it is to be found in any history or treatise of the first six centuries. On the other hand, the simplicity of its style and narrative is decidedly in its favour, and especially the absence of all that legendary matter which gathered round the history of the martyr in later times. Dr. Donaldson has called attention to this in his Introductory Notice, and illustrates it by reference to the legend which identified Ignatius with the child

The Martyrdom of Ignatius appears from internal evidence to have been written by some companions of the martyr, who accompanied him on his last voyage and were eye-witnesses of his death. At its close the writers describe a vision which they had received on the night following his passion in these words, "After we had fallen asleep a short time, some of us saw the blessed Ignatius suddenly standing at our side and embracing us: others beheld him again praying over us, whilst others saw him dropping with sweat, as though he had just come out of a great labour, and standing before the Lord."[1]

Now it cannot be denied that there is something antecedently improbable in the story, and much allowance must be made for the high pitch of excitement into which their feelings must have been wrought by the terrible scenes which they had been

The Martyrdom of Ignatius.

---

which Christ took up in His arms and set before the disciples, (S. MATT. xviii. 2), from which circumstance he is said to have obtained the name Theophorus :—"one carried by God." Now in the second chapter of this treatise Ignatius explains to Trajan that Theophorus is "one who has Christ within his heart," which no one would have written, at least without further explanations, after the traditional meaning given above had gained acceptance. Cf. *Apost. Ff. Ante-Nicene Libr.* 289.

[1] μικρὸν ἀφυπνώσαντες, οἱ μὲν ἐξαίφνης ἐπιστάντα καὶ περιπτυσσόμενον ἡμᾶς ἐβλέπομεν, οἱ δὲ πάλιν ἐπευχόμενον ἡμῖν ἑωρῶμεν τὸν μακάριον Ἰγνάτιον, ἄλλοι δὲ σταζόμενον ὑφ' ἱδρῶτος ὡς ἐκ καμάτου πολλοῦ παραγενόμενον καὶ παρεστῶτα τῷ κυρίῳ.—*Martyrium S. Ignatii,* c. vii.

called upon to witness; but whether any such vision was vouchsafed to them or not, the record they have left is a distinct expression of their conviction, that he, whose labours they had shared, and from whom they had so lately been separated in the body, was still associated with them by his spirit, and that he still remembered them in his prayers as he stood at the right hand of the Lord.

<small>Origen.</small>

The testimony of Origen is on the whole very decisive. He speaks on the subject perhaps more frequently than any of the Fathers, and only once that we are aware of with the least semblance of doubt. The passage to which we allude is as follows:—" Moreover, whether the saints, who being out of the body are with Christ, act and work at all for us, like the angels, who minister to our salvation; <small>Occasional ambiguity of his language.</small> or whether again the wicked, who are out of the body, act at all according to the purpose of their mind, like the bad angels, with whom it is said by Christ they will be sent into the eternal fire, let this too be held among the secret things of God, mysteries that ought not to be committed to writing."[1]

[1] "Jam vero si etiam extra corpus positi vel sancti, qui cum Christo sunt, agunt aliquid, et laborant pro nobis ad similitudinem angelorum, qui salutis nostræ ministeria procurant: vel rursum peccatores etiam ipsi extra corpus positi agunt aliquid secundum propositum mentis suæ ad angelorum nihilominus similitudinem, cum quibus et in æternum ignem mittendi dicuntur

In some places,¹ again, it is not quite clear whether his language may not refer to angels only; but in many there is no ambiguity: for instance, "It will not be out of place to say that all the saints who have departed this life, still retaining their love for those who are in the world, concern themselves for their salvation, and aid them by their prayers and mediation with God. For it is written in the Book of Maccabees thus: 'This is Jeremias the prophet of God, who always prays for the people' (2 MACC. xv. 14)."² *His general opinion clear and decided.*

Again: "It is my opinion that all those fathers who have fallen asleep before us, fight on our side and aid us by their prayers, for so also I heard one of the old masters say."³ He repeats the same language elsewhere.⁴

a Christo, habeatur et hoc quoque inter occulta Dei nec chartulæ committenda mysteria."—*Ep. ad Romanos Comment.* lib. ii. 4.

¹ Cf. *contr. Cels.* viii. 34; *de Oratione* xi.

² "Omnes sancti qui de hac vita decesserunt, habentes adhuc caritatem erga eos qui in hoc mundo sunt, si dicantur curam gerere salutis eorum, et juvare eos precibus suis, atque interventu suo apud Deum non erit inconveniens. Scriptum namque est in Maccabæorum libris ita: hic est Hieremias propheta Dei, qui semper orat pro populo."—*In Cant. Hom.* iii., *Erasm.* vol. i. p. 604.

³ "Ego sic arbitror, quod omnes illi qui dormierunt ante nos patres pugnent nobiscum et adjuvent nos orationibus suis; ita namque etiam quemdam de senioribus magistris audivi dicentem." —*In Jesu Nave. Hom.* xvi. cap. xiii.

⁴ *In Num. Hom.* xvi. cap. xxxi.

And when he would encourage Ambrose not to shrink from martyrdom through fear of leaving his family unbefriended, it is with the assurance that after death "he will have greater power to help them," and "will pray for them with greater wisdom."[1]

Once more: when Celsus had shown some inconsistency in the advice which he had given to the Christians, by telling them at one time that in all their actions and in all their words their soul should be constantly fixed on God, and by advocating at another an appeal to the favour of earthly rulers, Origen replies that if God is on their side they need have no fears, for the good-will of the angels and of spirits, who are the friends of God, will follow as surely as the shadow attends upon the body from which it is thrown; "they understand who are worthy of the Divine approval, and are not only well disposed to these themselves, but co-operate with them in their endeavours to please God: they seek His favour on their behalf, and with their prayers and intercessions for them they join their own." And yet further: "We may indeed boldly state that men who deliberately aspire after better

---

[1] παρρησίαν ἀναλαμβάνων πρὸς τὸ εὐεργετεῖν αὐτοὺς, φίλος γενόμενος θεῷ· τότε γὰρ . . . συνετώτερον περὶ αὐτῶν εὔξῃ. *Exhort. ad Martyrium*, 37, 38.

Intercession of the Saints.

things have ten thousand of sacred powers on their side, when they pray to God. These, even when not asked, pray with them and bring help to our perishable race, and, if I may so speak, take up arms alongside of it."[1]

And in connection with the same Father we have yet further testimony. During the persecution of Severus, some of the converts whom Origen had made became so deeply imbued with his spirit that they were enabled to finish their course by martyrdom. An account of their sufferings and constancy has been preserved to us by the Father of Ecclesiastical History, in which he dwells at length upon the case of Basilides, to whom the judges had committed the execution of the sentence of death upon the celebrated Potamiæna:—"No sooner had the word been spoken, and she had received the sentence of condemnation, than Basilides, who was one of the officers in the army, took her by the hand and led her away to die. But when the mob attempted to

[margin: Eusebius on the martyrdom of Potamiæna.]

---

[1] συναίσθονται γὰρ τῶν ἀξίων τοῦ παρὰ θεοῦ εὐμενισμοῦ· καὶ οὐ μόνον καὶ αὐτοὶ εὐμενεῖς τοῖς ἀξίοις γίνονται, ἀλλὰ καὶ συμπράττουσι τοῖς βουλομένοις τὸν ἐπὶ πᾶσι θεὸν θεραπεύειν καὶ ἐξευμενίζονται, καὶ συνεύχονται καὶ συναξιοῦσιν. ὥστε τολμᾶν ἡμᾶς λέγειν, ὅτι ἀνθρώποις, μετὰ προαιρέσεως προτιθεμένοις τὰ κρείττονα, εὐχομένοις τῷ θεῷ μυρίαι ὅσαι ἄκλητοι συνεύχονται δυνάμεις ἱεραί, συμπαρέχουσαι τῷ ἐπικήρῳ ἡμῶν γένει, καί, ἵν' οὕτως εἴπω, συναγωνιῶσαι. *Contr. Celsum*, lib. viii. 64.

annoy and insult her with violent abuse, he succeeded in keeping them off and restraining their insults, manifesting the greatest pity and kindness towards her, whereupon she, accepting the man's sympathy in her sufferings, bids him be of good cheer, for that after her departure she would obtain pardon for him from the Lord, and at no distant time would repay him for the good deeds which he had done for her." Basilides became a Christian, and when summoned before the tribunal confessed that he had seen a vision in the night, "Potamiæna placing a crown upon his head, and telling him that she had besought the Lord in his behalf, and that her prayer had been answered."[1]

S. Cyprian. S. Cyprian and his friend Cornelius, in talking upon death, and anticipating the pain of separation, experience some consolation in agreeing together, that the one who was to be first taken should remember in

[1] ἅμα δὲ λόγῳ τὸν τῆς ἀποφάσεως ὅρον καταδεξαμένην ὁ Βασιλείδης εἷς τις ὢν τὸν ἐν στρατείαις ἀναφερομένων, ἀπάγει παραλαβὼν τὴν ἐπὶ θανάτῳ· ὡς δὲ τὸ πλῆθος ἐνοχλεῖν αὐτῇ καὶ ἀκολάστοις ἐνυβρίζειν ῥήμασιν ἐπειρᾶτο, ὁ μὲν ἀνεῖργεν ἀποσοβῶν τοὺς ἐνυβρίζοντας, πλεῖστον ἔλεον καὶ φιλανθρωπίαν εἰς αὐτὴν ἐνδεικνύμενος, ἡ δὲ τῆς περὶ αὐτὴν συμπαθείας ἀποδεξαμένη τὸν ἄνδρα θαρρεῖν παρακελεύεται· ἐξαιτήσεσθαι γὰρ αὐτὸν ἀπελθοῦσαν παρὰ τοῦ ἑαυτῆς Κυρίου, καὶ οὐκ εἰς μακρὸν τῶν εἰς αὐτὴν πεπραγμένων τὴν ἀμοιβὴν ἀποτίσειν αὐτῷ.—Euseb. *Eccl. Hist.* vi. 5.

λέγεται εἰπεῖν ὡς . . . αὐτοῦ τῇ κεφαλῇ περιθεῖσα εἴη, φαίη τε παρακεκληκέναι χάριν αὐτοῦ τὸν Κύριον, καὶ τῆς ἀξιώσεως τετυχηκέναι.—*Ibid.*

prayer those who were left behind. These were the terms of the agreement: "Let us mutually be mindful of each other, with one heart and one mind. On both sides let us always pray for each other, let us relieve our afflictions and distresses by a reciprocity of love, and whichever of us goes hence before the other by the speed of the Divine favour, let our affection continue before the Lord, let not prayer for our brothers and sisters cease before the mercy of the Father."[1] And at the close of his treatise on Mortality, in which, during the plague which devastated Carthage in the year 252 A.D., he tried to animate his fellow-citizens with Christian hope, he speaks of "a large number of dear ones, parents, brothers, children, a goodly and numerous crowd longing for us, and while their own immortality is assured, still anxious for our salvation."[2]

And he concludes his directions on the Dress of

[1] "Memores nostri invicem simus concordes atque unanimes: utrobique pro nobis semper oremus, pressuras et angustias mutua caritate relevemus, et quis istinc nostrum prior Divinæ dignationis celeritate præcesserit, perseveret apud Dominum nostra dilectio, pro fratribus et sororibus nostris, apud misericordiam Patris non-cesset oratio."—*Ep.* lvii. *ad Cornel.* p. 206.

[2] "Magnus illic nos carorum numerus expectat parentum, fratrum, filiorum, frequens nos et copiosa turba desiderat, jam de sua immortalitate secura et adhuc de nostra salute sollicita."— *De Mortal. ad fin.*

Virgins with this exclamation : "Endure bravely, go on spiritually, attain happily, only remember us at that time, when the virgin-state begins to be honoured in your persons,"[1] that is, when they shall have received the crown of martyrdom.

S. Ephraem. S. Ephraem writes : "Blessed are they who toil and weary themselves in the Lord, for the delights of Paradise await them, and may it be granted to us to enjoy them, through the intercession of all those who have been acceptable to the Lord!"[2]

S. Gregory Nazianzen. S. Gregory Nazianzen, in his Funeral Oration on S. Basil, says, "He now abides in heaven, and there, as I think, offers sacrifice in our behalf, and prays for the people, for he did not so leave us as to have left us altogether."[3] And in that delivered over his father : "I am satisfied that he accomplishes this now by his prayers more than he did before by his teaching, just in proportion as he approaches nearer

[1] "Durate fortiter, spiritualiter pergite, pervenite feliciter: tantum mementote tunc nostri, cum incipiet in vobis virginitas honorari."—*De hab. Virgin. ad fin.*

[2] "Beati qui laboribus se fatigant in Domino : quoniam deliciæ eos paradisi manent : quibus concedatur nobis perfrui, intercessione omnium qui complacuerunt Domino."—*De Virtute,* cap. ix. *Lat. redd. Voss.*

[3] καὶ νῦν ὁ μέν ἐστιν ἐν οὐρανοῖς κἀκεῖ τὰς ὑπὲρ ἡμῶν ὡς οἶμαι προσφέρων θυσίας καὶ τοῦ λαοῦ προσευχόμενος. οὐδὲ γὰρ ἀπολιπὼν ἡμᾶς παντάπασιν ἀπολέλοιπεν.—*Funeb. Orat.* xx. *in laud. Basilii magni, ad fin.*

to God, after having shaken off the fetters of the body."[1]

S. Cyril writes: "We all of us supplicate Thee, and offer to Thee this sacrifice, that we may also commemorate those who have fallen asleep before us, first patriarchs, prophets, apostles, martyrs, to the end that God, by their prayers and intercessions, may accept our petition."[2] — S. Cyril of Jerusalem.

S. Chrysostom, in several of his Homilies, maintains the same truth: "May you by the prayers of this holy martyr, and of those who have wrestled as she did, retain an accurate recollection of these things, and of others that have been said to you."[3] — S. Chrysostom.

"Let us pray then together, . . . taking the blessed Meletius as an associate in this our prayer (for his power is greater now, and his love towards us more fervent), that this love may increase in us."[4]

[1] πείθομαι δὲ ὅτι καὶ τῇ πρεσβείᾳ νῦν μᾶλλον ἢ πρότερον τῇ διδασκαλίᾳ ὅσῳ καὶ μᾶλλον ἐγγίζει θεῷ, τὰς σωματικὰς πέδας ἀποσεισάμενος.—*Funeb. orat. in laud. Patris*, xix. ad init.

[2] δεόμεθά σου πάντες ἡμεῖς καὶ ταύτην προσφέρομέν σοι τὴν θυσίαν ἵνα μνημονεύωμεν καὶ τῶν προκεκοιμημένων . . . ὅπως ὁ Θεὸς εὐχαῖς αὐτῶν καὶ πρεσβείαις προσδέξηται ἡμῶν τὴν δέησιν.—*Catech. Mystag.* v.

[3] γένοιο δὲ εὐχαῖς τῆς ἁγίας ταύτης καὶ τῶν τὰ αὐτὰ ἠθληκότων αὐτῇ καὶ τούτων καὶ τῶν ἄλλων τῶν εἰρημένων ἀκριβῆ τὴν μνήμην ὑμᾶς κατασχεῖν.—*Hom. in S. Pelagiam*, lxvi.

[4] εὐξώμεθα δὴ κοινῇ πάντες . . . αὐτὸν τὸν μακάριον Μελέτιον κοινωνὸν τῆς εὐχῆς ταύτης λαβόντες (καὶ γὰρ πλείων αὐτῷ παρρησία νῦν καὶ θερμότερον πρὸς ἡμᾶς τὸ φίλτερον) αὐξηθῆναι ταύτην ἡμῖν τὴν ἀγάπην.—*Hom. de S. Meletio*, lxxvii.

And in praying for the long life of the Emperor Arcadius and his wife he calls upon his friends "to take the holy martyrs into partnership in their intercessions."[1]

S. Ambrose. S. Ambrose, overwhelmed with grief for his brother's death, expresses his bereavement in these words: "What other consolation is left me but this, that I hope to come to thee, my brother, speedily, and that thy departure will not entail a long separation between us; and that this favour may be granted me by thy intercessions, that thou mayest summon me, who long to join thee, more speedily."[2]

S. Jerome. S. Jerome speaks without hesitation. In writing to Paula respecting her daughter Blesilla, who was dead, he says, "She entreats the Lord for thee, and begs for me the pardon of my sins."[3] Again, to Heliodorus: "The day will come hereafter, when you will return victorious to your fatherland, where, crowned for your fortitude, you will enter the heavenly Jerusalem. Then you will be made a

---

[1] λαβόντες τοὺς ἁγίους μάρτυρας κοινωνοὺς τῶν εὐχῶν.

[2] "Quid enim mihi superest solatii, quam quod me citius ad te, frater, spero venturum, nec digressus tui inter nos longa divortia fore; tuisque intercessionibus mihi hoc posse conferri, ut citius desiderantem tui advoces."—*De excessu fratris sui Satyri*, Lib. ii. 1170; cf. *id.* Lib. i. 1118.

[3] "Pro te Dominum rogat mihique . . . veniam impetrat peccatorum."—*Ep.* xxv. *super obitu Blesillæ.*

fellow-burgher with S. Paul. There also you will seek for your parents the rights of the same citizenship. There too you will pray for me, who spurred you on to victory."[1]

And in a vigorous dispute with Vigilantius, who asserted that prayers and intercessions must cease after death, "for that even the martyrs, with all their entreaties, were unable to obtain revenge for their own blood," he answers, "if the Apostles and Martyrs, while still in the body, are able to pray for others when as yet they ought to be anxious for themselves, how much more may they do so after they have been crowned, and gained victories and triumphs. One man, Moses, obtains from God pardon for six hundred thousand men in arms: and Stephen, the imitator of his Lord, and the first martyr in Christ, begs forgiveness for his persecutors: and shall their power be less after they have begun to be with Christ?"[2]

[1] "Veniet postea dies ille quo victor revertaris in patriam; quo Hierosolymam cælestem vir fortis coronatus incedas. Tunc municipatiam cum Paulo capies. Tunc et parentibus tuis ejusdem civitatis jus petes. Tunc et pro me rogabis qui te, ut vinceres, incitavi."—*Ep.* i. *ad Heliodorum.*

[2] "Præsertim cum martyres ultionem sui sanguinis obsecrantes impetrare non quiverint. Si apostoli et martyres adhuc in corpore constituti possint orare pro cæteris, quando pro se adhuc debent esse solliciti: quanto magis post coronas victorias et triumphos. Unus homo Moyses sexcentis millibus armatorum impetrat a Deo veniam: et Stephanus, imitator Domini sui et primus martyr in

S. Augustine.

S. Augustine, in his sermon on the Feast-days of the martyrs Castus and Æmilius, expresses his belief that they pleaded the cause of the living, and he vindicates their intercession from the supposed idea that it may appear to trench upon the prerogative of the One "𝔄𝔡𝔳𝔬𝔠𝔞𝔱𝔢 𝔴𝔦𝔱𝔥 𝔱𝔥𝔢 𝔉𝔞𝔱𝔥𝔢𝔯, 𝔍𝔢𝔰𝔲𝔰 ℭ𝔥𝔯𝔦𝔰𝔱 𝔱𝔥𝔢 𝔯𝔦𝔤𝔥𝔱𝔢𝔬𝔲𝔰." The opinion with which he begins belongs to himself alone of the Fathers; at least we know of none others who have assigned such a special virtue to martyrdom, as to assert that it placed those who endured it in a sphere where the prayers of the faithful are no longer welcomed. "The righteousness of the martyrs," he says, "is perfect, for their very passion made them perfect. For this reason the prayers of the Church are not offered for them. For the rest of the faithful they are offered, not for martyrs, for they died so perfect that they are not our clients but our advocates. Neither are they this in themselves, but in Him to Whom they cleaved perfect members to the head. For He is truly the One Advocate Who intercedes for us, sitting at the right hand of the Father, but the One Advocate as He is also the One Shepherd . . . as Christ was a Shepherd, was not Peter a shepherd?

Christo, pro persecutoribus veniam deprecatur, et postquam cum Christo esse cæperint, minus valebunt?"—*Ep.* liii. *adv. Vigilantium.*

Yes, Peter also, and the rest like him, were undoubtedly shepherds."[1]

In another passage he looks for help from the prayers of S. Cyprian: "May Cyprian help with his prayers us, who are toiling in this mortal flesh as beneath some murky cloud, so that, if the Lord grant it, we may to the best of our ability copy his virtues."[2]

And elsewhere he explains the object of the commemoration of martyrs to be "to excite rivalry, and that we may be made partakers of their merits and be aided by their prayers."[3]

[1] "Martyrum perfecta justitia est, quoniam in ipsa passione perfecti sunt. Ideo pro illis in Ecclesia non oratur. Pro aliis fidelibus defunctis oratur, pro martyribus non oratur: tam enim perfecti exierunt, ut non sint suscepti nostri sed advocati. Neque hoc in se, sed in illo cui capiti perfecta membra cohæserunt. Ille est enim vere advocatus unus, qui interpellat pro nobis, sedens ad dextram Patris: sed advocatus unus, sicut et pastor unus . . . ut Christus pastor, Petrus non pastor? Imo et Petrus pastor et cæteri tales sine ulla dubitatione pastores."—S. Aug. *Sermo* cclxxxv. 5.

On Vincentian principles such a view as this must be rejected at once. "Whatsoever," he says, "any, though holy and learned, though Bishop, Confessor, and Martyr, hath holden otherwise than all or against all, let that be put aside from the authority of the common judgment, lest we follow the novel errors of some on man."—S. Vinc. *Common.* xxviii.

[2] "Adjuvet itaque nos Cyprianus orationibus suis in istius carnis mortalitate tanquam in caliginosa nube laborantes, ut donante Domino quantum possumus bona ejus imitemur."—*De Bapt. contra Donat.* vii. 1.

[3] "Ad excitandam imitationem et ut meritis eorum consocietur atque orationibus adjuvetur."—*Contr. Faust.* xx. 21.

The Council of Chalcedon.

We close the Patristic citations on this subject with two memorable cases connected with the Council of Chalcedon; the one referring to Flavian, who had been killed at the Robber Synod of Ephesus; the other to Proterius, who had met his death in the Baptistery at the hands of Timothy Ailurus. When, in a session of the Council, the name of the former was incidentally mentioned, the assembled Fathers cried out, "Flavian lives after death. The martyr will pray for us."[1]

And in the letter of the Bishops to the Emperor Leo, written at the same Council, they said that "Proterius had been admitted into the army of martyrs, and they prayed that God would regard his intercessions and show them mercy and favour."[2]

The foregoing testimony is sufficient on Vincentian principles to satisfy the mind of the Catholicity of the belief that the Saints in Paradise intercede for the Church on earth. There is not wanting, however, corroborative proof in the other sources of information which are open to us. The Early Liturgies appear to take less notice of the subject

Primitive Liturgies.

---

[1] Φλαυιανὸς μετὰ θάνατον ζῇ· ὁ μάρτυς ὑπὲρ ἡμῶν εὔξεται.—*Conc. Chalc. Act* xi.; Labb. et Cossart, vol. iv. p. 698.

[2] "Sanctissimum quidem Proterium in ordine et choro sanctorum martyrum ponimus, et ejus intercessionibus misericordem et propitium Deum nobis fieri postulamus."—*Ep. Episc. Europæ, apud Conc. Chalc.* cap. xxvii.: Labb. et Cossart, vol. iv. p. 907.

than perhaps we should have expected; for, upon the kindred question of prayers for the dead, their witness is both abundant and conclusive. The reason may be, that inasmuch as public forms of prayer and worship are for the most part designed to express the wants of the worshippers, and their own feelings in relation to God, to whom their thoughts are especially turned, little mention is made of any possible help to be derived from the intercession of others; whereas prayers for friends and relations, whether living or dead, being, as they not unfrequently are, expressions of some of our greatest needs, are fitly introduced, and that to a very large extent.

As soon as the thoughts were drawn off from God, as the sole Hearer of prayer, and the idea prevailed that subordinate spirits were conscious of men's deeds, and might be asked to exercise their influence and mediation with Him, invocations became frequent, and the intercessory nature of their occupation more generally acknowledged.

In the early forms, then, we look only for occasional and individual allusions to the doctrine, but, infrequent though they be, they are sufficient for our purpose, that is, as subsidiary testimony. The following are a few examples:—

The Syriac Liturgy of S. James.

In the Syriac Liturgy of S. James, which was probably the original Liturgy, we read, "Therefore we commemorate them, that while they stand before Thy Throne, they may remember our weakness and infirmity, and offer to Thee, in union with us, this tremendous sacrifice."[1]

The Liturgy of S. Basil.

In the Liturgy of S. Basil: "Now, Lord, by the command of Thine only begotten Son, we communicate with the memory of Thy saints, who pleased Thee from the beginning, . . . and of the saint whose memory we this day celebrate, and of the whole company of thy saints, by whose prayers and supplications do Thou have mercy upon us all, and deliver us, for the sake of Thy holy Name which is invoked upon us."[2]

Coptic Liturgies.

The same prayer, with only an occasional variety of expression, is repeated in the Coptic Liturgies of S. Gregory,[3] and S. Cyril,[4] and in the Alexandrian

---

[1] "Idcirco enim memoriam illorum agimus ut dum ipsi stabunt coram throno tuo nostræ quoque tenuitatis et infirmitatis meminerint, tibique nobiscum offerant sacrificium hoc tremendum." Cf. HAMMOND, *Litt. East and West*, p. 75.

[2] "Nunc, Domine, ex præcepto Filii tui unigeniti communicamus memoriæ Sanctorum tuorum, qui tibi placuerunt ab initio, . . . et sancti N. cujus hodie memoriam celebramus omnisque chori Sanctorum tuorum, quorum precibus et supplicationibus miserere nostrum omnium, et libera nos propter nomen tuum sanctum quod invocatum est super nos."—RENAUD. i.

[3] RENAUD. i. 34.   [4] *Id.* i. 42.

Liturgy of S. Basil,[1] and the Liturgy of S. James the Lord's brother.[2]

There can be little doubt that portions of the passages here referred to, for example the lists of saints commemorated, are additions or interpolations of much later date, but there is no reason to suppose that the words which speak of the intercession of the saints did not constitute part of the original forms, because there is sufficient corroborative evidence of the doctrine in the Fathers and Doctors of the age. In some cases there is an almost exact agreement between the language of a Liturgy and the expositions of the author whose name the Liturgy bears.[3]

---

[1] RENAUD. i. 12.   [2] *Id.* ii. 36.
[3] S. CYRIL. *Catechesis* xxiii. *Mystag.* v. *de Sacra Liturgia*, ix.

CHAPTER II.

Primitive Testimony to the Invocation of the Saints.

The results of the previous considerations.

THE application of the Vincentian test to the primitive belief in the Intercession of the Saints has satisfied us in respect of universality, antiquity, and consent. It has been shown to be not without witness in Holy Scripture; and the Fathers, in quite sufficient numbers to be considered as fairly representative of the Church Catholic, are seen to have expressed their views with such an entire absence of ambiguity or hesitation, that they may well be listened to as candid interpreters of the faith as it was held in the generations to which they belonged.

We turn now from this, where all is so decisive and convincing, to the consideration of evidence which, when impartially weighed, can hardly fail to leave a far different impression upon the mind.

In examining the Catholicity of the practice of addressing the saints in prayer, or asking for their intercessions, we propose to bring together all the passages with a distinct bearing upon it which are known to us, without any further comments than may be necessary by way of introduction, and in a subsequent chapter to consider separately and in detail whether there is anything either in the extracts themselves, or in other treatises by the same authors, which ought to depreciate the value of their evidence or neutralise its effect altogether.

The first quotation is one of some ambiguity, taken from a passage of Origen, in which he is distinguish- Origen ing different kinds of prayer. He writes thus: "It is not improper to offer supplication, intercession, and thanksgiving to saints: and two of these—I mean intercession and thanksgiving—not only to saints, but to mere men, but supplication to saints only, if any Peter or Paul can be found, that they may help us: making us worthy to enjoy the licence which was granted to them of forgiving sins."[1]

S. Basil addresses the Forty Martyrs, "O holy S. Basil. band, O sacred company, O unbroken phalanx, O

---

[1] δέησιν μὲν οὖν καὶ ἔντευξιν καὶ εὐχαριστίαν οὐκ ἄτοπον καὶ ἁγίοις* προσενῖγκεεν· ἀλλὰ τὰ μὲν δύο, λέγω δὴ ἔντευξιν καὶ εὐχαριστίαν οὐ μόνον ἁγίοις ἀλλὰ δὴ καὶ ἀνθρώποις, τὴν δὲ δέησιν μόνον ἁγίοις, εἴ τις εὑρεθείη Παῦλος ἢ Πέτρος ἵνα ὠφελήσωσιν ἡμᾶς ἀξίους ποιοῦντες τοῦ τυχεῖν τῆς δεδομένης αὐτοῖς ἐξουσίας πρὸς τὰ ἁμαρτήματα ἀφιέναι.—*De Oratione*, 14.

* Alia lect. ανθρωποις, the corruption arising from the contracted form ανοις.

common guardians of the human race, kind sharers in our anxieties, co-operators in prayer, most influential patrons."[1]

Again he expresses his belief in the utility of invocation by declaring his own practice: "I accept also the holy Apostles, Prophets, and Martyrs, and I call upon them for their supplication to God, that by them, that is by their mediation, the merciful God may take compassion upon me, and that there may be granted to me redemption for mine offences."[2]

And some of the results he led people to expect from the invocation of martyrs are evident from what follows:—"Commemorate the martyr (Mamas), all who in dreams have partaken of his benefits; all ye who meeting in this place have had him as a co-operator in prayer; all whom, when invoked by name, he has aided in their works; all wayfarers whom he has brought back to their homes; all whom he has restored from sickness; all to whom he has given back their children from the jaws of death;

[1] ὦ χορὸς ἅγιος, ὦ σύνταγμα ἱερόν, ὦ συνασπισμὸς ἀρραγής, ὦ κοινοὶ φύλακες τοῦ γένους τῶν ἀνθρώπων, ἀγαθοὶ κοινωνοὶ φροντίδων, δεήσεως συνεργοί, πρεσβευταὶ δυνατώτατοι.—S. Bas. Hom. in xl. Mart. § 8.

[2] δέχομαι δὲ καὶ τοὺς ἁγίους ἀποστόλους προφήτας καὶ μάρτυρας καὶ εἰς τὴν πρὸς Θεὸν ἱκεσίην τούτους ἐπικαλοῦμαι τοῦ δι' αὐτῶν ἤγουν διὰ τῆς μεσιτείας αὐτῶν ἵλεών μοι γενέσθαι τὸν φιλάνθρωπον Θεόν, καὶ λύτρον μοι τῶν πταισμάτων γενέσθαι καὶ δοθῆναι.— Ex Epistola ad Julian. Apostatam, ccv.

all for whom he has extended the boundaries of life. Gather it all together and frame a panegyric out of the common fund."¹

S. Gregory Nazianzen quotes a passage from an oration, in all probability falsely attributed to S. Cyprian, in which there is a distinct appeal to the Blessed Virgin for help, "beseeching the Virgin Mary to help a virgin in danger."² But though almost certainly apocryphal, it is nevertheless the evidence of a time anterior to the Father who narrates it.

S. Gregory Nazianzen.

The same Saint exclaims, "Hear, O soul of the great Constantius (if thou hast any faculty of perception), and ye souls of all the kings who before him loved Christ."³

Again, in a funeral oration delivered in honour of Gorgonia his sister,—"If thou have any regard for our affairs, and it be a privilege granted by God to holy souls to take cognisance of such things,

¹ μνήθητε μὲν τοῦ μάρτυρος, ὅσοι δι' ὀνείρων αὐτοῦ ἀπηλαύσατε, ὅσοι περιτυχόντες τούτῳ τῷ τόπῳ ἐσχήκατε αὐτὸν συνεργὸν εἰς προσευχήν, ὅσοις ὀνόματι κληθεὶς ἐπὶ τῶν ἔργων παρέστη, ὅσους ὁδοιπόρους ἐπανήγαγεν, ὅσους ἐξ ἀρρωστίας ἀνέστησεν, ὅσοις παῖδας ἀπέδωκεν ἤδη τετελευτηκότας, ὅσοις προθεσμίας βίου μακροτέρας ἐποίησεν, πάντα μὲν συναγαγόντες ἐγκώμιον ἐκ κοινοῦ ἐράνου ποιήσατε.—*De Martyre Mamante, Hom.* xxvi.

² Τὴν Παρθένον Μαρίαν ἱκετεύουσα βοηθῆσαι παρθένῳ κινδυνευούσῃ.—*Orat. in laud. S. Cypriani Mart.* xxiv. § 11.

³ ἄκουε καὶ ἡ τοῦ μεγάλου Κωνσταντίου ψυχὴ (εἴ τις αἴσθησις), ὅσαι τε πρὸ αὐτοῦ βασιλέων φιλόχριστοι. — *Adv. Jul. Imp. Invect.* i. *Orat.* iv. 3.

then, I pray you, accept this oration of ours."[1] And he thus appeals to S. Basil: "But do thou, O divine and sacred head, look on us from above, and either by thy intercessions take away the thorn in the flesh which afflicts us, or persuade us to bear it with fortitude."[2]

S. Gregory of Nyssa. S. Gregory of Nyssa, on the festival held in honour of Theodore, after describing the crowds who flocked to his shrine in such numbers that he could compare the appearance of the roads to nothing else than a busy ant-hill, appeals to the saint thus: "Come, to those who honour thee, an unseen friend: visit these rites, that thou mayest redouble thy thanksgiving to God. . . . We are in need of many favours: intercede with our common King for this country. . . . We are in expectation of troubles, and look for dangers: the blood-stained Scythians are not far distant, travailing with war against us. As a soldier fight for us: as a martyr use boldness of speech for thy fellow-servants. What though thou hast passed from this life, yet thou art cognisant of

---

[1] εἰ δέ τίς σοι καὶ τῶν ἡμετέρων ἐστι λόγος, καὶ τοῦτο ὁσίαις ψυχαῖς ἐκ θεοῦ γέρας τῶν τοιούτων ἐπαισθάνεσθαι, δέχοιο καὶ τὸν ἡμέτερον λόγον.—*Funeb. Orat. Sor.* viii. 23.

[2] σὺ δὲ ἡμᾶς ἐποπτεύοις ἄνωθεν, ὦ θεία καὶ ἱερὰ κεφαλή, καὶ τὸν δεδομένον ἡμῖν περὶ θεοῦ σκόλοπα τῆς σαρκὸς τὴν ἡμετέραν παιδαγωγίαν, ἢ στήσαις ταῖς σεαυτοῦ πρεσβείαις, ἢ πείσαις καρτερῶς φέρειν.—*Funeb. Orat. in laud. Basilii. Magni, ad fin.*

the sufferings and wants of humanity. Ask for peace, that these public assemblies may not cease: that the frantic and lawless barbarian may not rage against temples and altars: that the profane may not trample under foot the sacred things. For we who have been preserved unharmed, to thee we ascribe the boon: but we beg also safety for the future. And if there should be need for more numerous intercessions, assemble the company of thy brother martyrs, and petition together with them all; let the prayers of many just loose the sins of multitudes of the people."[1]

Again he writes: "Do thou (Ephraem), standing by the divine altar, and in company with angels

[1] ἧκε πρὸς τοὺς τιμῶντάς σε ἀόρατος φίλος. ἱστόρησον τὰ τελούμενα, ἵνα τὴν εἰς Θεὸν εὐχαριστίαν διπλασιάσῃς ... χρήζομεν πολλῶν εὐεργεσιῶν, πρέσβευσον ὑπὲρ τῆς πατρίδος πρὸς τὸν κοινὸν βασιλέα ... ὑφορώμεθα θλίψεις, προσδοκῶμεν κινδύνους, οὐ μακρὰν οἱ ἀλιτήριοι Σκύθαι τὸν καθ' ἡμῶν ὠδίνοντες πόλεμον. ὡς στρατιώτης ὑπερμάχησον· ὡς μάρτυς ὑπὲρ τῶν ὁμοδούλων χρῆσαι τῇ παρρησίᾳ. εἰ δὲ ὑπερέβης τὸν βίον, ἀλλ' οἶδας τὰ πάθη καὶ τὰς χρείας τῆς ἀνθρωπότητος. αἴτησον εἰρήνην ἵνα αἱ πολυηγόρεις αὗται μὴ λήξωσιν. ἵνα μὴ κωμάσῃ κατὰ ναῶν καὶ θυσιαστηρίων ἄθεσμος βάρβαρος. ἵνα μὴ πατήσῃ τὰ ἅγια βέβηλος. ἡμᾶς γὰρ ὑπὲρ ὧν ἀπαθεῖς ἐφυλάχθημεν, σοὶ λογιζόμεθα τὴν εὐεργεσίαν. αἰτοῦμεν δὲ καὶ τοῦ μέλλοντος τὴν ἀσφάλειαν. ἂν χρεία γένηται δὲ πλείονος δυσωπίας, ἄθροισον τὸν χορὸν τῶν σῶν ἀδελφῶν τῶν μαρτύρων καὶ μετὰ τούτων δεήθητε, πολλῶν δικαίων εὐχαὶ λαῶν καὶ δήμων ἁμαρτίας λυσάτωσαν.—S. GREG. NYSS. de S. Theodoro Mart., ad fin.

ministering to the all-holy **Trinity,** the Source of life, remember all of us, asking for us remission of sins and perfect enjoyment of the eternal kingdom in Christ Jesus our Lord."[1]

S. Ephraem Syrus.

S. Ephraem Syrus, in his panegyric on the Forty Martyrs, after dwelling upon the virtues of the mother of one of them, and the blessed state to which she had attained, concludes with an appeal for her prayers, "Wherefore, O holy and faithful and blessed, I beseech thee, supplicate the holy ones in my behalf, and say, 'Ye triumphant martyrs of Christ, intercede for Ephraem, the least, the miserable, that I may find mercy, and through the grace of Christ may be saved.'"[2]

In his praise of the whole army of martyrs he says, "We therefore call upon you, O most holy martyrs . . . that ye will pray the Lord in behalf of us miserable sinners, beset with the filthiness of sloth, that He will pour upon us His Divine grace, for the perpetual illumination of our hearts by the

---

[1] σὺ δὲ τῷ θείῳ παριστάμενος θυσιαστηρίῳ καὶ τῇ ζωαρχικῇ καὶ ὑπεραγίᾳ λειτουργῶν σὺν ἀγγέλοις Τριάδι, μέμνησο πάντων ἡμῶν, αἰτούμενος ἡμῖν ἁμαρτημάτων ἄφεσιν αἰωνίου τε βασιλείας ἀπόλαυσιν, ἐν Χριστῷ, κ.τ.λ.—*Vita S. Ephr. App.* iii.

[2] "Unde a te deposco, O sancta atque fidelis et beata, ora pro me sanctos dicens: intercedite O triumphatores Christi, pro minimo ac miserabili Ephraem, ut misericordiam inveniam Christique gratia salvus fiam."—*Encom. in sanctos xl. Martyres,* p. 562, ed. Voss.

rays of a holy love. For ye are pronounced truly blessed and glorious by the common voice of angels and men."[1] And he concludes the panegyric with a similar appeal to them to aid him by their prayers, that he may find mercy in the last dread hour, "𝔴𝔥𝔢𝔫 𝔊𝔬𝔡 𝔰𝔥𝔞𝔩𝔩 𝔧𝔲𝔡𝔤𝔢 𝔱𝔥𝔢 𝔰𝔢𝔠𝔯𝔢𝔱𝔰 𝔬𝔣 𝔪𝔢𝔫," and may share with them the enjoyment of eternal bliss. And he concludes his panegyric on S. Basil thus: "O faithful Basil, thou art accepted like Abel, and saved like Noah, called, as Abraham was, the friend of God. . . . Pray for me, who am exceedingly miserable, and recall me by thy intercessions, thou who art strong while I am weak . . . who hast laid up for thyself a store of all virtues, bring me back, who am wanting in every good work."[2]

Moreover, in a collection of prayers found in various manuscripts and assigned by traditions of

[1] "Obtestamur igitur vos, O sanctissimi martyres, . . . ut pro nobis miseris peccatoribus negligentiæ squalore obsitis Dominum deprecemini ut divinam suam in nos infundat gratiam quæ corda nostra sanctæ caritatis radio jugiter illustret . . . vos etenim vere nunc beati et gloriosi estis quos angeli pariter et homines una voce et consensu felices et beatos prædicant."—*In laud. omn. Sanct. Martyrum*, p. 570.

[2] "O fidelis Basil, velut Abel acceptus es, et sicut Noe salvatus, tamquam Abraham amicus Dei . . . deprecare pro me admodum miserabili et revoca me tuis intercessionibus pater fortis imbellem . . . qui thesaurizasti tibi thesaurum omnium virtutum me omnis boni operis inopem reducito."—S. EPHR. SYR. *Op.*, Voss. p. 556, *in Sanct. Basil. Magn.*

the Syriac Church to the pen of S. Ephraem, direct invocation of saints is of most frequent occurrence, but we have not brought them forward, as some suspicion has been justly cast upon their genuineness.

S. Chrysostom. S. Chrysostom, after encouraging the people to frequent the shrines of the martyrs, and speaking as though he thought them possessed of some great power and virtue, says, "Not on the day of this festival only, but also on other days, let us place ourselves beside them, let us beseech and implore them to become our patrons; for they have much boldness of speech, not merely when living, but also after death, yea, a great deal more after death. For now they bear the *stigmata* of Christ, and when they have pointed to these they can use all persuasion with the King. Seeing then that they have such influence and friendship with God, let us by our unfailing attendance and constant visiting of their shrines make ourselves as it were members of their household, and draw upon ourselves, through their intervention, the mercy of God; which may we all obtain by the grace of our Lord Jesus Christ."[1]

[1] καὶ μὴ μόνον ἐν τῇ ἡμέρᾳ τῆς ἑορτῆς ταύτης ἀλλὰ καὶ ἐν ἑτέραις ἡμέραις προσεδρεύωμεν αὐταῖς, παρακαλῶμεν αὐτάς, ἀξιῶμεν γενέσθαι προστάτιδας ἡμῶν. πολλὴν γὰρ ἔχουσι παρρησίαν οὐχὶ ζῶσαι μόνον ἀλλὰ καὶ τελευτήσασαι· καὶ πολλῷ μᾶλλον τελευτήσασαι. νῦν γὰρ τὰ στίγματα φέρουσι τοῦ Χριστοῦ. τὰ δὲ στίγματα ἐπιδεικνύμεναι ταῦτα. πάντα δύνανται πεῖσαι τὸν Βασιλέα. ἐπεὶ οὖν

Elsewhere, in a passage in which he contrasts the establishment of Christ's kingdom with that of the heathen Alexander, he says, "Christ then set up His Kingdom after He was dead. And why do I speak of Christ, seeing that He granted to His disciples also to shine after their deaths? For, tell me, where is the tomb of Alexander? Show it me, and tell me the day upon which he died. But of the servants of Christ the very tombs are glorious, seeing they have taken possession of the most royal city; and their days are well known, making festivals for the world. . . . And the tombs of the servants of the Crucified are more splendid than the palaces of kings; not for the size and beauty of the buildings (yet even herein they outstrip them), but, what is far more, in the zeal of those who frequent them. For he that wears the purple himself goes to embrace those tombs, and, laying aside his pride, stands entreating the saints to be his advocates with God, and he that hath the diadem implores the tent-maker and the fisherman, though dead, to be his patrons."[1]

τοσαύτη η δύναμις αὐταῖς καὶ φιλία πρὸς τὸν Θεὸν, τῇ συνεχεῖ προσεδρίᾳ καὶ τῇ διηνεκεῖ πρὸς αὐτὰς ἀφίξει καταστήσαντες ἑαυτοὺς οἰκείους αὐτῶν, ἐπισπασώμεθα δι' αὐτῶν τὴν παρὰ τοῦ Θεοῦ φιλανθρωπίαν ἧς γένοιτο πάντας ἡμᾶς ἐπιτυχεῖν χάριτι, κ.τ.λ.—*De SS. Bernice et Prosdoce, in fin.*

[1] ὁ δὲ Χριστὸς τότε αὐτὴν μάλιστα ἔστησεν ὅτε ἐτελεύτησε. καὶ τί λέγω περὶ τοῦ Χριστοῦ ὅπου γε καὶ τοῖς μαθηταῖς αὐτοῦ μετὰ τὸ τελευτῆσαι λάμψαι ἔδωκε; ποῦ γάρ, εἰπέ μοι, τὸ σῆμα Ἀλεξάν-

Again: "Knowing this, beloved, let us flee to the intercessions of the saints, and let us beseech them to pray for us; but let us not place confidence in their supplications alone, but order our own lives as is fit, and aim at constant improvement, that we may give full play to the intercession which is made in our behalf."[1]

S. Ambrose. S. Ambrose writes: "We must beseech the martyrs, whose patronage we seem to claim for ourselves from having their bodies as a kind of pledge. They are able to entreat for our sins, who by their blood have washed away whatever sins they had themselves; for they are God's martyrs, our leaders, the watchmen of our life and actions. Let us not

δρου· δεῖξόν μοι καὶ εἰπὲ τὴν ἡμέραν καθ' ἣν ἐτελεύτησε. τῶν δὲ δούλων τοῦ Χριστοῦ καὶ τὰ σήματα λαμπρά, τὴν βασιλικωτάτην καταλαβόντα πόλιν καὶ αἱ ἡμέραι καταφανεῖς, ἑορτὴν τῇ οἰκουμένῃ ποιοῦσαι ... καὶ οἱ τάφοι τῶν δούλων τοῦ σταυρωθέντος λαμπρότεροι τῶν βασιλικῶν εἰσιν αὐλῶν, οὐ τῷ μεγέθει καὶ τῷ κάλλει τῶν οἰκοδομημάτων μόνον· καὶ τούτῳ μὲν γὰρ κρατοῦσιν· ἀλλ', ὃ πολλῷ πλέον ἐστὶ τῇ σπουδῇ τῶν συνιόντων. καὶ γὰρ αὐτὸς ὁ τὴν ἀλουργίδα περικείμενος ἀπέρχεται τὰ σήματα ἐκεῖνα περιπτυξόμενος, καὶ τὸν τῦφον ἀποθέμενος ἕστηκε δεόμενος τῶν ἁγίων ὥστε αὐτοῦ προστῆναι παρὰ τῷ Θεῷ καὶ τοῦ σκηνοποιοῦ καὶ τοῦ ἁλιέως προστατῶν καὶ τετελευτηκότων δεῖται ὁ τὸ διάδημα ἔχων.—*In Epist.* ii. *ad Cor. Hom.* xxvi.

[1] ὅπερ εἰδότες, ἀγαπητοί, καταφευγῶμεν μὲν ἐπὶ τὰς τῶν ἁγίων πρεσβείας καὶ παρακαλῶμεν ὥστε ὑπὲρ ἡμῶν δεηθῆναι. ἀλλὰ μὴ ταῖς ἐκείνων ἱκεσίαις μόνον θαρρῶμεν, ἀλλὰ καὶ αὐτοὶ τὰ καθ' ἑαυτοὺς δεόντως οἰκονομῶμεν, καὶ τῆς ἐπὶ τὸ βέλτιον μεταβολῆς ἐχώμεθα ἵνα χώραν δῶμεν τῇ πρεσβείᾳ τῇ ὑπὲρ ἡμῶν γενομένῃ.—*In Genes. Hom.* xliv. 2.

be ashamed to employ them to intercede for our weakness, because they themselves experienced the weaknesses of the body, even when they conquered."[1]

There is but little countenance for appealing to the dead for aid to be found in the works of S. Augustine, except in connection with the tombs of the martyrs. He speaks in one place of the habit and the utility of praying near the shrines of the martyrs, and commending the souls of people in prayer to their special patronage, to be helped by their intercessions with the Lord.[2] {S. Augustine.}

Elsewhere[3] he vindicates the character of the miracles which are said to have been wrought at their tombs, and asserts that God, through the prayer and co-operation of the saints, performs them for the establishment of the faith, which maintains that they are not gods, but have one and the same God as ourselves. And in the same treatise, contrasting the Christian treatment of martyrs with

[1] "Martyres obsecrandi, quorum videmur nobis quodam corporis pignore patrocinium vindicare. Possunt pro peccatis rogare nostris, qui proprio sanguine, etiam si qua habuerunt peccata, laverunt; isti enim sunt Dei martyres nostri præsules spectatores vitæ actuumque nostrorum. Non erubescamus eos intercessores nostræ infirmitatis adhibere, quia ipsi infirmitates corporis etiam cum vincerent (*quædam edit.* etiam cum vivcrent) cognoverunt."—AMBROS. *de Viduis*, cap. ix. 55.
[2] *De Cura pro Mortuis*, 4.
[3] *De Civ.* xxii. cap. x.

that of demons by the heathens, he says: "To our martyrs we do not build temples as to gods, but 'Memorials' as to dead men, whose spirits live with God; nor do we raise altars there that we may sacrifice to martyrs, but to Him alone Who is the God of the martyrs as well as of us; and at this sacrifice their names are mentioned in their proper places and order as men of God, who overcame the world by confessing Him; they are not, however, invoked by the priest who offers the sacrifice."[1]

The story of Florentius of Hippo. He also narrates a story of an aged saint, Florentius of Hippo, who, having lost his cloak, and being unable from his poverty to replace it, prayed to the twenty martyrs of famous memory to help him in his difficulty. After his prayer, and as S. Augustine implies in answer to it, he discovered a fish cast upon the shore, in which on its being cut up was found a gold ring. It was put into his hand, says S. Augustine, with these words, "See how the twenty martyrs have clothed you!"[2]

[1] "Nos autem martyribus nostris non templa sicut diis, sed Memorias sicut hominibus mortuis, quorum apud Deum vivant spiritus, fabricamus ; nec ibi erigimus altaria in quibus sacrificemus martyribus, sed uni Deo et martyrum et nostro : ad quod sacrificem, sicut homines Dei, qui mundum in ejus confessione vicerunt, suo loco et ordine nominantur ; non tamen a sacerdote qui sacrificat invocantur."—*De Civ. Dei*, xxii. cap. x.

[2] *De Civ. Dei*, xxii. cap. viii. 9.

CHAPTER III.

The trustworthiness of the Patristic evidence for invocation tested.

BEFORE turning to other sources of evidence, it will be well to weigh carefully the value of that which has been put forward in the preceding pages. Its force will be very materially weakened by close examination.

We spoke of some ambiguity in the language quoted from Origen. The passage seems indeed to have been quite unjustly claimed in favour of addressing petitions to departed saints. It is next to certain, as the whole context shows, that he had in his mind none but living saints. Indeed, the parenthesis about the advantage likely to accrue if only a second Peter or Paul could be found to take up their cause, seems almost necessarily to restrict it to the living; for if he had believed that the saints in Paradise might be invoked, he would hardly have introduced such a clause as this. *Origen.*

Among those "who had come out of great tribulation," there were certainly others like them, ready, if they knew where it was needed, to lend efficient help; among the living, still compassed with infirmity and sin, there might be some, but they were not easy to find.

This interpretation is supported by what the author said in his arguments with Celsus, "For every prayer and supplication, and intercession and thanksgiving, is to be sent up to the supreme God through the High Priest, Who is above all the angels, the living Word and God."[1]

It is true he is speaking here of angelic ministries, but he could not have used such absolutely unqualified language had he held the doctrine with which he has been credited.

Moreover, in a passage already quoted, we have seen that he is far from considering appeals to the saints for their intercession in any way necessary, for he says that they join their prayers to ours and fight on our side without being invoked.[2]

S. Basil. As regards S. Basil's testimony, though one passage may well come into the category of

[1] πᾶσαν μὲν γὰρ δέησιν καὶ προσευχὴν καὶ ἔντευξιν καὶ εὐχαριστίαν ἀναπεμπτέον τῷ ἐπὶ πᾶσι Θεῷ, διὰ τοῦ ἐπὶ πάντων ἀγγέλων ἀρχιερέως, ἐμψύχου λόγου καὶ Θεοῦ.—*Contr. Celsum*, v. 4.

[2] *Contr. Celsum*, viii. 64 ; *vide* supra, p. 161.

rhetorical apostrophes, which are very far removed from the formal invocations of such frequent occurrence in the next generation, there can be no question that he regarded the practice as legitimate, and did not hesitate to adopt it himself, and encourage others to do the same.

In examining the value of the quotations from S. Gregory Nazianzen, we observe that even if the first could be proved to be genuine, it merely contains the statement of a fact, which is not indorsed or recorded with the distinct approval of the writer. And it has been ironically asked, "Is the conduct of a girl of like authority with an ecclesiastical statute, or of sufficient weight to fix our faith?"[1]

S. Gregory Nazianzen.

In the second and third there is clear indication that he had misgivings about the efficacy of the appeals which he was making; otherwise he would surely have been silent as to any possibility of their not being heard and regarded.

When he wrote the fourth, he appears to have had his doubts removed, and this passage may fairly be claimed in support of Invocation.

S. Gregory of Nyssa again must be ranked

S. Gregor of Nyssa.

---

[1] "*At puella ibi Virginem Mariam invocabat. Sed an factum puellæ statutum ecclesiæ? an ex puellarum factis, fidei nobis figenda regula est?*"—ANDREWES, *Responsio ad Cardinalis Bellarmini Apologiam*, sect. 42.

among its advocates. Nothing could be stronger than what he has written in the extracts which we brought forward, and none of his other writings, as far as we know, contain anything which could be alleged in diminution of its force.

S. Ephraem. S. Ephraem was a man of a fervid imagination and impassioned nature, especially given to apostrophising both people and things, and much that he says is in the language of panegyric, where men are not wont to measure their words as carefully as they may be expected to do in a theological treatise. But, all allowances made, we can hardly do otherwise than feel that, had occasion occurred to call forth a deliberate expression of his opinion, he would have written in support of the practice on doctrinal grounds.

S. Chrysostom. S. Chrysostom's writings supply sufficient evidence of a contradictory nature to weaken very considerably the force of the sentiments before expressed. "Thus then," he writes, "we do not appease Him when we make our request by the mouths of others so well as by our own. For inasmuch as He longs for our friendship, He does all He can to lead us to place our confidence in Him. When He sees us doing this, (praying) by our own mouth, then He is most inclined to yield assent."[1]

[1] οὐχ οὕτως οὖν αὐτὸν δυσωποῦμεν δι' ἑτέρων ἀξιοῦντες ὡς δι' ἡμῶν αὐτῶν. ἐπειδὴ γὰρ τῆς ἡμετέρας ἐρᾷ φιλίας, καὶ πάντα

In what precedes he had pointed out God's readiness to hear our petitions, contrasting it with the difficulty of obtaining access to the great ones of the earth, as is evident from his allusion to porters and stewards and watchmen, who bar the entrance; but he would hardly have spoken unreservedly of direct personal appeal to God, had he been quite satisfied of the value of invoking the intercession of saints. He makes precisely the same assertion in another place,[1] and frequently illustrates his principle by arguments drawn from the case of the Syrophœnician woman.

There is certainly no advocacy of the practice in question in either of the following passages, but they rather show marks of disapproval. "What a boon to find him of whom you ask a favour ready to grant you what you ask! What a boon not to have to go about in search of one to ask from, but to find Him ready! What greater blessing is there than this? For here is One Who is most willing to do anything, when we do not supplicate others. Like a sincere friend He upbraids us most for lack of confidence in His friendship, when we supplicate others to ask Him."[2]

ποιεῖ ὥστε ἡμᾶς αὐτῷ θαρρεῖν. ὅταν ἴδῃ δι' ἑαυτῶν τοῦτο ποιοῦντας, τότε μάλιστα ἐπινεύει.—*Expos. in Ps.* iv. 2.

[1] *In Genes. Hom.* xliv. 4.
[2] τίς σοι δῷ ἕτοιμον εἶναι τὸν ἀξιούμενον χάριν σοι ἔχειν ὅτι

"Thou hast no need of mediators with God, or of much running to and fro and of flattering of others. But even if thou be unbefriended and destitute of patrons; if thou beseech God thyself by thine own mouth, thou shalt certainly succeed. It is not His wont to assent, when others beseech Him in our behalf, so much as when we are ourselves the petitioners, even though we be laden with innumerable ills."[1]

S. Ambrose. In S. Ambrose we have been able to discover a single passage only in support of the practice, and this is counterbalanced by the expression of an adverse opinion in what follows. At least it shows that he could not have formed any settled and deliberate judgment upon it. "My heart is worn out, because a man has been snatched away, whose like we can hardly find again; but yet Thou alone,

---

ἀξιοῖς; τίς σοι δῷ μὴ περιϊέναι καὶ ζητεῖν τίνα ἀξιώσεις, ἀλλὰ εὑρεῖν ἕτοιμον; μὴ ἑτέρων δεῖσθαι ἵνα δι' ἐκείνων ἀξιώσῃς; τί τούτου μεῖζον; οὗτος γὰρ τότε μάλιστα ποιεῖ, ὅταν μὴ ἑτέρων δεηθῶμεν. καθάπερ φίλος γνήσιος τότε μάλιστα ἡμῖν ἐγκαλεῖ ὡς οὐ θαρροῦσιν αὐτοῦ τῇ φιλίᾳ, ὅταν ἑτέρων πρὸς αὐτὸν δεηθῶμεν τῶν ἀξιούντων.— *In Acta Apost. Hom.* xxxvi. 3.

[1] οὐ χρεία σοι μεσιτῶν ἐπὶ τοῦ Θεοῦ οὐδὲ πολλῆς τῆς περιδρομῆς καὶ τοῦ κολακεῦσαι ἑτέροις. ἀλλὰ κἂν ἔρημος ᾖς κἂν ἀπροστάτευτος, αὐτὸς διὰ σαυτοῦ παρακαλέσας τὸν Θεὸν ἐπιτεύξῃ πάντως· οὐχ οὕτω δι' ἑτέρων ὑπὲρ ἡμῶν παρακαλούμενος ἐπινεύειν εἴωθεν, ὡς δι' ἡμῶν αὐτῶν τῶν δεομένων, κἂν μυρίων ὦμεν γέμοντες κακῶν.— *Sermo. Philip.* i. 18.

O Lord, art to be invoked, Thou art to be entreated, that Thou mayst supply his place with his sons."[1]

It is quite impossible to doubt S. Augustine's approval of the practice of invoking the saints, at least when his opinions are fairly examined. But the invocation which he sanctioned was certainly under restrictions.

S. Augustine.

The words however, which have been quoted above—"they are not invoked by the priest who offers the sacrifice,"—have been held to forbid all invocation, for if not by the priest, why, it is said, by the people?

To accept such an interpretation as this would be to charge him, very unjustly we think, with glaring inconsistency. Either of the following explanations is sufficient to acquit him of this:—

Firstly, it may be that he regarded it simply as a pious practice, as a natural outcome of an intense realisation of the Communion of Saints, that we should continue to appeal to them after they had been taken away, just as we had done whilst they were with us, for their prevailing intercession. But he guarded himself with a most jealous care against

---

[1] "Conteror corde quia ereptus est vir, quem (*Rom. ed.* qualem) vix possumus invenire ; sed tamen tu solus, Domine, invocandus, tu rogandus, ut eum in filiis repræsentes."—*De obitu Theodosii Orat.* 1207.

appearing to sanction any the least encroachment upon the prerogative of God.

Invocation of different kinds.

To invoke or appeal to the saints in one way, he felt was only the unburdening of a soul deeply impressed with the conviction that those who cared and prayed for its welfare while they lived, must continue to do the same, and probably with greater energy and more prevailing importunity, when disencumbered from the trammels of the flesh.

To invoke them in another way, when the invocation was surrounded by all the circumstance of religious worship, would be at least of the nature of, and differing only in degree from, that which he was laying to the charge of the heathen; it would be like building altars to them for the offering of sacrifice, a trenching upon the honour of God, by giving to the creature a portion of that which was due to the Creator alone.

A difference between sacrificial and non-sacrificial prayers.

Or, secondly, he may have meant to draw a distinction between sacrificial and non-sacrificial prayers, and was not speaking against invocation in prayers altogether, but, as inconsistent with the characteristic features which he especially recognised in the Eucharistic service. It cannot fail to be noticed that in this it has, with the rarest exception,[1] been

[1] The second clause of the Angelic Hymn or Great Doxology is an exception, but in primitive times only the first clause, which

the common practice of the Church, both in ancient and modern times, to address prayers to the First Person of the Blessed Trinity alone. It arose out of the Catholic belief that there is a distinctly sacrificial element in the Service, consisting mainly in its being, as it is technically called, a pleading or re-presentation of the One Sacrifice upon the Cross before the Father, rather than a mere memorial designed to keep the recollection of Christ's Death before the eyes of men. If all looks to the Father, all praise, all prayers must be directed to Him. This principle, which is exemplified in all Liturgies, Eastern and Western alike, was indorsed by a Synod of Carthage,[1] at which a decree was passed that "when the priest stands at the altar, prayer should always be addressed to the Father." The invocation of the Holy Ghost for the sanctification of the

is addressed to the Father, was used to be sung. In the form however which is extant in the Apostolical Constitutions, Lib. vii. cxlvii., there is an ascription of praise to "the Lord Jesus, the Christ of the God of all created nature," but no such prayer as we have in the present Hymn. But in whatever form it has been used, it is to be noted that it has always been separated from the central portion of the Office, and been placed either at the beginning, as in the First Prayer-Book of Edward VI., and the earlier English and the present Roman Liturgies, or in the Post-Communion, as in the present Anglican Office.

[1] The Third Council, Can. 23; cf FORBES, *Considerationes Modestæ*, vol. ii. p. 257, *Anglo-Cath. Libr.*, from whom we have taken the reference.

Elements of Bread and Wine, which was almost universal till the Reformers omitted it in the Second Prayer-Book of Edward VI., though at first sight appearing to contradict this, will be found on investigation not to do so. Every form which we have met with is addressed, not like the "Veni Creator," directly to the Third Person, but to the Father Himself, to pour down the Spirit of sanctification upon the gifts set forth upon the altar.

We think then, on a full consideration of S. Augustine's teaching, that he may fairly be claimed as advocating appeals at least to the martyrs for their intercession, and that the passage, which has been supposed to express his judgment against the practice, may be explained either as deliberately separating it from the worship of God generally, or at any rate from Eucharistic worship. If we are right in what we have said about the universally admitted principle of restricting appeals in the latter to the Father alone, it seems little better than a simple truism for S. Augustine to assert that the saints might not be invoked then; and we must interpret his words as providing a safeguard against surrounding such invocation with undue honour.

A summary of results. To summarise the result of the preceding observations and criticisms, it appears that Origen cannot be claimed in favour of Invocation, that S. Chrysostom's contradictions are such as to lessen the force of his evidence, that S. Gregory Nazianzen speaks doubtfully, that S. Ambrose, in the little which he has said upon the subject, is inconsistent with himself; but that the testimony of SS. Basil, Gregory Nyssen, Ephraem, and Augustine remains so far unshaken.

CHAPTER IV.

The Primitive Liturgies and the Roman Catacombs.

The Liturgies.

WE look in vain for any corroborative evidence of the practice in the Primitive Liturgies or other Offices of the Church.

Accepting the principle that in the Commemorative Sacrifice all prayer and praise is directed to God the Father alone, we can hardly expect to find any trace of the Invocation of Saints in the Service. The AVE MARIA in the Liturgies of S. Mark and S. James is manifestly a late interpolation; even a cursory glance at the context will satisfy us of this. Nicephorus, who wrote the history of the Church of the first six centuries, failed to discover any such address to a saint in public worship till the close of the fifth century, and he assigned the introduction of the practice to Peter Fullo, the Eutychian Patriarch of Antioch.

Had it been held legitimate, though its absence from the Liturgies proper might be naturally accounted for, it would certainly have had a place in other Offices,—in the Litanies or Preces, or the Oriental Ectene; but in the oldest form still extant, that which is embodied in the Apostolical Constitutions,[1] there is no address or appeal to any saint or martyr.

<small>Other Offices.</small>

When we turn to the only other source of evidence which is open to us, viz. the Roman Catacombs, we are met with clear and unmistakable proof that those who made the inscriptions considered it lawful to ask the prayers of their departed friends. It may be said that the sentiments which find their expression in times of mourning and bereavement ought not to be strictly scrutinised; but a careful examination of these early Epigraphs reveals a singular absence of all fervid and exaggerated language, such as is so common in more modern times. We cannot therefore but believe that the following inscriptions may be taken as a fair index of the practice prevalent at the time when they were written, but some cause will be shown hereafter for not assigning to them an earlier date than the fourth century.

<small>The Catacombs.</small>

In the Catacomb of Prætextatus, on the Appian Way, especially familiar as the burial-place of S. Januarius, the following has been deciphered :—

[1] *Apostol. Constit.* lib. viii. capp. vi.-xi.

MI REFRIGERI JANUARIUS AGAPOTUS FELICISSIM MARTYRES.

Ye martyrs, Januarius, Agapotus, Felicissimus, refresh my soul, etc.

It has been conjectured that this was inscribed about fifteen centuries ago, as the prayer of one who was burying a friend or relative in close proximity to the resting-place of the martyrs mentioned.[1]

It is probable[2] that MI is IN and O the obliterated termination of the noun. Several instances of *in refrigerio* are found. If this be right, it is almost equivalent to *in pace*, and there is no necessity for interpreting it as a prayer or invocation.

This also indicates the idea of patronage:—

DOMINA BASILLA COMMANDAMUS TIBI CRESCENTINUS ET MICINA FILIA NOSTRA CRESCEN QUE VIXIT MEN X ET DIES. . . .

Saint Basilla, we, Crescentinus and Micina, commend to thee our daughter Crescentina, who lived ten months and . . . days.[3]

---

[1] Cf. *Catacombs of Rome*, by the author of *Buried Cities of Campania*, p. 31.

[2] I am indebted to Dr. Westcott for this conjecture.

[3] Cf. NORTHCOTE, *Epitaphs of the Catacombs*, p. 80, where it is given in facsimile.

Here is an appeal, probably by the parents and others, to the saints, with whom they felt assured the soul of their child was abiding:—

ΔΙΟΝΥΣΙΟΣ ΝΗΠΙΟΣ ΑΚΑΚΟΣ ΕΝΘΑΔΕ
ΚΕΙΤΕ ΜΕΤΑ ΤΩΝ ΑΓΙΩΝ ΜΝΗΣΚΕΣΘΕ
ΔΕ ΚΑΙ ΗΜΩΝ ΕΝ ΤΑΙΣ ΑΓΙΑΙΣ ΠΡΕΥΧΑΙΣ
ΚΑΙ ΤΟΥ ΓΛΥΨΑ ΤΟΣ ΚΑΙ ΓΡΑΨΑΝΤΟΣ.

Dionysius, a guileless infant, lies here with the saints. Do ye remember us also in your holy prayers, as well as him who carved and him who composed this inscription.[1]

The next two,[2] from the Catacomb of SS. Nereus and Achilles, are still to be seen *in situ*:—

ΑΥΓΕΝΔΕ
ΖΗΣΑΙΣ ΕΝ ΚΩ ΚΑΙ
ΕΡΩΤΑ ΥΠΕΡ ΗΜΩΝ.

Augenda, mayest thou live in the Lord, and do thou pray for us.

VIBAS IN PACE ET PETE
PRO NOBIS.

Mayest thou live in peace, and do thou pray for us.

---
[1] This is from the Kircherian Museum.
[2] These are quoted by Burgon in his *Letters from Rome*.

Of a similar kind is the following, from the cemetery of S. Callixtus:—

VINCENTIA IN CHRISTO PETAS PRO PHŒBE ET PRO VIRGINIO EJUS.

Vincentia in Christ, mayest thou pray for Phœbe and her husband.

The dates of the foregoing inscriptions unknown.   None of the above inscriptions bear any date, and there are indications which would lead us to fix most of them certainly after the opening of the fourth century. In the case of Basilla it could not possibly have been earlier, as she was martyred under Diocletian, after the fatal edict of 303 A.D.

Nearly the same date is usually assigned to the martyrdom of S. Januarius, and also to that of Agapotus mentioned with him on the inscription,— at least if he is to be identified with Agathopus, who witnessed to Christ a good confession in Thessalonica.

And in connection with this it may be observed that peculiar reverence for the graves of the martyrs, which led people to expect some special benefit to accrue to those whose bodies were laid in proximity to them, did not take any hold upon men's minds in general till this century.

With regard to those which contain the *pete pro nobis*, or the same abbreviated into the initial letters P.P.N., in the absence of all notes of time we have no other data to go upon than such as are furnished by contemporary evidence. This, as we have abundantly seen, carries the practice no further back than the middle of the fourth century.

CHAPTER V.

Patristic opinions on the extent of the knowledge possessed by the Saints.

IT will enable us to form a more accurate estimate of the Patristic notices of appeals to the saints, if we can arrive at the judgment of the writers upon the amount of knowledge of what is passing in the world, which they supposed to be possessed by those to whom they appealed. It will be shown hereafter that intercessory prayers may be offered, and may serve a very beneficial purpose even though the intercessors have no specific knowledge of the immediate wants of those for whom they plead.

The subject rarely touched upon.
Very few of the Fathers mention the subject at all; but in the case of those who do, their observations ought certainly to be taken into consideration in estimating the value of their testimony touching the utility of invocation. It will at least help us to decide whether they said what they did, with

their minds fully made up and under settled convictions, or whether they may not have been carried away by some strong impulse to speak unadvisedly.

Deny to the saints addressed all knowledge of the supplicant's needs, either attained by their own inherent faculties of perception, or communicated by some agency from without, and invocation is nothing more than a pious apostrophe. It may kindle the fervour and affection of him who employs it, but as a direct means of obtaining assistance it is valueless.

In the funeral oration of his sister Gorgonia, S. Gregory Nazianzen addresses her in these terms: "If thou hast any care at all for our speeches, and such honour be conceded by God to holy souls that they should take cognisance of such things, do thou also accept this speech of ours."[1] S. Gregory Nazianzen.

And he uses the same limitation in the beginning of one of the invectives which he wrote against the Emperor Julian, saying, "Hear, O thou soul of great Constantius, if thou hast any faculty of perception,"[2] upon which the Greek Scholiast[3] comments: He speaks "like Isocrates, meaning, if thou hast any power to hear the things that are here," alluding to

---

[1] Cf. note on p. 178. [2] P. 177.
[3] *Schol. Graec. in priorem Nazianzeni Invectivam*, p. 2, ed. Etonensis: εἴ τίς ἐστιν αἴσθησις τοῖς τεθνεῶσι περὶ τῶν ἐνθάδε.

a form of speech used by Isocrates in his Evagoras and Ægineticus. In other places, however, he makes no such reservation, appealing to S. Athanasius directly to look down with an eye of favour upon the people.[1]

Again, of Peter of Alexandria, Gregory writes: "Having departed this life in a good old age, after many struggles and labours, he looks down from above now, I well know, upon our affairs, and stretches out a hand to those who are toiling in the cause of what is right, and all the more because he is freed from trammels."[2]

And once more: "I am persuaded that the souls of the saints take cognisance of our affairs."[3]

S. Ambrose. The opinion of S. Ambrose upon the probability of appeals being heard by those to whom they were addressed may be gathered from what he says on the death of his brother, whom he apostrophises thus: "So full of compassion towards thy kindred was thy holy mind, that if thou knewest Italy to be threatened with so near an enemy, what groans

[1] *In laudem Magni Athanasii, Or.* xxi. *ad fin.*
[2] ἐν γήρῳ καλῷ καταλύσας τὸν βίον ἐπὶ πολλοῖς τοῖς ἀγωνίσμασι καὶ ἀθλήμασιν, ἄνωθεν ἐποπτεύει εὖ οἶδα νῦν τὰ ἡμέτερα, καὶ χεῖρα ὀρέγει τοῖς ὑπὲρ τοῦ καλοῦ κάμνουσι, καὶ τόσῳ μᾶλλον, ὅσῳ τῶν δεσμῶν ἐστὶν ἐλεύθερος.—In *Ægyptiorum Adventum, Orat.* xxiv.
[3] καὶ γὰρ πείθομαι τὰς τῶν ἁγίων ψυχὰς τῶν ἡμετέρων αἰσθάνεσθαι.—*Theclæ Epist.* 201.

thou wouldst utter! How wouldst thou grieve that the last hope of safety lay in the barrier of the Alps."[1]

S. Jerome, at a time when his country was suffering from invasion, finds some consolation in the thought that a dear friend in Paradise was spared the knowledge of what was happening. "Happy," he says, "is Nepotianus in that he does not see these things, happy in that he does not hear them."[2] And again: "Whatever I may say, it must seem as though I were dumb, inasmuch as he does not hear."[3]

S. Jerome.

S. Augustine, in considering the case of Judas, imagines some one suggesting that his punishment might be aggravated in the next world by his being conscious of the state of destitution to which his wife and children had been reduced in fulfilment of the predictions, "𝕷𝖊𝖙 𝖍𝖎𝖘 𝖈𝖍𝖎𝖑𝖉𝖗𝖊𝖓 𝖇𝖊 𝖈𝖔𝖓𝖙𝖎𝖓𝖚𝖆𝖑𝖑𝖞 𝖇𝖆𝖌𝖆𝖇𝖔𝖓𝖉𝖘, 𝖆𝖓𝖉 𝖇𝖊𝖌; 𝖑𝖊𝖙 𝖙𝖍𝖊𝖒 𝖘𝖊𝖊𝖐 𝖙𝖍𝖊𝖎𝖗 𝖇𝖗𝖊𝖆𝖉 𝖆𝖑𝖘𝖔 𝖔𝖚𝖙 𝖔𝖋 𝖙𝖍𝖊𝖎𝖗 𝕯𝖊𝖘𝖔𝖑𝖆𝖙𝖊 𝖕𝖑𝖆𝖈𝖊𝖘;" and to the questions

S. Augustine.

---

[1] "Nam qua cras sanctæ mentis misericordia in tuos, si nunc urgeri Italiam tam propinquo hoste cognosceres, quantum ingemisceres, quam doleres in Alpium vallo summam nostræ salutis consistere."—*De excessu Fratris sui Satyri,* i. 31.

[2] "Felix Nepotianus qui hæc non vidit, felix qui hæc non audit." —*Epist.* xxxv.

[3] "Quicquid dixero, quia ille non audit, mutum videtur."— *Ibid.*

proposed, whether any pain touches the dead in consequence of anything that may happen to their relations after his death, or whether they are supposed to be conscious of such things, he answers that it is indeed "a weighty question, and one which he cannot then discuss, as it calls for greater attention than he can give, whether, that is, or to what extent, and in what manner, the spirits of the dead are aware of what is passing around."[1]

When dealing directly with the case of the dead elsewhere, he answers the question, at least in part, expressing his belief that though the saints are of themselves incapable of knowing all that is going on in this lower world, yet that they are not left in ignorance, but receive information from different sources. "Therefore," he writes, "we must allow that the dead have no knowledge of what is being done here, but (this only) at the time whilst it is being done; afterwards, it is true, they hear from those who dying pass from hence to them; not indeed everything, but only what they are permitted to declare, who are permitted also to recall these things to remembrance, and such as those to whom they

Different modes of obtaining information.

---

[1] "Cui respondeo magnam quidem esse quæstionem, nec in præsentia disserendam, quod sit operis prolixioris, utrum vel quatenus vel quomodo ea quæ circa nos aguntur noverint spiritus mortuorum."—*Enarr. in Ps.* cviii. 17.

declare them ought to hear. It is possible also that the dead may hear something from the angels,[1] who are present at the things which are done here, may hear as much as He to whom all things are subject decides that each one of them ought to hear. . . . The spirits of the dead may learn also some things which are done here, which it is necessary for them to know, not merely what is past or present, but the future also, by a revelation of the Spirit of God."[2]

[1] From Holy Scripture it seems clear that the angels are themselves permitted to know the affairs of men. The language which the angel used to Daniel implies this: "Fear not, Daniel; for from the first day that thou didst set thine heart to understand and to chasten thyself before thy God, thy words were heard, and I am come for thy words" (DAN. x. 12).

From the conversation also in the beginning of the Prophecies of Zechariah it appears that the angel of the Lord is well acquainted with the condition of Jerusalem and the cities of Judah (Zech. i. 10-13).

And whatever doubt may hang over the full interpretation of the passage in S. Matthew's Gospel, with which the belief in guardian angels is associated, it at least indicates that the angels in heaven would be conscious of any contempt which the disciples might pour upon Christ's little ones here on earth (S. MATT. xviii. 10).

[2] "Proinde fatendum est nescire quidem mortuos quid hic agatur, sed dum hic agitur; postea vero audire ab eis qui hinc ad eos moriendo pergunt; non quidem omnia, sed quæ sinuntur indicare, qui sinuntur etiam ista meminisse; et quæ illos, quibus hæc indicant, oportet audire. Possunt et ab angelis, qui rebus quæ aguntur hic præsto sunt, audire aliquid mortui, quod unumquemque illorum audire debere judicat cui cuncta subjecta sunt. . . . Possunt etiam spiritus mortuorum aliqua quæ hic aguntur, quæ necessarium sit ea nosse, non solum præterita vel præsentia, verum etiam futura Spiritu Dei revelante cognoscere."—*De Cura pro Mortuis gerenda*, xv.

And in the case of martyrs, who were generally believed to have an exceptional concern in the affairs of the living, he states that it must be through the agency of some divine power, because it was against the nature of the dead to have it of themselves.[1]

And again in a similar strain: "Although this question, how the Martyrs aid those who it is certain are aided by them, surpasses my power of comprehension; whether they themselves are present at the same time in places so different and so far distant from each other, . . . or whether they themselves, being removed from all intercourse with mortals in a place suited to their deservings, and yet praying in general terms for the wants of their suppliants (as we pray for the dead, with whom we certainly are not present, nor know where they are nor what they are doing), Almighty God . . . hearing the prayers of the martyrs, bestows by means of angelic ministries spreading in every direction those consolations upon such men as He judges worthy to receive them in the misery of this life." [2]

[1] *De Cura pro Mortuis gerenda.*
[2] "Quamquam ista quæstio vires intelligentiæ meæ vincit quemadmodum opitulentur martyres in quos per eos certum et adjuvari; utrum ipsi per se ipsos adsint uno tempore tam diversis locis et tanta inter longinquitate discretis, . . . an ipsis in loco suis meritis congruo ab omni mortalium conversatione remotis et tamen

The result then at which we arrive is, that S. Conclusion. Gregory Nazianzen, though several times expressing himself in very decided terms, must have had misgivings; that SS. Ambrose and Jerome comforted themselves in the belief that the saints were precluded from all knowledge of this lower world; while S. Augustine was evidently much perplexed, wishing no doubt to satisfy himself that they were aware of what was going on, but unable to do so without interposing some means of communication outside of themselves.

generaliter orantibus pro indigentiis supplicantium (sicut nos oramus pro mortuis quibus utique non præsentamur, nec ubi sint nec quid agunt scimus), Deus omnipotens . . . exaudiens martyrum preces, per angelica ministeria usquequaque diffusa præbeat hominibus ista solatia, quibus in hujus vitæ miseria judicat esse præbenda."—*De Cura pro Mort.* xvi. 20.

CHAPTER VI.

The Testimony of Holy Scripture upon the same Subject.

<small>The probable reason why the Fathers said so little.</small>

IT would seem that the comparative silence of the Fathers respecting the possession by the saints of any knowledge of what is being done upon earth was enforced upon them by an almost entire absence of direction in Holy Scripture. Without Divine guidance in a matter of this kind they felt, no doubt, that their own opinions must be purely speculative, so very little is or can be known about the nature of spirits. Who can say, for instance, whether, when freed from their connection with material bodies, they remain as before subject to laws of space, or whether they share the properties of angels, and are to be numbered with those of whom the poet sang?

"Millions of spiritual creatures walk the earth
Unseen, both when we wake and when we sleep."[1]

<small>The Old Testament.</small>

In the Old Testament there are a few casual observations indirectly bearing upon the subject, but from the manner in which they are introduced they cannot be expected to have much weight in

[1] MILTON, *Par. Lost*, iv. 677, 678.

the settlement of a controverted question; however, such as they are, they must be put into the scale against the view of those who would endow departed spirits with a specific knowledge of mundane affairs.

In the Historical Books we find Solomon, at the dedication of the Temple, appealing to God in heaven as alone able to read the thoughts of men on earth.

The Historical Books.

"Then hear thou in heaven thy dwelling-place, and forgive, and do, and give to every man according to his ways, whose heart thou knowest; (for thou, even thou only, knowest the hearts of all the children of men.)"[1]

Again, when Huldah the prophetess is directed to offer some consolation to King Josiah in view of the desolation, which she was charged to predict, she does it in these terms:—

"Thus saith the Lord God of Israel, . . . Behold, therefore, I will gather thee unto thy fathers, and thou shalt be gathered into thy grave in peace; and thine eyes shall not see all the evil which I will bring upon this place."[2]

Now this may have no connection at all with his state after death, but may be simply an assurance that he personally would not be involved in the calamities which were approaching, but would be

[1] 1 Kings viii. 39.   [2] 2 Kings xxii. 18, 20.

taken away before the city was destroyed and the land devastated. But, as the king fell fighting amidst the tumult and carnage of battle, it is quite possible that the peace of the grave, foretold by the prophetess, was spoken, not of the manner of his death, but of that which would follow, that is, his removal to a sphere of existence where he would be exempted from all participation in his country's misery, because he would have no knowledge of its condition.

The Prophetical Books.
In the Prophetical Books there is a single reference. The Church appeals to God by His love, as the only help in time of trouble. "Look down from heaven, and behold from the habitation of thy holiness and of thy glory: . . . Doubtless thou art our Father, though Abraham be ignorant of us, and Israel acknowledge us not: thou, O Lord, art our Father, our Redeemer; thy name is from everlasting."[1]

With all their pride of descent from Abraham, they felt that he was powerless to relieve them, and it would be idle to appeal to him, or to Jacob,

[1] ISAIAH lxiii. 15, 16. The rendering and punctuation of the A. V. are inaccurate. The meaning of the Hebrew would be better expressed by translating thus:—"Because thou art our Father, seeing that Abraham is ignorant of us, and Israel does not acknowledge us. Thou, O Lord, art our Father; our Redeemer is thy name from of old."

because they felt that they had passed beyond the reach of communication with earth, and were in ignorance of the present needs of their descendants.

In the New Testament, except in the case of Dives and Lazarus, nothing is said till we come to the Epistles, and here too there is little certainty. In one place S. Paul speaks as clearly as possible of a marvellous increase of knowledge being imparted to the soul at some time after death; but we can only gather by general considerations whether the time referred to is before or after the resurrection. If it could be proved that he spoke of the disembodied state, we should have no difficulty in attributing to the saints in Paradise a knowledge of what is passing in the world, for nothing could be stronger than the language which he uses. The contrast between the present and future knowledge is very striking, and the Apostle endeavoured to impress this on the mind of his converts by employing a double figure to illustrate it: "Now we see through a glass, darkly; but then face to face."[1]

The New Testament.

S. Paul.

[1] 1 Cor. xiii. 12. S. Paul here uses a phrase which was quite familiar to the Jews in his time. To distinguish the clearness of the prophecy of Moses from the visions of other prophets, they said that he saw through "the glass which shineth," אספקלריא המאירא, but they only through one "which does not shine," אספקלריא שאינה המאירא. Cf. Numb. xii. 6, 7, 8, and Hosea xii. 11.

In the first figure the present capacity for knowledge is represented as of one who sees things reflected in a mirror. For the right understanding of the comparison it must be borne in mind that the metal surfaces which formed the mirrors of those times were very inadequate for the purpose of clear reflection. The future capacity would be so vastly developed that all intervening objects between the knowing and the known would be completely removed, and the soul would see everything face to face.

In the second figure he expresses the same truth, but apparently has in his mind that comprehension which is exercised more by hearing than by seeing; for the expression "darkly" would be more fitly rendered, "in a riddle," or, "in a dark saying."[1] There is probably an allusion to God's promise, that He would talk with Moses, not "in riddles" or obscure prophecies, as He did to so many of His servants, to whom only a portion of what He said could be intelligible, but would explain the meaning of His words, and talk with him as a man talketh with his friend.

Then the Apostle leaves the metaphor, and concludes, "Now I know in part; but then shall I

[1] NUMBERS xii. 8.

know even as also I am known,"—"I shall know fully," to translate more accurately,[1] with that complete knowledge, which can be compared to nothing less than that which the Omniscient God possessed of everything which had transpired in his own life, —"even as I myself was fully known."

But we have no grounds for supposing that this stupendous change in his intellectual powers, which the Apostle looked forward to, would precede the coming of the Lord. It was upon that event that his eye was constantly fixed as the goal, when he would receive the consummation of joy in his risen and glorified body.

It was moreover at Christ's appearing, and at no time previous to it, that S. John expected to be conformed to His likeness, and it is quite inconceivable that he could become possessed of any faculty perfect and complete before the Divine image had been fully restored. "Beloved," he says, "now are we the sons of God, but it doth not yet appear what we shall be; but we know that when he shall appear, we shall be like him: for we shall see him as he is."[2] The exact interpretation

S. John.

---

[1] ἐπιγνώσομαι καθὼς καὶ ἐπεγνώσθην. In the A. V. the force of the compound is ignored as well as the aorist tense by which S. Paul places himself in the future, and looks back to his life as passed.

[2] οὔπω ἐφανερώθη τί ἐσόμεθα. οἴδαμεν ὅτι ἐὰν φανερωθῇ, ὅμοιοι αὐτῷ ἐσόμεθα, κ.τ.λ. (1 S. JOHN iii. 2.) It seems natural at first

may not be expressed in our translation, but it is quite evident that the future condition, which he had in view, was to follow the manifestation of God at the final judgment. At no time before that would he have been justified in expecting it, as S. Paul teaches in the words: "𝕺𝖚𝖗 𝖈𝖔𝖓𝖛𝖊𝖗𝖘𝖆𝖙𝖎𝖔𝖓 𝖎𝖘 𝖎𝖓 𝖍𝖊𝖆𝖛𝖊𝖓, 𝖋𝖗𝖔𝖒 𝖜𝖍𝖊𝖓𝖈𝖊 𝖆𝖑𝖘𝖔 𝖜𝖊 𝖑𝖔𝖔𝖐 𝖋𝖔𝖗 𝖙𝖍𝖊 𝕾𝖆𝖛𝖎𝖔𝖚𝖗, 𝖙𝖍𝖊 𝕷𝖔𝖗𝖉 𝕵𝖊𝖘𝖚𝖘 𝕮𝖍𝖗𝖎𝖘𝖙: 𝖜𝖍𝖔 𝖘𝖍𝖆𝖑𝖑 𝖈𝖍𝖆𝖓𝖌𝖊 𝖔𝖚𝖗 𝖛𝖎𝖑𝖊 𝖇𝖔𝖉𝖞, 𝖙𝖍𝖆𝖙 𝖎𝖙 𝖒𝖆𝖞 𝖇𝖊 𝖋𝖆𝖘𝖍𝖎𝖔𝖓𝖊𝖉 𝖑𝖎𝖐𝖊 𝖚𝖓𝖙𝖔 𝖍𝖎𝖘 𝖌𝖑𝖔𝖗𝖎𝖔𝖚𝖘 𝖇𝖔𝖉𝖞."[1]

The intermediate state is an imperfect one: it is a period of longings unsatisfied and hopes deferred; it would be a manifest contradiction, therefore, to admit the possibility therein of anything so near perfection as is implied in seeing all things face to face, and knowing as fully as we are known by God.

Conclusion. We conclude, then, that the future condition spoken of by the Apostle is that in which with the risen and glorified body the soul shall be admitted into the very presence of God, and shall behold the unveiled brightness of His glory, and partaking in the fullest manner of the fruits of conformity to His likeness, shall know with a perfect knowledge.

sight to refer to the preceding clause for the subject of $\phi\alpha\nu\epsilon\rho\omega\theta\hat{\eta}$, and translate the passage, "if it were manifested," especially with $\dot{\epsilon}\grave{\alpha}\nu$ instead of $\ddot{o}\tau\alpha\nu$. But just before, in ii. 28, according to the best MSS., the reading is $\dot{\epsilon}\grave{\alpha}\nu$ $\phi\alpha\nu\epsilon\rho\omega\theta\hat{\eta}$, and the meaning, "if God should be manifested," and in iii. 5 the word is used of the manifestation of God.   [1] PHIL. iii. 20.

CHAPTER VII.

The Beatific Vision not yet attained by any of the Saints.

OF the souls of men in general there can be little question that they are not yet admitted to the Beatific Vision of God. Are there any exceptions to the rule, for it is the state of all the dead in Christ, which we are considering? It is well known that one portion of the Church Catholic maintains that there are, and makes it an article of faith that the martyrs who suffered with Christ on earth do already reign with Him in heaven.[1] *The view of the Roman Church.*

It is of the utmost importance that we should test the Catholicity of this belief, because nearly all the recorded instances of invocation in primitive times are more or less connected with martyrs.

Let us appeal then to the judgment of antiquity.

---

[1] At the Council of Florence, A.D. 1439, the Roman Church repudiated the opinion which the Greeks had maintained, viz., that the Beatific Vision has not yet been vouchsafed to any. It was indirectly rejected also at the Council of Trent, A.D. 1545-1563, Sess. xxv., by the decree respecting the Invocation of Saints who were held to be already reigning with Christ.

S. Augustine. S. Augustine[1] held that the righteousness of the martyrs had been perfected by their passion, and forbade the offering of prayers in their behalf, as for the rest of the dead. Now it was the general belief of antiquity that prayers should be offered for all the faithful upon whom the final judgment had not yet been passed.

S. Cyprian. S. Cyprian, in his exhortation to martyrdom, in describing the rewards which will be obtained by a patient endurance of conflicts and sufferings on earth, uses language which certainly supports the idea of an anticipated judgment: "What a dignity it is, and what a safeguard, to go gladly from hence, to depart gloriously in the midst of tribulations and afflictions, to close in a moment the eyes, with which men and the world were looked upon, and to open them at once for the vision of God and Christ!" And of the martyr in will, who was called away before he had an opportunity of displaying the constancy for which he was prepared, he adds, "his reward is given, without loss of time, by the judgment of God."[2]

---

[1] *Sermo* cclxxxv. 5.

[2] "Quanta est dignitas et quanta securitas exire hinc lætum, exire inter pressuras et angustias gloriosum ; claudere in momento oculos, quibus homines videbantur et mundus, et reperire eosdem statim ut Deus videatur et Christus. . . . Sine damno temporis merces, judice Deo, redditur."—*De exhort. Martyr.* xii. *in fine.*

But such an opinion was very far from being generally indorsed. Tertullian, with the intense admiration which he felt for martyrdom, never dreamed of exempting those who endured it from the intermediate state of expectation and waiting. It is true he assigns to them special honours, for while maintaining that the souls of the rest of mankind were detained in Hades, he assigned to the martyrs the peculiar privilege of being translated at once to Paradise,[1] by which however he does not mean the Presence and Vision of God, but that place in which S. John saw the souls of the martyrs, viz., under the Altar. "The only key to unlock Paradise is your own life's blood."[2] He asks, moreover, "How shall the soul mount up to heaven, where Christ is already sitting at the right hand of the Father, when as yet the archangel's trumpet has not been heard by the command of God? . . . To no one is heaven opened; . . . when the world indeed shall pass away, then the kingdom of heaven shall be opened."[3]

Tertullian.

[1] "Nemo enim peregrinatus a corpore statim immoratur penes Dominum nisi ex martyrii prærogativa, scilicet Paradiso non Inferis deversurus."—*De Res. Carnis,* c. 43.

[2] "Tota Paradisi clavis tuus sanguis est."—*De Anima,* cap. lv.

[3] "Quomodo ergo anima exhalabit in cœlum, Christo illic adhuc sedente ad dexteram patris, nondum Dei jussu per tubam archangeli audito. . . . Nulli patet cœlum terra adhuc salva . . . cum transactione enim mundi reserabuntur regna cœlorum."—*Ibid.*

Origen. Origen records his opinion that all the faithful are still waiting their consummation of bliss; "not even the Apostles," he says, "have yet received their joy, but even they are waiting, in order that I too may become a partaker of their joy. For the saints departing hence do not immediately receive all the rewards of their deserts; but they wait even for us, though we be loitering and dilatory. For they have not perfect joy as long as they grieve for our errors or mourn for our sins."[1] And he says that this opinion is not his own merely, but was held by the great Apostle of the Gentiles, as is plain from what he said of the holy fathers, who had been justified by faith: "These all having obtained a good report through faith, received not the promise, God having provided some better thing for us, that they without us should not be made perfect."[2]

---

[1] "Nondum enim receperunt lætitiam suam, ne Apostoli quidem, sed et ipsi expectant, ut ego lætitiæ eorum particeps fiam. Neque enim decedentes hinc sancti, continuo integra meritorum suorum præmia consequuntur; sed expectant etiam nos, licet morantes licet desides. Non enim sit illis perfectia lætitia, donec pro erroribus nostris dolent et lugent nostra peccata.—*In Levitic. cap. x. Hom. vii.*; ORIGEN. *Opera per Erasm. versa,* i. 151.

[2] EP. TO THE HEB., xi. 39, 40.—Origen seems here, as well as in other places, to speak of the Epistle unreservedly as S. Paul's, but it will be well to quote his deliberate opinion, which he expressed in one of his latest works. In the *Homilies on the Hebrews,* of which Eusebius (*Eccl. Hist.* vi. 25) has preserved a passage bearing on the authorship, he writes—"The Epistle does not exhibit that plainness of diction which belongs to the Apostle, . . .

But it is unnecessary to multiply quotations; suffice it here to mention that some of the most learned controversialists,[1] who would gladly have arrived at an opposite result, have been compelled to admit that there is no sufficient evidence from Patristic writings to show that any saints are yet admitted to the Beatific Vision.

Justin Martyr would hardly have written the following passage had he believed that any exception was made as regards admission into heaven before the Judgment: "If you have fallen in with

<small>it is more pure Greek in the composition of its phrases, as every one who knows how to judge of differences of style would admit. . . . If I were to give my own opinion I should say that the thoughts belong to the Apostle, but the diction and phraseology to some one who wrote from memory the Apostle's teaching, and commented so to speak on that which his master had said. If then any Church holds this Epistle to be from Paul, let it be commended for this, for not without reason have the men of olden time handed it down as his. But who it was that really wrote the Epistle, God only knows."</small>

<small>[1] "Olim controversium fuit num animæ sanctorum usque ad diem judicii Deum viderent et Divina visione frui cum multi insignes viri et doctrina et sanctitate clari tenere viderentur, eas nec videre nec frui usque ad diem judicii; donec receptis corporibus una cum illis divina beatitudine perfruantur. Nam Irenæus, Justinus Martyr, Tertullianus, Clemens Romanus, Origenes, Ambrosius, Chrysostomus, Augustinus, Lactantius, etc., hujus referuntur fuisse sententiæ."—FR. PEGNA *in part* 2 *Direct. Inquis.* 21, quoted by Ussher.</small>

<small>To this may be added the testimony of Stapleton, who gives almost a similar list, omitting, however, and as we think rightly, the name of Augustine.—*Def. Eccles. Author. contra Whitaker*, l. 2.</small>

any persons called Christians, who do not admit this (the resurrection), but dare to blaspheme the God of Abraham, the God of Isaac, and the God of Jacob, and say that there is no resurrection of the dead, but that their souls at the time of their death are taken up to heaven, do not regard them as Christians."[1]

<small>Why special honours were assigned to the Martyrs.</small>
We can hardly be surprised, however, that some of the Fathers, as we have seen, should have made an exception in assigning unequalled honour to the martyrs. If we go back in imagination to the early Church, and thus to try place ourselves alongside of those who lived in the days of persecution and dire distress, we shall see what an unique position the martyrs held. It must have been felt, by all thoughtful men, that the value of their testimony could hardly be over-estimated; that had they drawn back in those critical times the very existence of the Faith must have been imperilled. No wonder then that some at least of those who realised the momentous influence of their conduct upon the

---

[1] εἰ γὰρ συνεβάλετε ὑμεῖς τισὶ λεγομένοις χριστιανοῖς καὶ τοῦτο μὴ ὁμολογοῦσιν ἀλλὰ καὶ βλασφημεῖν τολμῶσι τὸν θεὸν 'Αβραὰμ καὶ τὸν θεὸν 'Ισαὰκ καὶ τὸν θεὸν 'Ιακὼβ οἳ καὶ λέγουσι μὴ εἶναι νεκρῶν ἀνάστασιν, ἀλλὰ ἅμα τῷ ἀποθνήσκειν, τὰς ψυχὰς αὐτῶν ἀναλαμβάνεσθαι εἰς τὸν οὐρανὸν, μὴ ὑπολάβητε αὐτοὺς χριστιανούς. —*Dialog. cum Tryphone*, p. 306; ed. Paris, 1615.

destiny of the Church should have wished to bestow upon those who resisted unto blood privileges and rewards of a distinctly exceptional kind—to place them on a pinnacle of glory which none beside could reach,—to suppose, in short, in their case, an immediate fulfilment to the promise, "If we suffer, we shall also reign with Him."[1]

But let us turn to the teaching of Holy Scripture on this point. When our Lord was talking with His disciples on the difficulty which the rich must ever experience in attaining to the kingdom of God, S. Peter interrupted Him with the question, "Behold, we have forsaken all and followed Thee, what shall we have therefore?" And this was the answer which He gave: "Verily I say unto you, that ye which have followed me, in the regeneration, when the Son of Man shall sit in the throne of His glory, ye also shall sit upon twelve thrones, judging the twelve tribes of Israel."[2]

The evidence of Holy Scripture.

Now most of those to whom this promise was given died the martyr's death; they were the leaders

---

[1] 2 Tim. ii. 12.

[2] S. Matt. xix. 27-28. ἐν τῇ παλιγγενεσίᾳ has been by some connected with what precedes, and referred to the new order of things which was inaugurated by Christ at the first Advent. In the earliest printed texts the punctuation favoured this interpretation, but the Elzevirs changed it, and most succeeding editors have followed them. There can be little question that they are right.

P

in that noble army which contended and shed their blood for the Faith; but there is not a word of any anticipation or forestalling of their reward; they are not encouraged to look for any immediate or near exaltation, but they must wait for its realisation till the "regeneration," that second birth of the world at "the restitution of all things," when there would be "new heavens and a new earth." Then, but not till then, would they obtain the superior privileges which they were destined to enjoy, then only be elevated to royal dignity and reign with Christ in glory.

S. John. Again, in the mysterious visions which S. John was permitted to see, the condition of the martyrs was revealed to him: "I saw under the altar the souls of them that were slain for the Word of God, and for the testimony which they held: and they cried with a loud voice, saying, How long, O Lord, holy and true, dost thou not judge and avenge our blood on them that dwell upon the earth? And white robes were given unto every one of them; and it was said unto them, that they should rest yet for a little season, until their fellow-servants also, and their brethren, that should be killed as they were, should be fulfilled."[1]

[1] Rev. vi. 9, 10.

It is clear from this description that the martyrs no less than others are detained in an intermediate state; their judgment has not been anticipated, neither is there any possibility of their longings being satisfied till the roll of martyrdom is complete.

In another vision[1] he sees those "which came out of great tribulation," and "they are before the throne of God, and serve Him day and night in His temple." Apart from the consideration that this is taken from a distinct prophecy of the Church in its glorified state, it has been shown[2] by a comparison of the Temple at Jerusalem, from which the imagery is taken, that the throne, which was the ark of the Covenant overshadowed by the Cherubim, was not seen by those who worshipped without in the Court.

From all this it is clear that the Fathers and Doctors of the Early Church were right in their conclusion, that the souls of the saints, whether martyrs or others, will not see God and be admitted to the Beatific Vision till after the Day of Judgment. It follows also that the perfect knowledge of which S. Paul spoke must be still in the future, and dependent on the same manifestation.

Conclusion.

[1] Rev. vii. 14, 15.
[2] Cf. THORNDIKE, *Laws of the Church*, vol. iv. p. ii. Lib. iii. c. xxvii.

CHAPTER VIII.

Conclusions drawn from the foregoing Testimony.

NOW that all the evidence from antiquity within our reach has been put forward and subjected to examination, it only remains to gather up the conclusions which are to be drawn from it. In doing this it will be most convenient to take separately the two parts,—the intercession of departed saints, and the practice of addressing them in prayer.

The doctrine of the Intercession of the Saints held to be Catholic.

Firstly, then, ought the belief in their intercession to be accounted Catholic on Vincentian principles? There can be little hesitation in replying in the affirmative. A large number of Primitive Doctors, in divers portions of the Church, amply sufficient at least to be regarded as fairly representative of the whole community, are shown to have expressed their opinion in support of it, and there is no trace of any countervailing or contradictory views. It is true there is but little in the way of corroborative

Summary of Patristic evidence in favour of it.

evidence forthcoming from the other sources to which we look for early information, but there are reasons to account for its absence; and it is the less desiderated as the doctrine is not without witness in Holy Scripture. We can hardly stop, however, with the bare statement of this conclusion. After what has been said of the ignorance of the saints touching the affairs of this world, it seems almost imperative upon us to add something in explanation of the probable nature and extent of their intercessions for the living. We conceive that their prayers are of a twofold character: they are both general and particular: the latter, however, only within a limited compass, and based mainly, as far as we can be certain, on the recollection of the past, which may enable them in some measure to comprehend the wants of the present.[1]

<small>Upon what their intercessions are based.</small>

There can hardly be a question that the saints in Paradise retain the power of memory. It is im-

<small>Memory retained in the disembodied state.</small>

[1] There are indications in Scripture that the powers of memory will be developed and quickened into the fullest energy by the separation of the soul from the body: that between death and the Judgment the soul will have its recollection of the past intensified almost beyond our conception. Some such belief is necessary to account for that which would be otherwise impossible,—except, at least, by the exercise of miraculous power, of which no intimation is given,—viz. that when called before the tribunal of God we shall give an account of ourselves and confess with our own lips the deeds and words and thoughts of a life long passed. Cf. ROM. xiv. 12; S. MATT. xii. 36.

possible to imagine the soul preserving consciousness during its disembodied state without admitting that it possesses also the faculty of remembrance; to deny it this would be to rob it of much of that which makes consciousness worth having, and which is absolutely indispensable, if they are right who think that the intermediate state is a time for growth in holiness, and all that can fit the pardoned soul for the Presence of God. This admission is forced upon us from two quarters. There is, to begin with, an instinctive conviction in the heart that death cannot destroy the link which binds the soul to the past. Can anything, short of positive proof that it sleeps after death, ever convince us that it will in an instant forget those whom, up to the very moment of its departure, it thought of, and cared for, and loved above all else in the world? And the voice of nature finds its echo in the teaching of Holy Scripture. However we may understand the parable of the rich man and Lazarus, we believe it equally with the rest to be "𝔴𝔯𝔦𝔱𝔱𝔢𝔫 𝔣𝔬𝔯 𝔬𝔲𝔯 𝔩𝔢𝔞𝔯𝔫𝔦𝔫𝔤," therefore substantially true. Now we read that Abraham reminded the rich man of the past,—"𝔯𝔢𝔪𝔢𝔪𝔟𝔢𝔯 𝔱𝔥𝔞𝔱 𝔱𝔥𝔬𝔲 𝔦𝔫 𝔱𝔥𝔶 𝔩𝔦𝔣𝔢𝔱𝔦𝔪𝔢 𝔯𝔢𝔠𝔢𝔦𝔳𝔢𝔡𝔰𝔱 𝔱𝔥𝔶 𝔤𝔬𝔬𝔡 𝔱𝔥𝔦𝔫𝔤𝔰;" and we know that he exercised the faculty of remembrance, for he

The parable of Dives and Lazarus.

showed himself mindful of the brethren whom he had left behind; he recalled their old mode of life, and dwelt upon the particular temptations to which they had been exposed, and, acting upon the fears which the recollection of his father's house engendered, he interceded for the deliverance of those who had survived him there.

It is quite obvious, however, that such prayers as this can only be very restricted; the time must inevitably come, and that very speedily in most cases, when all those whom the departed soul remembered in life will have joined its ranks in the place of disembodied spirits.

If, therefore, the intercession of the saints be the great reality which we would fain believe, and which the importance attributed to it by the early Fathers appears to justify, its range must be far more comprehensive than this, and certainly it cannot be circumscribed by anything so narrow as the bonds of earthly friendship. *The restricted nature of prayers for individuals.*

The theme of their prayers must be the whole company of the baptized, the Church militant of every nation and people and tongue, wherever its members are struggling with the same temptations and enduring the same labours as they themselves experienced in their earthly pilgrimage. Normally *The whole Church the object of intercession.*

the power of intercession is exercised for the whole body of the redeemed; exceptionally, and in a far less degree, for individual Christians.

Of the possibility of the area in the latter case being widened by a revelation of present wants through some angelic or Divine agency,[1] no opinion is here expressed; it is all purely speculative, and we are not dealing with "pious beliefs," however attractive and fascinating, so much as with the well-supported and widely-recognised credenda of the Primitive Church.

The practice of Invocation.

Secondly, what conclusions does the foregoing testimony enable us to draw respecting the Catholicity of the practice of invoking or addressing in prayer departed saints? The direct evidence from the Fathers is undoubtedly slight. There are a few distinct examples of appeals by name, but it must be noted that most of them are of a highly impassioned kind, uttered in moments of deep religious emotion, and, in some cases, at the very graves or "memorials" of martyrs on the anniversary of their deaths. Of these, too, there is not one which can carry back the first beginning of the practice beyond the middle of the fourth century,

Patristic evidence opposed to its Catholicity.

---

[1] Cf. S. AUG. *de Cura pro Mortuis*, cap. xv.; PET. LOMBARD. *Sent.* Lib. iv. dist. 45.

if indeed so far. The indirect evidence is of importance as exhibiting some want of confidence in the efficacy of such appeals, arising out of the extreme uncertainty whether the saints appealed to possessed any capacity for hearing the prayers of their petitioners. The real value of invocation, for the furtherance at least of the object immediately sought for, must stand or fall with the possession of this. So long as doubts existed upon this point, it is quite inconsistent with reason to suppose that it could have been widely practised. In isolated cases perhaps the intensity of a man's wishes may have completely overridden all sober conviction, but anything like a general practice could never have grown up in the midst of doubts and misgivings, which strike at the very root of its utility.

The Catacombs, as we have seen, are not wanting in illustrations of this practice; but though we may be disposed to attach no little importance to any testimony which they may exhibit with sufficient frequency to give it a general character, that which concerns the present question is practically unavailable, owing to an entire absence of chronology on the particular monuments brought under notice. If any corroborative evidence were forthcoming to

The evidence of the Catacombs unavailable.

establish the existence of the practice in the third and second centuries, there would be no impropriety in claiming them as records of the same period. But where there is so much uncertainty, it would be manifestly unreasonable and arbitrary to assert that their testimony is older than that supplied from other sources.

Primitive Liturgies, so far as they afford evidence, are adverse to the practice.

The public forms of Primitive worship lend no support to invocation of any kind; we could hardly expect that they would contain anything resembling the rhetorical appeals encouraged by some of the Fathers, while the very nature of the Liturgies discouraged the introduction of religious interpellations of any other than God the Father, before Whom alone the Commemorative Sacrifice of the Son is pleaded. But apart from this, it seems that the early services of the Church supply the strongest evidence we can possibly have against the doctrine, short of positive and distinct expressions of disapproval. The Primitive Liturgies which have come down to us, almost without exception, contain prayers for the saints. Is it reasonable to maintain that persons who prayed to God for the light and rest and refreshment of the spirits in Paradise, could in the same breath appeal to them as hearers of prayer, or as able to give to those who invoked them their special advocacy and patronage?

Lastly, Holy Scripture nowhere hints even at the utility or lawfulness of addressing appeals for spiritual help of any kind to other than the Three Persons of the Blessed Trinity. *Holy Scripture is silent.*

While, then, it has been shown that the doctrine of the Intercession of the Saints is able to bear the Vincentian test of "universality, antiquity, and consent," the Catholicity of the practice of invocation breaks down when subjected to the same ordeal. *Conclusion.*

SUPPLEMENTARY CHAPTER.

A.

Is a fuller recognition of the practice of praying for the dead desirable or not?

Arguments in favour of a fuller recognition of a primitive practice.

HAVING now exhausted the records of the past, as far as we are familiar with them, in gathering proofs or indications of the early practice of praying for the departed, we proceed to consider the arguments of those who advocate its fuller recognition, both in public worship and in private devotion.

On the ground of its antiquity and Catholicity.

The first argument is that with which so many of the previous pages have been especially concerned, viz., its undoubted claim to be regarded as primitive and Catholic. It is quite impossible to weigh the evidence adduced without being convinced that it satisfies the Vincentian test most completely; and in consideration of the great importance of the subject of this chapter, it may be advisable to dwell a little upon the nature of the evidence upon which so much rests.

The Catacombs, which carry us back almost to the foundation-days of the Faith, set forth in their rude simplicity the accepted belief of the early generations of Christians touching the comfort to be derived from continuing to pray for departed friends. Those monumental records of pious affection, in which the expression of the feelings was so held in check that the keenest pain of bereavement is said to have found vent in nothing more demonstrative than the simple word "dolens," can never be justly accused of containing anything unreal or fanciful. Indeed, the epitaphs are so brief and simple, so devoid of all exaggeration, that when they speak we feel sure that they only express that which the calm and deliberate judgment of the age would completely indorse. And no one can deny that they do speak in language of prayer for the peace and light and refreshment of the souls which are at rest with God and Christ. *The Catacombs.*

Again, the early Fathers and Doctors of the Church exhibit in their writings a perfect *catena* of confirmatory testimony. Men of differing habits of thought, trained in diverse schools and countries, and often holding upon important questions of doctrine and *The Fathers.*

practice widely divergent opinions, yet unite in bearing common witness to the propriety and advantage of praying for the dead. But if any one, with a view to depreciate the value of their judgment, should raise the objection, that after all they are only entitled to the consideration which other irresponsible individuals receive, then we may fall back upon the fact, that the matter was brought under discussion before a representative assembly, summoned from the whole Church,[1] whose deliberations and decrees command the acceptance of all Catholic Christians.

<small>Primitive Liturgies.</small> And lastly, we have a great collection of Primitive Liturgies testifying to the use of such prayers in the public services,—Liturgies, be it observed, composed for countries and Churches differing by a variety of circumstances the one from the other. And nothing, we feel confident, could have been used, or been suffered to continue for any length of time, in Forms of common worship, which did not receive the unwavering assent of the Church at large.

<small>Its inherent usefulness.</small> A second argument rests upon the simple ground of its usefulness. The objects for which our public services are framed are twofold: that the creature may pay to the Creator the homage which is due

---

[1] The Council of Chalcedon; see p. 98.

unto His Name; and that he may pray for the supply of his necessities, and the well-being of his body and soul in time and eternity. Leaving out of consideration here the primary object, it is obvious that the Forms of public prayer ought to be such as are able to satisfy the cravings of nature, when at least those cravings are for things not forbidden by God's Word. Now it is impossible for the mourner, who goes up to the house of God in times of sorrow and bereavement, not to feel an aching void in the Church's prayers. We may pray for our Queen, our relations and friends, for the heathen and unbelievers and the enemies of our peace, in short, for all conditions of men who are still in the flesh; but even though we come fresh from the chamber of death, with the heart full and overflowing with longings for the happiness of one that is gone, we can find no outlet for our yearnings in those utterances which ought to be as comprehensive models, providing for the expression of all our best desires and the truest wants of the human heart. If the instinct of nature prompt us to pray for the departed, if the Great Teacher Himself gave His tacit approval to the practice, if the purest ages of Christianity freely adopted it, there can hardly be any question that it has in itself some elements of usefulness, and the Church

The effect produced upon the mourner by the void in the public services.

may well foster them for the benefit and comfort of those who look to her for guidance.

<small>Its influence in the controversy with Rome.</small>

A third argument is that it would place us in a stronger position in our disputes with Rome. The Church of England claims, as it is now constituted, to be the Church of the early ages of Christianity, the same Church, only stript of mediæval accretions by which her rites and ordinances had been overlaid and disfigured; but, it is retorted upon us by those whose interest it is to disallow her antiquity, that at the Reformation, the English divines, though their original intention of destroying nothing which was ancient, was laudable enough, yet suffered themselves to be so overborne by the foreign Protestants[1] that in some cases they made no distinction between what was primitive and what was mediæval, but involved both alike in indiscriminate condemnation; and the consequence of this is, that some familiar features of the Church of the first five centuries are no longer visible.

<small>Attempts to gloss over the Reformers' omissions.</small>

There are writers on the Liturgy who maintain that prayer for the dead is by no means excluded, and one of the most widely read at

---

[1] How little Peter Martyr and Martin Bucer, who did not even know the English language, were fitted to undertake the Reformation of the English Church, and how alien the minds of Calvin and John à Lasco were to Catholic doctrine, is well known.

the present day sums up his observations on the subject in these words: "It must be considered a great matter for thankfulness that in all the assaults made upon the Liturgy of the Church of England by persons holding a more meagre belief in things unseen, the Providence of God has preserved the prayer for the whole Church, departed as well as living, in the prayer for the Church militant."[1]

But however much men may try to satisfy themselves by reading mentally between the lines, or persist in interpreting the expression "that with them we may be partakers" as though it were equivalent to "that they, as well as we," the Roman Catholic will always point triumphantly to the unanswerable rubric, "militant here on earth,"[2] with which the prayer was fenced and guarded at the very time

---

[1] The *Annotated Book of Common Prayer*, p. 176, notes, by J. H. BLUNT.

[2] This was added in the Second Prayer-Book of Edw. VI., 1552, by Bucer and Calvin, when the following prayer of commendation was omitted:—"We commend unto Thy mercy, O Lord, all other Thy servants, which are departed hence from us with the sign of faith, and now do rest in the sleep of peace. Grant unto them, we beseech Thee, Thy mercy and everlasting peace, and that at the day of the general resurrection we, and all they which be of the mystical body of Thy Son, may altogether be set on His right hand, and hear that His most joyful voice: Come unto Me, O ye that be blessed of My Father, and possess the kingdom, which is prepared for you from the beginning of the world."—*First Prayer-Book of Edw.* VI.

that the distinct petition for God's mercy to be shown to the dead and for their everlasting peace was withdrawn from it.

This passage, therefore, must be clearly abandoned in so far as it may have been supposed to afford any evidence of the retention of prayers for the dead in our public services. But there are two other places where traces do still remain. The first is the Prayer of Oblation, in which we pray in these terms: "that by the merits and death of Thy Son, Jesus Christ, and through faith in His blood, we and all Thy whole Church may obtain remission of our sins and all other benefits of His passion." Now Bishop Cosin, one of the revisers of the Prayer Book, be it remembered, makes this refer to the departed as well as the living. His words are, "By 'all the whole Church' is to be understood, as well those that have been here before, and those that shall be hereafter, as those that are now members of it." And again, "The virtue of this sacrifice (which is here in this Prayer of Oblation commemorated and represented) doth not only extend itself to the living and those that are present, but likewise to them that are absent and them that be already departed."[1]

The Prayer of Oblation.

---

[1] Cosin's *Works*, vol. v. 351, 352.

The second is the prayer in "The order for the Burial of the Dead," "beseeching Thee, that it may please Thee of Thy gracious goodness, shortly to accomplish the number of thine elect, and to hasten Thy kingdom; that we, with all those that are departed in the true faith of Thy holy name, may have our perfect consummation, and bliss, both in body and soul, in Thy eternal and everlasting glory."[1] Here, "we with all those," must be equivalent to "we and all those," for if not the order of words must have been changed and would have run thus, "that we may have our perfect consummation and bliss with all those," etc. *The Burial Service.*

If we are right in our reading of these prayers, we see in the retention of these somewhat ambiguous expressions a manifestation of the desire which the Revisionists must have felt to preserve, if they possibly could, here and there in the public service, some trace of the primitive practice. *Sufficient traces preserved to satisfy us of its existence in the Liturgy.*

It is enough to satisfy us that the Church has not entirely abandoned the usage, but we can hardly be surprised if the Roman Catholic takes a different view and calls for that clear and unmistakable recognition of the principle, which was manifested in the pre-Reformation services.

[1] *Id.* 377.

Such then are the chief grounds upon which those who desire to see prayers for the faithful dead restored to our Forms of public worship, rest their claims to be heard. Let us look for a moment at the other side. The doctrine, it is urged, is liable to abuse. So early as the close of the fourth century Aerius laid great stress upon this, and though the Fathers treated his objections with disdain, and Epiphanius, who took upon himself to advocate the prevailing usage, did not even condescend directly to answer them, later ages have borne ample testimony to the realisation of his worst fears. History tells us how in lapse of time the true doctrine became obscured, and a novel estimate of its object was suffered to grow up unchecked, and the pious aspirations and ardent longings for the light and refreshment and peace of souls which had departed in the faith, were perverted into petitions and masses, which might be bought and sold like common wares, for deliverance from Purgatorial pain and torment. We who interpret Christ's promise to be with His Church "alway even unto the end of the world" as implying that He overrules and directs all the changes and vicissitudes to which it is subject, for its ultimate good, may well believe that in the temporary obscuration of the primitive practice, and

Arguments on the opposite side.

The abuse of doctrine in mediæval times.

the almost complete withdrawal of what is confessedly a most consolatory doctrine, we can see a distinct sign of a punitive purpose, and a visitation on this and preceding generations for other men's sins.

With this view it must be the anxious care of our leaders, whenever any revision of the Liturgy shall be undertaken, to ascertain whether the period of punishment may not have run its length, or whether the liability to corruption, notwithstanding all the safeguards[1] which the experience of the past would suggest, is still so great that the restoration of a primitive and Catholic usage cannot yet be safely recommended.

But whatever objections may be raised against

---

[1] The language of the Primitive Liturgies should be most carefully adhered to. However strong a belief may exist that the process of sanctification and the effacement of the stains of sin, may be advanced by the prayers of survivors, it found no such support from primitive times, no such general expression in the Primitive Liturgies, as to justify its acknowledgment in public forms of prayer. Whatever finds a place in these must rest upon nothing less than Catholic recognition. The only forms of petition which were universally accepted were for the light, or rest, or peace, or refreshment of those who had departed in the true faith.

To pray for these is the rightful privilege of the Church Catholic, and whatever questions of expediency may arise for the time, and have weight with those who are in authority, it cannot be permanently alienated from public worship without serious harm and loss.

No such objection can be made against its use in private.

the re-introduction into public worship, no such arguments, as have been stated above, have force in reference to the practice in the private devotions of individual Christians. The examples of the pious divines, whose names form a long and goodly array from the Reformation to our own time, is quite sufficient guarantee for its continuance apart from Common Prayer. They realised truly the exact position. They felt that the Church had been compelled to take the steps, which she had taken, in regard to certain forms which amidst the prevailing ignorance were so liable to misconstruction and abuse; but being at the same time satisfied that though withdrawn the prayers had never been condemned or pronounced illegal[1] by any authoritative tribunal whatever, they held themselves perfectly free to use them privately.

The non-jurors.

The non-jurors did not hesitate to enforce them 'as a bounden duty,'[2] and in consequence of the value which they attached to the practice it has not uncommonly been supposed that it was confined to them; but there is no ground for the supposition. Long before they restored the obliterated prayers to their Form of Service, individual bishops of no

---

[1] Cf. note on p. 253.
[2] LATHBURY, *History of the Non-jurors*, p. 298.

little weight and influence expressed their approval of them.

Bishop Andrewes in the intercessory portion of his *Private Devotions*, prays, <small>Bishop Andrewes' Devotions</small>

> "O Thou Who didst die and rise again,
> To be Lord both of the dead and living,
> Live we or die we,
> Thou art our Lord;
> Lord, have pity on living and dead."[1]

And again,

> "Remember, O Lord, our God,
> All spirits and all flesh,
> Which we have remembered, and which we have not."[2]

Bishop Cosin recommended it both by precept and by practice; he refers to it again and again, as we have already shown in his notes on the Prayer Book, and writes at some length upon it in explanation of the prayer in the Burial Service, "That we with this our brother and all other,"[3] etc. "The <small>Cosin.</small>

---

[1] "Ὦ εἰς τοῦτο ἀπὸ θανὼν καὶ ἀναζήσας,
ἵνα καὶ νεκρῶν καὶ ζώντων κυριεύσῃς,
ἐάν τε ζῶμεν, ἐάν τε καὶ ἀποθνήσκωμεν,
Κύριος ἡμῶν σύ.
ζῶντας καὶ θανόντας ἐλέησον, ὦ κύριε.
Preces Privatæ, Diei primæ.

[2] Μνήσθητι, Κύριε, ὁ Θεός,
πάντων πνευμάτων καὶ πάσης σαρκός,
ὧν ἐμνήσθημεν καὶ ὧν οὐκ ἐμνήσθημεν.
Id. Diei quartæ.

[3] These words were altered at the Revision of 1662 to their present form.

Puritans think that here is prayer for the dead allowed and practised by the Church of England and so think I; but we are not both of one mind in censuring the Church for so doing. They say it is Popish and superstitious; I for my part esteem it pious and Christian."[1]

Barrow. Isaac Barrow, than whom it would be absolutely impossible to find one more capable of exercising a sound and temperate judgment, was in the pregnant language of his biographer "mighty for it."[2]

Bishop Barrow. The inscription on the monument of his uncle, Bishop Barrow, in S. Asaph Cathedral testifies to the practice, by inviting those who entered that house of prayer to pray for their fellow-servant, that he might find mercy at the last day.[3]

Thorndike. The learned Thorndike expressed doubts about the present existence of prayers for the dead in the Services of the Church of England, with especial

---

[1] This passage is erroneously attributed to Bishop OVERALL by Dr. F. G. LEE in *The Christian Doctrine of Prayers for the Dead*, p. 156, and to judge by the note, Nichols was guilty of the same mistake. It is to be found in *Notes and Collections in an interleaved Book of Common Prayer*, by Bishop COSIN, 1619, of the Anglo-Catholic Library, Vol. v. 169.

[2] *Hearnianæ Reliquiæ*, ii. 188.

[3] "O vos transeuntes in domum Domini, in domum orationis, orate pro conservo vestro ut inveniat misericordiam in die Domini."

Special stress was laid upon this circumstance in the decision of the Dean of Arches, referred to on p. 253.

reference to the petition in the Litany for deliverance "in the hour of death, and in the day of judgment," or in the post-communion prayer of oblation that "we and all the whole Church may obtain remission of our sins and all other benefits of His Passion," on which opposite views have been taken. He felt that the mediæval forms had departed so far from the original sense of the Church that a reformation was needed, but he maintained that the proposal of the Puritans would tend to break the Church in pieces; "to take away all prayer for the dead is not paring off abuses but cutting to the quick."[1]

The epitaph which he wrote for his own tombstone is the clearest evidence of the value he set upon the practice. It concluded with the words: "Do thou, reader, pray for rest and a happy resurrection in Christ for Herbert Thorndike."[2]

Two illustrations from the non-jurors will suffice.

The pious Bishop Ken, whose last will and testament witnessed to his adherence to Catholic truth "as it stands distinguished from all Papal and Puritan innovations," has left us amongst his prayers a form which he composed and used in behalf of

Bishop Ken.

---

[1] THORNDIKE, *The Laws of the Church*, III. xxix.
[2] BOWLES' *Life of Bishop Ken*, ii. 308.

those who were "in the flesh or sleeping in Christ."[1] Furthermore, in a letter written in 1677, on the death of a valued friend, he concludes with the prayer, "and may his soul rest in peace."[2]

Hickes.

Dean Hickes when asked by a correspondent for the explanation of his views in consequence of some apparent contrariety between the doctrines which he was generally supposed to hold, and what he had expressed in his recommendations to the Duchess of Ormond on the education of a daughter, asserts that he had been guilty of no inconsistency, but was as zealous as ever in support of the practice of "praying for the dead who depart in the faith and fear of God, and in the peace of the Church."[3]

John Wesley.

John Wesley was equally decided, and when it was alleged as a serious charge against him that he had adopted the practice in his daily devotions, he maintained its legality, and explained to his accusers the grounds upon which he had formed his conviction that it was perfectly justifiable, viz., "The earliest antiquity, and the Church of England."[4]

---

[1] "Tu lector requiem ei et beatam in Christo resurrectionem, precare."—BRETT, *Dissertation appended to Liturgies*, p. 425.

[2] "Cujus anima requiescat in pace."

[3] Letter from Rev. J. M—n to Dr. George Hickes, and Dr. Hickes' answer.—Anglo-Cath. Libr., iii. 471, 483.

[4] *Answer to Lavington*, Works, ix. 55.

This *catena* of quotations [1] we cannot close better than by recording the opinion of two of the most esteemed men of this century,—Reginald Heber and John Keble. They did not hesitate to give their matured judgment, based on an attentive consideration of the whole subject, in favour of the usage. "I have accordingly," Heber writes, "been myself in the habit for some years of recommending on some occasions, as after receiving the Sacrament, my lost friends by name to God's goodness and compassion, through His Son, as what can do them no harm, and may, and I hope will be of service to them."[2] But even though he appears to have had a settled conviction, we are hardly surprised to find that with that modesty and self-depreciation which so characterised him, the possibility of his being mistaken led him, at the same time that he offered his petitions for the

Bishop Heber.

[1] It would be very easy largely to supplement the list by extracts from Archbishops Ussher, Laud, Juxon, Wake, and Sheldon, or Bishops Forbes, Jeremy Taylor, Patrick, Gunning, Smallridge, and Bull ; or historians, such as Jeremy Collier ; or laymen, such as Robert Nelson, or Dr. Johnson ; or in our own times, Mr. Tennyson.

Again, in the *Hierurgia Anglicana*, there is a vast collection of monumental inscriptions illustrative of the practice as it prevailed between 1547 and 1782, and it is greatly supplemented and brought down to our own times in Appendix xi. of Dr. F. G. Lee's work.

[2] *Diaries of a Lady of Quality*, p. 196. This reference is taken from Dr. F. G. Lee, but we well remember reading the passage at the time of its publication.

dead, to ask forgiveness for himself, if unknowingly he had not prayed in accordance with God's will.

Keble. While to one in bereavement Keble sends a form of prayer which he acknowledged to have used for years with far greater comfort than he deserved:—
"Remember thy servants and handmaidens which have departed hence in the Lord, especially ——— and all others to whom our remembrance is due; give them eternal rest and peace in Thy heavenly kingdom, and to us such a measure of communion with them as Thou knowest to be best for us. And bring us all to serve Thee in Thine eternal kingdom when Thou wilt and as Thou wilt, only without shame or sin. Forgive my presumption and accept my prayers, as Thou didst the prayers of Thine ancient Church, through Jesus Christ our Lord."[1]

Conclusion. The conclusion from a full consideration of the foregoing arguments is, that the practice of praying for the faithful dead was universally adopted in primitive times; and though, as we have seen, for wise reasons it was allowed to drop almost entirely out of our public worship, yet such a state of things cannot possibly be regarded as permanent.

The restoration of the primitive usage to its proper place in the Prayer-Book, though surrounded

[1] *Letters of Spiritual Counsel*, p. 46.

with difficulties, which past experience forbids us to ignore, is yet an object to which men may look forward hopefully, and while striving to attain to it have no misgivings that they are acting in a spirit of true loyalty to the Church.

For their guidance in their private devotions they have the example of a long line of men, eminent alike for learning and piety, to encourage them, as well as the decisions of the Ecclesiastical Courts[1] to establish the perfect legitimacy of the practice.

Whatever doubts then may be felt touching the advisability at present of giving to the practice of praying for the dead a fuller recognition in public,[2]

---

[1] In 1838 the case of Breeks v. Woolfrey was tried before the Arches Court. The charge was that the inscription on the tombstone—
> Pray for the soul of J. Woolfrey.
> 'It is a holy and wholesome thought to pray for the dead.'
> 2 Macc. xii. 26.

—was "contrary to the Articles, Canons and Constitutions, as to the doctrine and discipline of the Church of England."

The decision of Sir Herbert Jenner Fust was as follows:—

"I am of opinion that the offence imputed by the articles has not been sustained; that no authority or canon has been pointed out by which the practice of praying for the dead has been expressly prohibited; and I am accordingly of opinion that if the articles were proved, the facts would not subject the party to ecclesiastical censure, as far as regards the illegality of the inscription on the tombstone."

[2] In the Scotch Liturgy, 1637, the following prayer is used:—
"Most humbly beseeching Thee, that we may have grace to follow

we feel perfectly justified, with the countenance of so many honoured names, in adopting it in private, with the conviction, moreover, that in so doing we are by no means reviving something which had ever been absolutely dropt, but are rather continuing that for which there is unbroken testimony from the beginning down to our own time; and we have little doubt that those who accustom themselves to pray for departed friends, will find the pains of bereavement lessened, and the bond of union between the Church on earth and the Church in Paradise more tightly drawn.

the example of their steadfastness in Thy faith and obedience to Thy holy commandments: that at the day of the general resurrection we and all they which are of the mystical body of Thy Son, may be set on His right hand," etc.

The Committee of Bishops, at the last Revision in 1662, accepted these words, but when they were laid before Convocation, those at present in use, "and we also bless Thy holy name," etc., were substituted for them.

For a full account of the successive editions of the Prayer Book, the Articles, and the Homilies in reference to this subject, the reader is referred to the *Church Quarterly Review* for April 1880.

SUPPLEMENTARY CHAPTER.

B.

Is it lawful or desirable to practise invocation of Saints in any form or not?

WHEN we turn from Prayers for the Dead to the practice of Invocation, all is changed. Those who desire to be guided by Vincentian principles, find that the very arguments which establish Catholicity in the one case, disprove it in the other.

There are, it is true, examples of appeals to the dead for prayers and intercessions on the monuments in the Catacombs, but none have yet been brought to the light in inscriptions bearing a date. It is, of course, quite possible that the antiquity of the instances adduced may be as great as that of some which were used to illustrate prayers for the dead, but we have no proof of it, and those investigators. *The threefold testimony to Invocation insufficient to establish its Catholicity.*

who have the strongest claims to be heard, have determined otherwise. No argument, therefore, based upon the opposite theory, can expect to meet with anything more than very partial assent.

The testimony of the Fathers is wholly insufficient to establish the practice. Out of the entire number of those who wrote during the first four centuries, only four can be said to have used or expressed an unreserved approval of Invocation.

The Liturgies, Litanies, and Services which have always reflected more or less the prevalent beliefs, lend no countenance to it, till long after[1] the time to which we look back as primitive.

Maintaining then as we do so great a regard for antiquity, we find it quite impossible to sympathise with those who desire to introduce Invocations into the Forms of public worship.

Article xxii. not condemnatory of every kind of invocation.

There can be little question that the Invocation of Saints, which the twenty-second Article describes "as a vain thing fondly invented," was that form which was accompanied with worship; it is argued, therefore, that a prayer addressed to them without worship is permissible. Much, no doubt, may be

---

[1] The first introduction was in the time of Peter Fullo, the Eutychian Bishop. But the first recognition by the Church was not till the episcopate of Gregory the Great, 590–604 A.D.

said in favour of "oblique prayer" or "pious apostrophes of the dead;" in themselves they may be not only harmless, but actually beneficial; men's faith in the Communion of the Saints may be quickened thereby, and their religious fervour increased; but Catholic antiquity offers little support to their use, and the great Anglican divines show few signs in their writings of having adopted them. There are, it is true, some men of eminence since the Reformation who have not hesitated to approve of invocation, where it could be clearly distinguished from the Roman form, but they are so few that their names may be counted on the fingers. Reformers,[1] such as Luther and Erasmus and Bucer, expressed themselves as not opposed to the practice, within certain limitations. Bramhall, in his answer to the Epistle of M. de la Milletière, shows that he was prepared to accept some kind of invocation as a help to devotion, but not as necessary. "If," he writes, "your Invocation of Saints were not such as it is, to request of them patronage and protection, spiritual graces and celestial joys, by their prayers and by their merits; . . . yet it is not necessary, for two reasons: first, no Saint doth love us so well as

Opinions of the Reformers

Bramhall

---

[1] Cf. FORBES, *Considerationes Modestæ*, vol. ii. pp. 267, 269, 281.

Christ; no Saint hath given us such assurance of his love, or done so much for us as Christ; no Saint is so willing or able to help us as Christ: and secondly, we have no command from God to invocate them."[1]

Thorndike's distinctions.

Thorndike is not unfrequently claimed as an advocate, but on wholly insufficient grounds. He distinguishes three forms. The first is a prayer that God will grant certain blessings by and through the merits and intercessions of His saints. The second is an appeal to the saints in the same terms as to Christ: "we beseech thee to hear us." The third, when exactly the same blessings, spiritual or temporal, are sought from them, as all Christians seek from God.

Of these he says, "the first kind seems to me utterly agreeable with Christianity,"[2] and from this avowal he is claimed as a supporter of invocation; but very little consideration will show that what he advocates is not an appeal to the saints at all, but only a making mention of their intercessions, and a prayer that they may avail for the desired object, a course which the conclusions arrived at above[3] naturally prompt us to adopt.

[1] BRAMHALL'S *Works*, vol. i. 57.
[2] *Works*, vol. iv. Part ii. p. 770; Anglo-Cath. Library.
[3] Part ii. Chap. i.

We can bring forward no other divines of note in the 17th and 18th centuries; but if we were to extend the list so as to embrace men of an inferior position, and if we were to come down to our own generation, in which there are unquestionably advocates of no mean authority, the whole combined testimony would be of far less weight than that which we appealed to in support of a recognition of prayers for the dead in post-Reformation times.

And before we bring this investigation to a close, we would express even more strongly than we did at the outset our firm conviction that the Vincentian Canon offers the only safe anchorage in such troublous times of doubt and controversy as the present. Once drift away from primitive antiquity, from the avowed principles of the great Fathers and Doctors of the Church, and it is impossible to say where the tide may carry us. *Conclusion.*

It matters not that developments of doctrine have gained the adherence of holy and pious men: or that devotional usages, unknown to the Christians of Primitive times, have attained importance in the eyes of those who have been led to adopt them; if the Catholicity which belonged to undivided Christendom is to be established against all objectors, if its revival is to be marked by that unity and consistency of purpose, which alone can command success, individual sacrifices must be made for the common good of the Church; and the most prominent among them, as it seems to us, is the practice of appealing to the dead in prayer.

THE END.

TABLE OF FATHERS, COUNCILS, AND OTHER AUTHORITIES REFERRED TO, WITH THEIR RESPECTIVE DATES.

Aerius,	Flourished about	A.D. 360
Ambrose,	Died	397
Apostolic Constitutions,	Written before	325
Arnobius,	Flourished about	300
Athanasius,	Died	373
Augustine,	,,	430
Barrow,	,,	1677
Basil,	,,	379
Beveridge,	,,	1708
Bramhall,	,,	1663
Bull,	,,	1710
Cassian,	,,	448
Celsus,	Flourished about	230
Chrysologus,	Died	451
Chrysostom,	,,	407
Clemens Alexandrinus,	,,	218
Clemens Romanus,	,,	100
Clementines,	Written before	325
Cosin,	Died	1672
Council of Bracara or Braga,	Held	561
,, Carthage,	,,	419

Council of Chalcedon, . . . *Held* . . .	A.D.	451
,, Constantinople, . . ,, ...		381
,, Ephesus, ... ,, . . .		431
,, Florence, ... ,, . . .		1439
,, Nicæa, ... ,, . . .		325
,, Trent, ... ,, . . .	1545-	1563
Cyprian, ... *Died* . . .		258
Cyril, Bishop of Jerusalem, . . ,, . . .		386
,, ,, Alexandria, . . ,, . . .		444
Epiphanius, ... ,, . . .		403
Ephraem Syrus, ... ,, . . .		379
Eusebius, ... ,, . . .		338
Fabricins, ... ,, . . .		1736
Faustus, ... ,, . . .		490
Flavian, ... ,, . . .		450
Fullo, Peter, ... ,, . . .		488
Gelasius, ... ,, . . .		496
Gregory the Great, . . . ,, . . .		604
,, of Nazianzum, . . ,, . . .		389
,, of Nyssa, . . . ,, . . .		396
Hickes, ... ,, . . .		1715
Hooker, ... ,, . . .		1600
Ignatius, ... ,, . . .		107
Irenæus, ... ,, . . .		202
Isidore of Seville, . . . ,, . .		633
Jerome, ... ,, . . .		420
Leo the Great, ... ,, . . .		461
Mabillon, ... ,, . .		1707

Table of Fathers, Councils, etc.

Macarius,	Died	A.D. 391
Maimonides,	,,	1205
Optatus of Milevi,	Flourished	370
Origen,	Died	254
Peter Lombard,	,,	1164
Rufinus,	,,	410
Taylor, Jeremy,	,,	1667
Tertullian,	,,	218
Theodore the Interpreter,	Flourished	390
Theodoret,	Died	456
Thorndike,	,,	1672
Usher,	,,	1655
Vincentius,	,,	448
Waterland,	,,	1740

PASSAGES OF SCRIPTURE EXPLAINED OR QUOTED IN THE PRECEDING PAGES.

Reference		PAGE	Reference		PAGE
Deuter.	xvi. 10, 16,	59	1 Corinth. xiii. 12,		215–216
	xxi. 8,	60		xv. 29,	73
1 Kings	viii. 39,	213		xv. 51,	42
2 Kings	xix. 34,	144	2 Corinth.	v. 10,	45
	xxii. 18, 20,	213		xii. 2-4,	35
Psalms	vi. 5,	143	Ephesians	i. 20, 21,	71
	cix. 10,	155		ii. 12,	77
Proverbs	xi. 7,	123	Philipp.	i. 23,	142
Eccles.	ix. 10,	44		iii. 20, 21,	218
	xi. 3,	43	1 Thess.	iv. 13,	138
Isaiah	lxiii. 15, 16,	214		iv. 15,	41
	lxiv. 4,	70	2 Timothy	i. 16, 17, 18,	78
Jerem.	xxxiv. 4-5,	90		i. 18,	79
S. Matthew	v. 17,	65		ii. 12,	225
	vi. 2,	60		iv. 19,	78
	xii. 31, 32,	67	Hebrews	xi. 39, 40,	46, 222
	xvi. 18,	10	S. James	v. 16,	51
	xix. 27, 28,	225	1 S. Peter	ii. 1,	131
	xxi. 22,	68		iii. 18, 19,	33, 47
	xxvi. 24,	139	1 S. John	iii. 2,	217
	xxviii. 20,	244	S. Jude	iii. 13,	8–15
S. Mark	iii. 29,	71	Revelation	v. 6-8,	154
S. Luke	xvi. 25,	230		vi. 9, 10, 11,	226–248
	xxii. 31,	51		vi. 9, 10,	155
S. John	ix. 4,	45		vi. 11,	48
	xvi. 13,	10		vii. 14, 15,	227
Romans	ii. 16,	131		viii. 3, 4,	155
	viii. 26,	52		x. 6,	38
	xv. 4,	230		xxi. 1,	226
1 Corinth.	i. 8,	76		xxi. 27,	39

GENERAL INDEX.

ADEN, epitaph discovered at, 62, 63.
Advent, the Second, S. Paul's views on, 49.
Æmilius the martyr, 168.
Aerius, objections of, to prayers for the dead, 133, 244.
—— evidence of, to be distrusted, 134.
—— Hooker's estimate of, 135.
Ailurus, Timothy, 170.
Andrewes, devotions of, 247.
Angelic hymn, the, 194, 195.
Apocryphal books, their place in history, 53.
Apostolical Constitutions, 131.
Arcadius, 166.
Arenariæ, 81, 82.
Articles, the xlii. of Edward vi., 29.
Article xxii. not necessarily condemnatory of all invocation, 256.
Atonement, Jewish means of procuring, 59.
Ave Maria, interpolated in the Liturgies, 193.

BAPTISM, witness to, in the Catacombs, 86, 87.
—— for the dead, 73.
—— —— censured by S. Chrysostom and Epiphanius, 73.
Barrow, on prayers for the dead, 243.
—— epitaph on tomb of, 243.
Basilides, 161.
Beatific vision of God not yet attained by the Saints, the, 219.
—— testimony of S. Augustine, 220.
—— —— of S. Cyprian, 220.
—— —— of Tertullian, 221.

Beatific vision, testimony of Origen, 222.
—— —— of Justin Martyr, 223.
—— —— of Jesus Christ, 225, 226.
—— —— of S. John, 226, 227.
—— the views of the Roman Church on, 219.
Beveridge on the value of the Fathers, 23.
Blesilla, 166.
Bracara or Braga, Council of, 148.
Bramhall on the value of the Fathers, 24.
—— on invocation of saints, 257.
Bucer, Martin, 240.
Bull on the perceptions of a disembodied soul, 34.
Burial Service, Bishop Cosin on the, 243.

CANONS, the, 21, 22.
Cassian's story of the hermit Hero, 147.
Castus the martyr, 168.
Catacombs, the origin of, 81.
—— period covered by the inscriptions of, 84.
—— dated inscriptions in, 85.
—— simplicity of the inscriptions in, 86.
—— sacramental teaching in, 86, 87.
—— testimony of, how used, 89.
—— inscriptions of, void of exaggeration, 237.
Catechumens who died without baptism, 140.
Catholic, the title misapplied, 3.
—— Emancipation Act, 3.
Catholicity, a recognised test of, needed, 4.
Cerinthians, the, 74.

Church, methods of ascertaining the voice of, 10.
Church Militant Prayer, 241.
Christ's coming the goal of the Christian, 48.
—— S. Paul's expectation of, 49.
Chroniclers of events, the Fathers as, 17.
Chwolson, Dr., on Crimean tombstones, 63.
Clementine Constitutions, 107.
Columbaria, 82.
Commemoration of souls, Jewish, 57.
Commonitorium of Vincentius, 7, 15, 16.
Communion of Saints, 12, 13.
—— the belief in, when first expressed in a public formulary, 13.
Constable on Hades, 31, 32.
Constantius, 177.
Cornelius, the friend of S. Cyprian, 162, 163.
Cosin on the Burial Service, 242, 243, 247.
Council of Bracara, 148.
—— Carthage, the third, 195.
—— Chalcedon, 6, 99, 170.
—— Constantinople, 12, 13.
—— Ephesus, 13.
—— Florence, 219.
—— Nicæa, 6, 12.
—— Trent, 41, 219.
Councils, General, guided by Vincentian principles, 12.
Cranmer on the value of the Fathers, 22.
Creeds, the construction of, 9.
—— illustrations from, 11.
—— Latin, 13.
—— of Irenæus, Tertullian, Cyprian, the Aquileian, 13.
—— Greek, 13.
—— of Eusebius, Arius, Epiphanius, Cyril, etc., 13.

De Rossi on inscriptions of the Catacombs, 81, 91.

Development of interpretation different from development of doctrine, 15.
Dioscurus before the Council of Chalcedon, 99.
Dispensation, the old and new, connection between, 65.
Dives and Lazarus, the parable of, 26-29, 230, 231.
Döllinger on baptism for the dead, 75, 76.
Drake on the symbolism of the paintings in the Catacombs, 88.
Dress of Virgins, the, by S. Cyprian, 164.

Edward vi., the First Prayer-Book of, 195.
—— the Second Prayer-Book of, 196.
Ephesus, Council of, *see* Councils.
—— the Seven Sleepers of, 37.
Epiphanius' answer to Aerius, 133, 135, 244.
Epitaphs in the Catacombs, 91.
—— to Libera, 91.
—— to Fortunatus Eumenes, 92.
—— to Zosima, 93.
—— to Fortunata, 93.
—— to Cervonia Silvana, 93.
—— to Hilaris, 94.
—— to Kalameros, 94.
—— to Bolosa, 94.
—— to Heraclea Roma, 94.
—— to Venus, 95.
—— to Timothea, 95.
—— to Hygeia, 95.
—— to Irenæa, 95.
—— to Chresime Victoria, 96.
—— to Marius Vitellianus, 96.
—— to Januarius and Agapotus, 200.
—— to Basilla, 200.
—— to Dionysius, 201.
—— to Augenda, 201.
—— to Vincentia, 202.
Era of Contracts, 62.
—— the Seleucides, 62.
Eusebius as an Arian, 13.

General Index.   267

Faber on Sanctification, 40.
Fabricius on the seat of Onesiphorus' labours, 78.
Fasts of Embertide, 20.
Fathers, *see* Primitive.
Flavian, 170.
Florentius Hippo, 186.
Forty Martyrs, Panegyric on the, 180.
Fullo, Peter, 198, 256.
Furni, letter of S. Cyprian to the people of, 145.

General Councils, the decisions of, guided by Vincentian principles, 12.
Geminius Faustinus, 145.
Geminius Victor, 145.
Gibbon on the legend of the Seven Sleepers, 37.
Gorgonia, funeral oration on, 177, 205.

Hades, by Constable, 31, 32.
Haskarnth Neshamoth, 57.
Heathen symbols in the Catacombs, 82.
—— Dean Stanley on, 84.
—— J. H. Parker on, 83.
Heliodorus, 166.
Hero the Hermit, story of, 147, 148.
Hickes on Interpolations in Liturgies, 106.
Hooker on Justification and Sanctification, 40.
—— on the character of Aerius, 135.
Hymns Ancient and Modern, quotation from, 44.

Ἰχθύς, explanation of the symbol of, 88.
Ignatius, the martyrdom of, 157, 158.
—— the genuineness of the treatise, 157.
Infant Baptism, silence about, in Holy Scripture, 65, 66.
Inhumation, the original mode of burial, 82.
Inscriptions, *see* Catacombs.
Intercession, the principle of, 50, 51.

Intercession of the Saints, testimony to, 153.
—— —— of the Apocalypse, 154.
—— —— of Origen, 158, 159, 160, 187, 188.
—— —— of Eusebius, 161, 162.
—— —— of S. Cyprian, 162.
—— —— of S. Ephraem, 164.
—— —— of S. Gregory Nazianzen, 165.
—— —— of S. Cyril, 165.
—— —— of S. Chrysostom, 165, 166.
—— —— of S. Ambrose, 166.
—— —— of S. Jerome, 166, 167.
—— —— of S. Augustine, 168, 169.
—— —— of the Council of Chalcedon, 170.
—— —— of the Liturgies, 171.
—— —— of S. James (the Syriac), 172.
—— —— of S. Basil, 172.
—— —— of the Coptic Liturgies, 172.
—— —— of S. Gregory, 172.
—— —— of S. Cyril, 172.
—— —— of the Alexandrian Liturgy of S. Basil, 173.
—— —— of S. James the Lord's brother, 174.
Intercession of the Saints, upon what based, 229.
—— —— for individuals, 231.
—— —— for the whole Church, 231, 232.
Invocation absent from Primitive Liturgies, 189, 234.
—— in the Catacombs, 199, 233, 234.
—— in the epitaph of Januarius, 200 202.
—— of Basilla, 200.
—— of Dionysius, 201.
—— of Augenda, 201.
—— of Vincentia, 202.
Invocation of Saints, testimony to, 174.
—— —— of Origen, 175, 187, 197.
—— —— of S. Basil, 175, 176, 189.
—— —— of S. Gregory Nazianzen, 177, 178, 189, 197.
—— —— of S. Gregory of Nyssa, 178, 179, 189, 190, 197.

Invocation of Saints, testimony to, of
S. Ephraem, 180, 181, 190, 197.
—— —— of S. Chrysostom, 182, 183,
184, 190, 191, 197.
—— —— of S. Ambrose, 184, 192, 197.
—— —— of S. Augustine, 185, 193, 196,
197.
Invocation of Saints, of different kinds,
194.
—— what its value depends on, 233.
—— not Catholic, 232, 235.
—— is the practice of, desirable in any
form? 254.
—— opinions of the Reformers on, 257.
—— Bramhall on, 257.
—— Thorndike on, 258.

JAMNITES, the, 54.
Jesus Christ, the Godhead of, 11.
Jewel on the value of the Fathers, 23.
Jewish services, 56.
—— prayers for the dead in divers
countries, 57.
—— means of atonement, 59.
—— tombstones and inscriptions, 61.
Judas Maccabeus, 54, 56.
Julian the Emperor, 205.
Justin Martyr a Millennarian, 18.

KADDISH, the, 56.
Keble on Prayers for the Dead, 249.
Ken, Bishop, on Prayers for the Dead, 249.
Knowledge, the extent of, possessed by
the Saints, 204.
—— S. Gregory Nazianzen on, 205.
—— S. Ambrose on, 206.
—— S. Jerome on, 207.
—— S. Augustine on, 207-211.
—— as taught in Scripture, 212.
—— in the Historical Books, 213, 214.
—— in the Prophetical Books, 215.
—— in the New Testament, 215.
—— in S. Paul's writings, 215-217.
—— in S. John's writings, 217, 218.
—— obtained by the Saints in different
ways, 208, 209.
—— the, of Angels, 209.

LAZARUS, etymology of the name, 27.
—— the Parable of, 26-29, 230, 231.
—— Irenæus on, 26.
—— S. Chrysostom on, 27.
—— S. Cyril on, 27.
—— S. Augustine on, 27, 28.
—— Tertullian on, 26, 27.
—— S. Ambrose on, 27.
Leo, the letter of the Bishops to, 107.
Lightfoot on "the world to come,"
68, 69.
Liturgical Service, the primal form of,
103.
—— traces of, in Apostolical writings,
103.
Liturgies, Primitive, divided into
groups, 104.
—— —— the uncertainty of the text,
105.
—— —— the arguments upon which
their date is approximately determined, 105.
—— —— examples of interpolations in,
106, 107.
—— —— the variety of, 233.
—— —— on Prayers for the Dead, 108.
—— —— the meaning and objects of
the petitions, 115, 116.
Liturgy of S. James (the Syriac), on
prayers for the pardon of sins of infirmity, 118.
Liturgies, the Jacobite, 119.
Liturgy of S. John the Evangelist, 119.
—— of S. Peter, 119.
—— of S. James the Less, 120.
—— of S. Dionysius, 120.
—— of Theodore the Interpreter, 121.
—— of S. Leo, 121.
—— of S. Gelasius, 122.
—— of S. Gregory, 122.
Liturgy, future revision of the, 5, 245.
—— traces of prayers for the dead still
left in, 243.
Liturgy of S. James, 108, 109.
—— the Clementine, 109.
—— of S. Mark, 110.

General Index.   269

Liturgy of S. Cyril, 111.
— the Gallican, 112.
— the Mozarabic, 112.
— the Ambrosian, 113.
— of S. Gregory, 113.
— of SS. Adæus and Maris, 114.
Lumby, Dr., on the early form of the Western Creed, 12, 13.

MACARIUS on instantaneous sanctification, 41.
Maccabees, the Second Book of, 54.
Maimonides' Precepts of Repentance, 69, 70.
— on the word "Memory," 63.
Mamas the martyr, 176.
Marchi, Padre, 81.
Marcionites, the, 74.
Martensen on a spiritual purgatory, 126.
Martyr, Peter, 240.
Martyrdom of Potamiæna, 161.
Martyrs, special honours assigned to, 168, 225.
Mason, W., "Spiritual Treasury," 41.
Memory in the disembodied state, 229, 230.
Memory, Memorial, Jewish meaning of, 63.
Midrash, the, on the books of Moses, 60.
Misapplied texts from Ecclesiastes, 43, 44.
— S. John, 45.
— S. Paul, 45.

NEPOTIANUS, 207.
Nestorian Liturgies, 104, 114.
Newman, Dr., on development of doctrine, 15.
— on the coming of Christ as the Christian's hope, 49.
Nonjurors on Prayers for the Dead, 246, 249, 250.

OBLATION, Prayer of, 242.
Odullam, 54.

Old Catholics on baptism for the dead, 75, 76.
Onesiphorus, prayers for, 77, 78.
— whether alive or dead when S. Paul wrote, 78.
Origen as a Platonist and Allegorist, 18.

PACE, IN, explained in divers ways, 90, 91.
— examples in the Catacombs, 91.
Pagan inscriptions and symbols in the Catacombs, 83.
— Dean Stanley on, 84.
Parable of Dives and Lazarus, 26-29, 230, 231.
Paradise, S. Paul caught up into, 35.
Parker, J. H., on the Catacombs, 81.
Pegna on the Beatific Vision, 223.
Pete pro nobis, P.P.N., 203.
Peter of Alexandria, 206.
Pollock, "Out of the Body," 28.
Prayer-Books of Edward VI., 195, 196.
Prayers for the Dead, 50.
— testimony of the early Fathers, 98.
— — of the Acts of the Council of Chalcedon, on, 98, 99.
— — of S. Augustine, 99.
— — of S. Ambrose, 100.
— — of Epiphanius, 100.
— — of S. Chrysostom, 100.
— — of Eusebius, 100.
— — of Arnobius, 101.
— — of Tertullian, 101, 102.
Prayers for the Dead, their object, 115, 116.
— advocated by Anglican divines :—
— — Jeremy Taylor, 80.
— — Bishop Andrewes, 247.
— — Barrow, 248.
— — Thorndike, 248.
— — Ken, 249.
— — Hickes, 249.
— — Wesley, 250.
— — Heber, 251.
— — Keble, 251.

General Index.

Prayers for the Dead, according to the Ecclesiastical Courts, 253.
—— unknown before the Captivity, 53.
—— abundant in Mediæval times, 244.
Prayers for the Dead, is a fuller recognition of, desirable? 236.
—— on grounds of utility, 239.
—— in controversy with Rome, 240.
—— no objection to them in private, 246.
Prayers for the pardon of sins of human infirmity, *see* Primitive Liturgies.
—— views of the early Fathers on, 123.
—— of S. Jerome, 123.
—— of Theodoret, 123.
—— of S. Augustine, 124.
Prayers for those who die in wilful sin, 127.
—— the example from the Apocrypha considered, 128, 129.
—— the Apostolical Constitutions on, 130.
—— S. Cyril on, 131.
—— Aerius on, 132.
—— Epiphanius' answer to his objections on, 135.
—— S. Augustine on, 137.
—— S. Chrysostom on, 139, 144, 147.
—— S. Cyprian on, 145.
Precepts on repentance, by Maimonides, 69.
Primitive Fathers as independent chroniclers, 17.
—— as credible exponents of doctrine, 18, 70.
—— errors of, how far injurious to their nfluence, 19.
—— the weight of the authority of, recognised in the Prayer-Book, the Ecclesiastical Canons, the Homilies, and the writings of the Reformers, 21, 22.
Proterius, 170.
Protestants, foreign, influence of, in the Reformaton, 240.

Purgatory, a spiritual, views on by a Lutheran divine, 126.

REFORMATION, changes brought about by the, 4.
Reformers, the foreign, 5.
Robber Synod of Ephesus, 170.

SACRAMENTAL teaching in the Catacombs, 86, 87.
Sacramentary of S. Gregory, 118, 122.
—— of S. Leo, 121.
—— of S. Gelasius, 122.
Sacrificial and non-sacrificial prayers, 194.
Saint Ambrose on the spirits in prison, 47, 48.
—— Augustine on special rewards of martyrdom, 168.
—— —— on S. Matt. xii. 31-33, 72.
—— —— Retractations of, 19.
—— Basil, funeral oration on, 164, 181.
—— —— on the Forty Martyrs, 176.
—— Chrysostom on baptism for the dead, 73.
—— —— on Onesiphorus, 79.
—— —— on the sin of delaying baptism, 147.
—— Epiphanius on baptism for the dead, 73.
—— Isidore on S. Matt. xii. 31-33, 72.
—— Jerome, censured by S. Augustine, 19.
—— —— on the effects of Christ's descent into Hades, 48.
—— Paul's anticipations of the Second Advent, 31, 32.
Saints, memory retained by, after death, 229, 230.
Sanctification, Hooker on, 40.
—— Faber on, 40.
—— Council of Trent on, 41.
—— S. Macarius on, 41.
—— Mason, 41.
—— in the disembodied state, 36.
—— distinct from Justification, 40.

Saphir, R. Jacob, travels of, 61.
Schiller-Szinessy, Dr., Manual for young Rabbis by, 59.
—— on the dates of Jewish inscriptions, 62.
Scripture, Holy, the sufficiency of, 9.
—— countenancing the theory of change in Hades, 46, 47, 48.
Sermon on the Mount, reference in, to the commemoration of the dead, 59, 60.
Silence of our Lord on prayers for the dead, 52.
Siphrè, the, 60.
Sleep of the soul, the, 29.
Stapleton on the Beatific Vision, 223.
Stier on the spiritual capacities of a disembodied soul, 34, 35.
Stanley, Dean, on baptism for the dead, 74, 76.
Suicides not commemorated by the Church, 146.
Syrophœnician woman, the, 191.
Swanison, Dr., on the Creeds, 13.

TALMUD, the, on S. Matt. xii. 31-33, 71.
Taylor, Jeremy, on the Catholic Church,
—— on Onesiphorus, 80.

Tertullian as a Montanist, 18.
—— on Symbols of Baptism, 87.
—— on the First Resurrection, 102.
—— on ἰχθύς, 88.
—— on the symbolism of the bird with a branch in its beak, 77.
Texts of Scripture misapplied, 43.
Theodore, Festival in honour of, 178.
Thief upon the Cross, the, 30.
Tombstones, Jewish, 62, 63.

VIGILANTIUS' dispute with S. Jerome, 167.
Vincentian Canon explained, 7.
—— its value as a test, 8.
—— its relation to Holy Scripture, 8.
—— objections to, of Roman Catholics, 14, 15.
—— —— of Protestants, 14.

WATERLAND on the value of the Fathers, 24, 25.
Wesley, John, on prayers for the dead, 250.
Wordsworth, Bishop, on baptism for the dead, 74.
World to come the Jewish meaning of, 68, 69.

www.ingramcontent.com/pod-product-compliance
Lightning Source LLC
Chambersburg PA
CBHW032103220426
43664CB00008B/1111